Professionals and Paraprofessionals

Professionals and Paraprofessionals

Michael J. Austin, Ph. D

School of Social Work
University of Washington

HUMAN SCIENCES PRESS
72 Fifth Avenue / 3 Henrietta Street
NEW YORK, New York 10011 / LONDON, WC2E 8LU England

Library of Congress Catalog Number 77-26273

ISBN: 0-87705-305-7

Copyright © 1978 by Human Sciences Press
72 Fifth Avenue, New York, New York 10011

Printed in the United States of America
289 987654321

HV
41
A87

Library of Congress Cataloging in Publication Data

Austin, Michael J.
  Professionals and paraprofessionals.

  Bibliography: p.
  Includes index.
  1. Paraprofessionals in social service. 2. Social service—Vocational guidance.
3. Social workers.
I. Title.
HV41.A87   361' .0023   77-26273
ISBN 0-87705-305-7

CONTENTS

FOREWORD

My first field instruction placement at Tulane University School of Social Work was at Kingsley House settlement. Most of my early practical learning about social group work came from a neighborhood paraprofessional who helped me organize a young boys' group. She taught me how to deal with the youngsters' families; how to gain access to the settlement's facilities and how to use them well; how to create some order with youngsters at their chaotic age. And she demonstrated to me, not formally but through my observation of her work, how one organized a ballgame, a field trip, a snack period, and an unstructured playground program with young children. After we had worked together for two weeks, I told her how grateful I was. She told me that she and many of her neighborhood colleagues knew a great deal about the work of the settlement. They had grown up in the neighborhood, used the settlement, and made friends with most of the families. Despite limited formal education, they knew the settlement house program and the people and were proud of their effectiveness.

That woman provided me with my introduction to what have come to be called "paraprofessionals," and my experiences with her came to mind when I was asked to prepare this foreword. What has evolved as the paraprofessional movement in social work and defined as a new movement in the field is really a long and honorable part of the history of social welfare. For many years and for a variety of reasons, agencies, particularly settlement houses, community centers, and residential institutions have employed persons knowledgeable about the special problems of the clientele being served, often because of direct experience with the neighborhood or the clients. One reason for using paraprofessional staff has been the shortage of professionally educated social workers to carry all of the social work responsibilities. Even if funds were unlimited, it would be questionable whether persons formally educated as social workers need to perform all the tasks that are carried out in social agencies. It has long been believed and confirmed in the practices of many agencies that untrained workers and volunteers may have greater skills for selected activities than trained workers.

The paraprofessional movement in social work in the 1960s was no more than a rediscovery, an enlargement, and a reconceptualization of personnel who had always been a part of social welfare history. This book provides us with the first comprehensive effort to document the motives for the use of paraprofessionals in the 1960s and their impact upon the social profession. Reasons for the expanded use of paraprofessionals included the sizeable growth of social service programs, the shortage of trained social workers, the realization that people with backgrounds other than social work could serve clients, the national priority to eliminate discriminatory practices in agency personnel policies, and the emerging theory that clients are better served by people who share their cultural backgrounds and live in similar neighborhoods.

It is interesting to note that the trend to employing paraprofessionals has had its greatest impact on the social work professional rather than on the legal, medical, and education professions, where similar client contact exists. While there is a strong paramedical movement, the high educational requirements of a bachelor's or master's degree limit paraprofessional involvement. The same is true in legal services where legal work continues to be done by attorneys with minimal paraprofessional involvement in clerical and/or social work-related responsibilities. In the field of preschool education—Head Start programs—paraprofessionals have assumed important functions based on legislative mandates, but their impact on   the   education profession has been limited. Many public school teachers have been unable to recognize and effectively utilize paraprofessionals in the classroom.

Perhaps the impact on social work has been greatest for a variety of reasons that are peculiar to social work itself. For example, social work has never had the licensing protection as a profession that education, law, and medicine have had. The 1967 Harris Amendments to the Social Security Act requiring the use of community service volunteers and community service aides in public welfare programs to assist in improving services and to provide employment opportunities was generally supported by the social work profession. However, it soon became clear that these were the only personnel in public welfare that were ever legislatively mandated. All of the other personnel requirements had been administratively required and enforced. The requirements of the 1950s and 1960s that there be persons with master of social work degrees in key public welfare positions was a requirement of administrative law, not legislation. And by the 1970s those administrative regulations had been eliminated by the federal government. State after state dropped its requirements for professional social work training in major public assistance and child welfare positions.

So the paraprofessional movement's major impact on social work may have resulted more from social work's vulnerability as a profession than it did from any conviction that social work required the participation of paraprofessionals more than other professions. The network of state licensing regulations and professional standards in education, law, and medicine clearly set the entrance requirements for those professions and automatically excluded paraprofessionals.

Another reason, of course, for paraprofessionals to have had such an impact on social work is that many social work clients were and are from lower income groups. Education, law, and medicine serve people at all socioeconomic levels. While the social work profession also serves all socioeconomic levels of society, a larger proportion of its clients are from the lower socioeconomic classes. Therefore, the logic of using representatives from the community, particularly the low-income community, was persuasive.

Paraprofessionalism has also brought attention to the difficult problem of ill-defined goals and objectives in social welfare. For a variety of reasons, the goals of social welfare programs are frequently unclear, unstated, or so broad that it is difficult to measure their attainment. In education, law, and medicine, the objectives are generally agreed upon and lend themselves to measurement. In social work that is rarely the case. Social workers and social agencies are not incapable of knowing what they are doing or specifying their goals, although such accusations are often made by those who are not fond of the field. In fact, social workers and social agencies have the talent and the kinds of personnel to be capable of explicit goal statements. However, there are often disincentives for social workers to state their goals clearly. In fact, there are major disagreements about the appropriate goals of social welfare programs and social workers. Is it the goal of social work, for example, to obtain a minimum standard of living for every citizen through direct grants? Or is it the goal of social agencies to change the socioeconomic situation in ways that will eliminate poverty? All of these are implicit objectives of social work in various agencies. There is no unanimity among social workers about those objectives or any priority ranking among them.

Another contested issue in any discussion of paraprofessionals is the role of educational preparation in equipping people to provide human services. There are many who believe that some people without any professional education can practice social work as effectively as those with bachelor's or master's degrees in social work. It can probably be documented that some people with no formal preparation in social work have performed and continue to perform social work tasks effectively, but there are some confounding elements in any such discussion. For example, effective performance of specific tasks does not make a professional. It does not guarantee subscription to a code of ethics, generalized knowledge about a field endeavor, or any of the other attributes of professions. It is possible that one might find an excellent general practitioner of medicine, a highly skilled nurse, or a talented attorney among those who have never prepared for those roles in professional schools. Perhaps societies should find ways of awarding such talented individuals with professional credentials.

Professional education is simply society's way of certifying to the public that a person has been prepared for the practice of a profession. It is also an effective but crude screening device testifying to the competence of an individual for professional practice. It may be that not all persons who are certified are the equal of all persons who are not certified. Professional credentials testify to the fact that the person has completed an appropriate planned program of formal study which has been sanctioned by an accrediting body and the person's potential skill as a practitioner is attested to by an educational institution. Social agency employers know, within a relatively narrow range, what they can expect from professionally educated social workers, just as other employ-

ers know what to expect from professional educators, law-
yers, and physicians. That is of major importance because it
is an efficient means of identifying competent workers. The
alternative would be the screening of thousands of individuals
on a case-by-case basis for their knowledge of and competence in professional practice.

The paraprofessional movement may also have been one
of the many attempts by persons from a variety of per-
suasions—from officials in the liberal Kennedy and Johnson
administrations to those in the less liberal Nixon administration—to discredit social work as a profession. It may have
been one means designed to reduce federal funding for the
preparation of social workers and salaries for social work professionals. That effort represented a retreat from the commitment to social welfare funding in the 1950s and the 1960s.
But these were realistic possibilities at any time in history,
because social work has throughout its history been unpopu-
lar with many groups. It is assaulted with some regularity by
conservatives, liberals, the radical poor—although there is
some evidence that low-income social work clients have a
rather high degree of respect for social work professionals,
members of other professions, some social scientists, and, in
some ways, by social workers themselves. That should not be
surprising. Social work throughout its existence has dealt
with the least popular members of societies: the poor, the
deviant, the handicapped, the very young, and the very old.
Perhaps social workers should accept the dislike of the profession in some elite quarters or even by some members of
low-income populations, some of whom are led by members
of elite groups.

It is interesting to note that social work has gained support
and increasing interest from college students and others in recent years. The size of the profession continues to grow,
largely because the kinds of problems society wants to resolve require the services of social workers for their resolu-

tion. Fortunately one's skills can be used and recognized for their value even when one is not loved.

Dr. Austin's book is one of the few systematic analyses of the paraprofessional-professional relationship in social welfare. It is an important book for the coming decades. Social welfare programs will continue to be staffed by people from a variety of backgrounds. To supervise staff and to be supervised requires systematic thinking, information, and analysis. This book will be useful to those engaged in social work staff development, education, and supervision because of its comprehensive treatment of the personnel issues in social work. It is a welcome piece of work for a variety of reasons, not the least of which is its focus on the profession itself rather than on social problems, social systems, or other dimensions that have been the focus of so many social work volumes in recent years.

The profession of social work, which is a large and crucial factor in American society, has not received sufficient analysis, and helpful research findings have too infrequently been disseminated. In particular, too little has been written about the profession from an intelligent, scientifically based point of view. This book has helped to fill that knowledge gap and should prove to be an important contribution to the literature of social work, as well as to literature on occupations and professions. Social work owes a debt to Dr. Austin for his research and for its dissemination in this volume.

LEON H. GINSBERG
Dean, School of Social Work
West Virginia University
Morgantown, West Virginia

PREFACE

The introduction of paraprofessionals into the midst of the social work profession in the mid-1960s provides an unique opportunity to study the social psychology of organizational change in the deployment of social service staff. Like the entrance of a new family into the neighborhood, the entry of paraprofessionals recruited primarily from low-income neighborhoods produced anxiety, accommodation, and acceptance among the ranks of both professional social workers and paraprofessionals.

This book was begun as a study of the relationship between professionals and paraprofessionals employed in health and social services. Many of these workers had been involved in delivering services supported by funds from the War on Povery Community Action Program and the Model Cities Program. As a group, professionals and paraprofessionals represented an emerging social movement related primarily to the new organizations—Head Start Centers, Neighborhood Health Centers, Neighborhood Service Centers, and Multiservice Centers—which emerged from the flood of social legislation throughout the 1960s.

In the early 1970s it became apparent that the introduction of paraprofessionals into social service programs would produce many unanticipated consequences. Both public and private agencies which had traditionally employed only trained social workers began to recognize the potential contributions of paraprofessionals to their agencies. For some agencies, paraprofessionals represented a source of cheap labor; for others, the involvement of paraprofessionals represented an opportunity to raise the quality of service based on a special knowledge of client populations and a multi-ethnic approach to staffing service programs.

The most profound impact of paraprofessionals upon the network of social services appeared in the area of personnel administration. As a result of inadequate in-service training and dead end jobs, paraprofessionals focused attention upon agency personnel practices which were recognized by many as archaic and unresponsive to the needs of all levels of workers. Rallying around the concepts of "career ladders" and "career lattices," professionals and paraprofessionals alike began to recognize the need to create career opportunities within agencies and between agencies for all levels of staff.

Planning for career advancement required renewed effort to analyze the nature of work in order to appropriately deploy staff with different levels of competence, experience, and education. The social work profession began to legitimate new levels of practice through the recognition of the bachelor's-degree-trained social worker as a social service generalist and the master's-degree-trained social worker as a specialist. In a similar fashion paraprofessionals began to organize themselves for purposes of recognition among the many human service professions. In some cases they followed the traditional method of staff differentiation by credentials, thereby encouraging paraprofessionals to acquire high school diplomas and community college associate degrees.

The emphasis on educational credentials also received considerable criticism throughout the early 1970s. New approaches to higher education as seen in various study commission reports, including that of the Carnegie Commission, gave credence to time-shortened college degrees and universities without walls. These visions of the future gave impetus to agency training staff to explore new methods of in-service training so that personnel might benefit from nontraditional forms of education in order to advance within the agency. These new approaches to education and training remain to be fully tested by the realities of the job market and the ability of staff trained in innovative education programs to produce effectively on the job.

This study traces the evolution of paraprofessionalism and the impact of paraprofessionals on professional social workers. Part I includes a discussion of the paraprofessional roots of the social work profession, the dilemmas of determining future social service manpower needs, and the emergence of a social movement stemming from the employment of paraprofessionals.

Part II addresses the implications of staffing social service programs with different levels of personnel. This analysis includes the motives behind employing paraprofessionals, methods of analyzing jobs, approaches to staff training based on the principles of adult learning, and new dilemmas in staff supervision. This section concludes with a discussion of functional job analysis and the future demands for career planning which should prove to be a major thrust of social service personnel management into the 1980s.

Part III includes a study of paraprofessionalism. Specific attention is given to the factors impinging on the working relationship between professionals and paraprofessionals. Research data for the study was gathered in six eastern cities from over four hundred professionals and paraprofessionals. The study provides new insights into the "psychic stretch" experienced by paraprofessionals caught between the agency and the client community and the "occupational stretch" experienced by professional social workers caught between the needs of an emerging profession and the increasing demands of clients.

Acknowledging the help of others is both a privilege and and opportunity to personalize. The development of my early thinking on the nature of occupations and professions began at the University of California where Andrew Billingsley, Scott Briar, and Ralph Kramer contributed immensely to my inquiry into the nature of professional social work practice. Building upon this foundation, I was greatly assisted by Joseph Eaton, William Hall, and Edmund Ricci at the University of Pittsburgh in expanding my knowledge of the social sciences and my skills in research. Through the support and encouragement of L. Diane Bernard and Bernhard Scher at Florida State University I was able to continue my research interests into the nature of professional and paraprofessional practice at the Florida Board of Regents under the helpful guidance of Travis Northcutt. In addition, many of the ideas developed in chapters six through ten reflect the insights and assistance of my very able colleague at the Board of Regents, Alexis Skelding.

A special note of thanks goes to a very talented researcher at the University of Alabama School of Social Work, Robert Teare, who has contributed significantly to the field of social welfare research and authored chapters four and five which represent a valuable addition to this study. In addition, chapter two represents a modified version of an article which appeared in *Arete*, the journal of the University of South Carolina Graduate School of Social Work (Spring 1973), and chapter eight represents a modified version of a chapter in *Approaches to Innovation in Social Work Education*, published by the Council on Social Work Education (1974).

Many people have contributed to the completion of this book. The several hundred professionals and paraprofession-

als who took the time to respond to questionnaires and interviews deserve a considerable note of thanks. I am most grateful to my skillful manuscript editor, Millicent Shargel, and to
Shirley Abdallah for her help with the index. I also greatly
appreciate the patience and thoroughness of my secretaries,
Beverly Harness, Nancy Holaday, and Mary Harvey. A
special note of appreciation goes to Dr. Steven Danish who
guided this book through the publishing process.

The research for the case study was supported by grants
from Community Action Pittsburgh, Inc., the United States
Children's Bureau, and the National Institute of Mental
Health. And finally, this book was supported by the love,
patience, and understanding of my wife, Sue, and my children, Marc and Kimberlee, to whom I dedicate this labor of
love.

MICHAEL J. AUSTIN
School of Social Work
University of Washington
Seattle, Washington
April 1977

INTRODUCTION

The potential for conflict rests in the dilemma of modern professionalism, which is self-perpetuating and accountable only to itself,.but which today faces great pressure to give the poor a voice and a place in social service. This is a dilemma which all of us have to face, for without a change in the nature of professionalism the nonprofesssional new careers movement is in danger of being aborted. Without such a change the best that can be hoped for is the creation of a new caste of persons who, although employed, are still powerless, still rejected, still disenfranchised, and still resentful recipients of professional service. [1]

Part I

PARAPROFESSIONALISM - A BACKGROUND

Chapter 1

HISTORICAL ROOTS

For the past decade there has been a renewed interest in channeling new types of manpower into the human services.[1] The strategies for introducing new workers into agency staffing patterns have varied in style and intensity in different professions and occupations. In certain areas of the human services where expertise may not be clearly defined and socially sanctioned, the need for credentials has been called into question.

This attack on credentialism occurs at a time when the labor force as a whole is increasing its technological stratification. More and more skill is required for even the simplest jobs. Building maintenance men become stationary engineers. Garbagemen become sanitation workers. Former secretaries are executive assistants. In the human services, however, we find an opposite trend. In fact, many believe that much technological stratification is basically irrelevant. Lines of demarcation are blurring. When health aides make home visits they are working in the traditional domain of public health nurses. Case aides follow up on released hospital patients, formerly the role of the social worker. Information and referral specialists with no formal training carry out tasks traditionally reserved for community organizers and planners.

What do these developments imply? Are the skills that professionals once thought to be necessary really exaggerated? Can there be a division of labor in which a good deal of what professionals have been doing can be done by untrained paraprofessionals? Or is this an illustration of the phenomenon of political considerations taking precedent over professional domain? These questions will be explored in the light of what professionals and paraprofessionals think of each other's effectiveness in fulfilling their respective duties.

The attack upon credentialism in the human service field is based in part on the reality that many tasks which were traditionally the domain of professionals are being performed by untrained persons. The status of the professional has been further called into question as doubt has been cast on the ability of persons with middle-class backgrounds and traditional credentials to understand and serve the needs of lower-class people. For example, the social work profession has been forced to confront the issues of credentialism and social class bias as they watched and in some cases participated in the transformation of their clients into colleagues.

Health, education, and welfare programs have recently expanded their work forces to include new faces, in some cases their former consumers, the working and the nonworking poor. The largest number of newcomers is found in the work force of paraprofessionals. The paraprofessionals are those persons who tend to live in the areas of our cities needing the greatest improvement in human services, whether in the hospitals, schools, or social agencies. Some of the paraprofessionals have high school diplomas; some do not. Many are black people; some are not. Many of them have had personal experience with poverty, and the majority have come to recognize their extensive knowledge of their neighborhoods or communities.[2] Reawakened minority groups have contributed to this recognition, in which Black Power and Black Pride served as the rhetoric of change.

The period of the 1960s also represented a time of proliferating credentialism in the human services. The World War II baby boom had hit the campuses. More professionally trained people were entering the labor market than ever before. College credentials became the *sine qua non* in the human service sector of the economy. These developments coincided with the successes of the civil rights movement which contributed to a rising sense of social conscience among blacks and whites. A reverse psychology developed around academic qualifications; lack of academic credentials qualified the working poor for paraprofessional jobs.[3]

Because of this reverse psychology, many paraprofessionals gained entrance into the labor force of the human services by political means in spite of their lack of academic credentials. They soon began to feel engulfed by the demands of organizations and professionals.[4] At the same time that increased technological demands contributed to a greater demand for graduate degrees, the nation became aware of the vast numbers of disenfranchised persons, both black and white, and of the tide of the rising expectations of poor people to share economically and politically in our society.

There was pressure for a new division of labor to emerge in the human services. Traditionally, the administrative staff in an organization determined how tasks were to be subdivided into functional specializations. This mode of operation changed radically as both professionals and paraprofessionals began to define new roles and tasks in the division of labor by their actions. Old services were under attack as being insufficiently responsive to human needs, while new services were developing overnight.

As a result of these developments, the most committed, the indifferent, and, in some cases, the naive in the social work profession found themselves on the firing line supervising, training, and consulting with the new paraprofessionals. These social workers soon emerged as new specialists without roots.[5] It was soon discovered that supervising paraprofessionals was quite different from supervising other trained social workers. Issues of class, race, income level, and lifestyle became increasingly important.

In recent years social work education has undergone considerable change, change related in part to the pressure generated by the demonstrated abilities of untrained workers to perform social work tasks. The goals of graduate education are undergoing reassessment as the emergence of paraprofessionals and graduates of undergraduate social welfare programs add fuel to the debate over what constitutes professional practice. There is a drastic shift underway in the nature of professional education and therefore of the social work profession. The shift is related to the emergence of an ideological change: the relevance of professional training as the important and only ingredient of professional action has been questioned. Professional training is being affected by the belief that the client culture has become more relevant than ever before and that being indigenous to the population in need is a worthwhile quality. Similar attitudes are reflected in the changing membership requirements of the National Association of Social Workers, which in 1970 admitted workers with less than a master's degree for the first time.

With these trends in mind, it is important to put the phenomenon of paraprofessionalism into a historical perspective. The roots of social work practice can be traced to the period of paraprofessional activity preceeding formal university training programs. The study of the development of professions provides a useful context for analyzing the emergence of the contemporary paraprofessional. An outline of the paraprofessional roots of the social work profession serves as the basis for further analysis of the professional-paraprofessional relationship.

PROFESSIONALISM DEFINED

What is a profession? How does it differ from an occupation? How do professions relate to the division of labor in large organizations? What is involved in maintaining professions? These questions tend to reappear in the literature as writers attempt to understand people and their work. One of the earliest attempts at a definition was developed in 1915 when Flexner commented on social work and focused on the following criteria for professions:[6]

1. They involve essentially intellectual operations
2. They derive their raw materials from science and learning
3. They work up this raw material to a practical and definite end
4. They possess an educationally communicable technique
5. They tend toward self-organization
6. They are becoming increasingly altruistic in nature

Greenwood approached the study of professions by elaborating on five main attributes which an occupation seemed to require in order to be a profession: (1) a systematic body of theory; (2) authority over a clientele; (3) community sanction through support, licensing, and accrediting; (4) a code of ethics; and (5) a subculture reflecting unique values, norms, symbols, and language.[7] Other writers, such as Marshall, have stressed the less tangible aspects of a profession by noting that it is merely an idea based upon the real character of certain services, and that the major professions—law, medicine, and others—were products of circumstance.[8] The history of professions seen from this perspective could be described as the evolution of services carried out in an informal way by paraprofessionals into services performed in a formal way by specialists. These specialists have then been regarded as professional since their occupation has attained a special standing among occupations.

According to Hughes, one major contributor to a further understanding of professions, professions serve as a means by which men judge others and judge themselves.[9] There is a certain dynamism in the continuing efforts to professionalize an occupation. By studying the process of work, Hughes notes that the delegation of dirty work was part of the process of occupational mobility and thereby of professionalization. This ongoing process in the division of labor is characterized by the upgrading-downgrading phenomenon in which menial tasks are downgraded and more complex tasks are upgraded and moved into the realm of professional activity.[10] As Hughes notes, the division of labor implied interaction in which different tasks, whether professional or not, are parts of a whole accomplishment. The problems in resolving what is professional arise whether one is doing "for" or "to" people. A related issue is the problem of client vulnerability in which it is difficult to determine if a client is better served by a professional or a paraprofessional.

In an effort to resolve such problems, each profession using its own set of rationalizations attempts to select and socialize its prospective members, police its members through licensing and legislation, remain free of lay evaluation and control, and secure the necessary power, income, and prestige both to gain community sanction and to appeal to prospective members. As Goode points out, these activities are designed to institutionalize various role relationships between the professional and his society in order to prevent encroachment on the profession and to protect both the profession and the community from charlatans.[11]

In recent years the impact of technology and new knowledge on professions has resulted in the process of specialization.[12] New movements developing within professions seek special recognition. This process has exploded the myth ususally sold to the public of united, cohesive professions and has demonstrated that professions tend to be loose amalgamations of segmented coalitions. While this process of diversification goes on, it is interesting to note

the degree to which the professions maintain a unity of agreement on the issue of competence. Goode describes this process as both protecting the inept and protecting the profession from the inept in which "the inept create a 'floor,' a lowest permissible level of competence . . . . To some degree, the mediocre 'need' the really inept."[13]

The following discussion of the social work profession is designed to highlight the attributes of an occupation in the process of becoming a profession characterized by a predominance of females, service to the public, rising social status, increasing licensing and legal status, and a significant contribution of manpower to health, education, and welfare programs which together receive one of the largest segments of support from the federal budget.

HISTORICAL PERSPECTIVE

Social work has its roots in the industrialization era of the late 1800s and the concern of middle-class volunteers—"Lady Bountifuls"—for the poverty-stricken and the handicapped.[14] It was in the early 1900s that a concern for professionalism led to the development of university training, spurred by the Flexner report which highlighted the lack of a knowledge base for social work. Mary Richmond's *Social Diagnosis* was a major response to this push.[15]

The post-industrialization era prior to 1920 has been characterized as a period of social reform. It was this period, distinguished by society's concern for the poor, that provided the beginning phase of the social work profession. Lubove notes that:

> The professionalization of social work was associated not only with the quest for a differentiating skill, but also with the establishment of a subculture or community where members shared a group identity and values.[16]

The next era of professionalization, roughly 1920-1950, focused heavily on the teachings of Freud. It has been characterized as the clinical era, highly influenced by medicine and psychiatry. In the post-World War II era there was renewed interest in social reform and institutional change.[17] Social work literature reflects a recurring concern with instilling values, developing a knowledge base, and learning how to interrelate with other helping professions. In this sense, early in its development social work assumed a professional stance and has concerned itself since with solidifying that stance in the community of professions. Social work has also been characterized as one of the "socially oriented professions."[18]

Some social workers were recruited from universities and the church; others rose spontaneously from a community of humanely motivated citizens. The profession began with broad concern for problems of social institutions and economic organization. Lurie notes that:

> In social work the focus of concern has been the individual as a whole or at least the individual in his social setting, whereas in the other professions the focus has been on the concrete aspects of individual health, education, or legal relationships.[19]

With this background, social work has been charactized as: (1) an agency based profession; (2) a career that attracts upwardly striving lower class people; (3) a profession with lower status than medicine, law, and theology; (4) a profession which is committed to social change; (5) a specialty that is highly exposed to public scrutiny; and (6) a profession whose knowledge has been developed from experience, not from academic origins.[20] Social work developed out of societal needs for individual adjustment and for institutional change. The practice of social work was also closely tied to the democratic principles of individual dignity, freedom of speech, and the inalienable rights of individuals to choose and achieve their own destiny. [21] This attempt to combine practice and principles has been described as the attempt to "wed science and ethics."[22]

On review, the literature of social work's past reflects a blend of the historical and the idealistic approach.[23] The early preoccupation with values and the pursuit of a base of knowledge has been followed in. recent years by the return with increased vigor to its earlier commitment to institutional change.[24]

Since most social work was practiced in organizations, both large and small, assessment of the organizational factors affecting social workers can be examined in part in terms of the "supervision complex."[25] The constraints of bureaucracy and the push for specialization affected the practice of social work to such an extent that close supervision is perhaps more pervasive here than in any other profession.

Blau and Scott found that the supervision was primarily authoritarian and typified by: (1) constant checking with supervisor by subordinates; (2) unwillingness of subordinates to assume responsibility and initiative; (3) emphasis on the detached, formal role of supervisors, resulting in social distance from subordinates; (4) stress on following procedures; and (5) importance given to consistency of work patterns.[26]

In addition to these observations about a restrictive supervisory posture, it was found that the professional objectivity of supervisors was heavily influenced by the dependence and loyalty of subordinates.

As with prevalent organizational role behaviors, the interpersonal relations in social work are unique among professions. Social workers generally tend to interpret both colleague and client behavior in professional terms. This pattern is seen as a reflection of a "fledgling, self-conscious profession as well as an uncertain state of knowledge."[27]

Other interpersonal relations are viewed as part of professional behavior: (1) being aware of the limited competence of one's own specialty; (2) honoring the claims of other specialties; and (3) being ready to refer clients to more competent colleagues.[28] While these characteristics have contributed to solidifying a professional group and subculture, they have inhibited the exposure of professional operations and techniques for description and testing.[29] In addition to emphasis on proper interpersonal relations within the profession, social work has put equally strong emphasis on coordination with other professions.[30]

When viewing the personal attributes of social workers, it is important to note the self-critical strain that pervades social work practice. Professional problems, complaints, or mistakes are not aired in public. It might be hypothesized that increased professionalization comes primarily with in-group evaluation not subject to public scrutiny. This line of reasoning seems to hold true in the cases of medicine and law, which are considered "full" professions.[31]

The occupational identity of social work can be described as: (1) emotional neutrality; (2) impartiality; and (3) commitment to the service ideal.[32] However, despite these professionalizing traits, social workers experience certain role conflicts. Wilensky and Lebeaux comment on the conflict that arises between the agency and the profession primarily over the developing work standards and other norms that may deviate from those enforced by the agency. A second role conflict may exist between the social worker's humanitarian sentiments and the rules and regulations of a traditional agency, such as a public assistance agency or correctional facility.[33]

As compared with other professions, social workers also closely reflect the conformity found in the general society which leads to a general reluctance to pioneer and a striving toward professional respectability and social acceptance.[34] This reluctance was quite prevalent in the 1940s and has shifted to a somewhat less conforming stance in the 1960s. It has been hypothesized that conformity might be more readily assumed as a positive value by a profession in a minority position as a way of gaining greater status.[35]

The effects of the 1960s on the social work profession have come not only through developments in the world of scholarship, but through the impact of large federal programs devoted to health, education, and efforts against poverty. Efforts to strengthen the weakest element in the professional repertoire of the social worker—the knowledge base—have resulted in bridges being built to the various social sciences. This has been accompanied by a cautious awareness developed out of practical experience with the danger inherent in overselling the implications drawn from the underdeveloped state of the social sciences.[36]

THE ROLE OF WOMEN

In view of the rising interest in the liberation of women and of the predominance of females in the social work profession, it seems important to comment briefly on the history of the status of women in this country as it relates to the development of this profession. After being forced out of the economic process of the industrial revolution, middle- and upper-class women fought vigorously from approximately

1880-1920 to gain equality among the sexes. During this period "every professionally active woman felt herself to be continuously on trial."[37] There was much pseudoscientific comparison during this period producing such statements as that whereas men excelled in mechanics, women excelled in linguistics; and whereas men excelled in physical strength, women excelled in dexterity.[38] This phase of women's fight for equality ended with World War I. It was in this period of American history that the social work profession began to push vigorously for professional recognition.

Parallels can be drawn with the emergence of indigenous paraprofessionals during the intense civil rights campaigns of the 1960s. The civil rights movement of the late 1950s and early 1960s contributed not only to the enactment of the Economic Opportunity Act of 1964, which included funding for many paraprofessional jobs, but gave many minority group members the confidence to seek out and maintain human service positions.

After World War II, women had attained their political equality, and it was the strong lower- and middle-class females who began to enter careers in earnest. They had gained their right to education and their full rights of citizenship. It was at this time that combining family and career was first legitimized. This demonstration of strong conviction and commitment contributed to the further professionalization of social work, because many women entered professional practice while raising families.

*****

Like other emerging professions, social work has neither sufficient community sanction nor a sufficiently systematic body of theory to be considered a full profession at the level of medicine or the law. While medicine and law meet the first order critical functions demanded by society—maintaining life and maintaining law and justice, respectively—the social work profession tends to meet second order critical functions demanded by society—improved health and education, and adjustment of life's economic, social, and psychological stresses. While the definition of professions continues to fall short of precision and empirical validity[39]   and as the number of new professions increases annually,[40] it seems appropriate to conclude with a still timely comment by two of the early scholars in the sociology of professions, Carr-Saunders and Wilson:

> Professionalism has its problems of organization. It has its weaknesses and its dangers. But taking all in all the growth of professionalism is one of the hopeful features of the time. The approach to problems of social conduct and social policy under the guidance of a professional tradition-ally raises the ethical standards and widens the social out-look.

Despite the difficulty in establishing adequate definitions of professional practice, the social and physical needs of people continue to require our attention. Planning to meet those needs through the deployment of trained and untrained manpower is the focus of the next chapter.

Chapter 2

PROFESSIONALIZATION

AND MANPOWER PLANNING

Manpower planning for a profession like social work conjures up many different images for those concerned with the aspects of manpower supply and demand. For some, manpower planning requires a comprehensive view or a systems model which encompasses recruitment, training, utilization, and retention.[1] For others, it takes a highly rational form—the search for statistical data, interpretation, and the realignment of supplies with geographical or political demand.[2] However, manpower planning for a particular profession is only part of a larger manpower planning dilemma facing this country, a problem characterized by fragmentation of manpower information, plans, and programs at the federal, state, and local levels that is further exacerbated by the general ineffectiveness of the public employment service with its different jurisdictions.[3] Manpower planning is also complicated by the dramatic social shift from a goods production economy to a service economy resulting from recent technological innovations that make different manpower demands.[4]

BUREAUCRACY AND THE SERVICE ECONOMY

The social work profession finds itself operating primarily in "non-market bureaucracies."[5] This means that it is both difficult to quantify the raw materials and the end products, and that neither of them is subject to the economic market of competition among products. While recent efforts have been made to approach quantification through cost-benefits analysis,[6] the social work profession continues to face the dilemma of not knowing when manpower is actually well utilized.

The social work profession has both shaped and been shaped by the forces of bureaucratization. Social workers as a manpower pool might be characterized as "functionaries" in four distinct ways.[7] Howton notes that the functionary is an "organization man," in the sense noted by Whyte,[8] who is both *in* the organization and *of* the organization. Second, a functionary is ubiquitous, since organizations must act through commissioned agents mandated to seek organization efficiency. The functionary is prototypic and has become a pattern and mold for all occupations, an occupational type, and a symbol of the culture of modern society. Fourth, a functionary is an elitist, or a member of a select group, and has become the owner of the means to do things—for example, to care for the poor, the ill, the handicapped, and the disturbed.

The characterization of functionary merely highlights the organizational constraints laid upon social work manpower. The logical extension of this characterization is found in the irony that "a man who does well in his line of work is rewarded by being compelled to leave it, to move up into a higher occupation (or echelon) and this is precisely how functionaries are recruited."[9] This evolution, which aptly applies to social work, produces continuous manpower vacancies at the lower levels of its service delivery system.

It is the element of service delivery that raises questions about the very nature of a service economy. While the social work profession has always operated in the service sector, the overall service economy has grown to the point where two out of every three workers in the United States work in the service sector rather than in the goods-producing sector. Ginzberg characterizes the service economy in the following way:

1. It tends to use more highly trained people than the industrial sector
2. Access to education and training become crucial
3. Rapid technological progress leads to rapid skill obsolescence
4. Pace of change requires training for more than entry level jobs
5. It has a high proprotion of women with special characteristics (different attachment to work; part-time, enter-leave-return attachment to work)
6. It is under-represented by trade unions
7. It has generally low wages, poor working conditions, and a limited range of fringe benefits[10]

The organizational constraints of bureaucratization and the overall nature of the service economy provide a background for a closer look at professionalization and newism as key elements of manpower planning related to the social work profession.

PROFESSIONALIZATION

It has only been in the period since World War II that serious attention has been given to the problems of social work manpower. The social work manpower shortages of the 1950s and early 1960s are reflected in the 1965 national social work manpower study and in the 1964 conference on researching manpower issues in social work.[11] These systematic efforts to lend validity to the nature and extent of manpower problems in social work also tend to reflect two significant postwar trends, the rise of the "employee society" and the rise of professional ideologies.[12]

While the social work profession has traditionally been based in organizations, both large and small, it is only in the past several decades of rapid technological change that the society as a whole has become an employee society. The decline of small business and the reduction of manpower needs in agriculture have contributed to this shift. It may be hypothesized that this shift toward an employee society has helped increase awareness in the social work profession of the importance of understanding the organizational context of an individual's work and life stress. What has been neglected is an understanding of the extent to which the very nature of organizational life has affected social work as a profession.[13]

The rise of professional ideologies has also been a feature of the postwar period. Bensman and Rosenberg highlight this development and note:

> Prestige, power, and income are claimed by and granted to those specialized groups whose spokesmen manage to convince a large number of people that they are functionally indispensable. Professional ideologies, seeking recognition and domination on the basis of skill and efficiency, have come to the fore. As spcecialization increases, so do professional ideologies, and the ensuing clamor is so considerable that most of their claims are drowned in noise.[14]

The noise in this case is caused in large part by those human service professions deeply immersed in professionalizing their occupation in order to recruit candidates and secure their knowledge base in legitimate practice.[15] The essence of "functional indispensability" appears to be a cry for superior efficiency, and it is this ideal of efficiency in service delivery and manpower utilization which seems to be the ideological key to large-scale organizations in an employee society.

In the context of the trends towards an employee society and increased professionalization ideologizing, it is only recently that recognition has been given to the social work profession's vested interest in establishing its own functional indispensability and to the significant conflict which the profession.[16] The nature of this conflict, whether or not it is clearly perceived, makes effective utilization of manpower still more difficult. As some have suggested, social work manpower policy ought to view the profession as one of the objects of its policy.[17] In approaching manpower policy, such questions need to be raised as whether the definition of present professional function is valid, whether there should be a different balance between professional and paraprofessional responsibility than is currently conceived, or if the present balance best achieves the overall purposes of our service system.[18]

Assessment of effective manpower utilization raises serious questions in relation to what we know about the human behavior of professionals. Clark and Wilson have noted that few professionals give up their tasks willingly, not being eager to end an activity that rewards them, no matter now routine it may be—perhaps, indeed, because it is routine and easily carried out.[19] Gurin has recently reaffirmed the well-established notion that occupational groups, when first approaching full professional status, are particularly jealous of their claims to specialized knowledge, societal mandate, and esoteric skills. He equates the vitality of such occupational groups with those social movements which have difficulty tolerating certain forms of innovation or deviance.[20]

The process of professionalization can be viewed from many different perspectives. It can be analyzed internally in terms of recruitment, training, standards, and membership, or externally in terms of organizational factors, relationships with other professions, and manpower allocation.[21] It is the manpower utilization approach that constitutes the focus of the remainder of the chapter. The introduction of paraprofessional personnel into the human services will be analyzed in the next section in the context of newism, keeping in mind an observation by Mencher:

> The history of social work, even in periods of manpower consciousness, has demonstrated a continuous displacement of nonprofessionals and at best a grudging delegation of inconsequential function.[22]

NEWISM AND THE PARAPROFESSIONAL

The concept of newism evolved out of Eaton's study of the introduction of group therapy techniques into the California prison system.[23] As a concept it has several elements that can be applied to the introduction of paraprofessionals into the human service industry, namely innovation and belief, validation, combating organizational ritualism, and the self-fulfilling prophecy. Newism is defined as the presumption that new developments of practices are superior to those not quite as new.

In the case of paraprofessionals, a new manpower pool was defined primarily in conjunction with the innovations of the War on Poverty programs, and a belief was promulgated that poor people with backgrounds similar—economic, ethnic, social, or whatever—to those of recipients or potential recipients of social welfare services ought to be hired to serve such target populations.[24] This belief, because it was new and had few connections with the past, generated a faith that services would greatly improve, a faith that tended to support the period of experimentation. This belief contributed to the atmosphere of experimentation by helping to make the experiment acceptable, if not necessarily effective, and enhanced the status of those involved, both professionals and paraprofessionals. The belief of improved services fit in with the cultural norm of a society which strongly endorsed experimental innovations.

The contribution of paraprofessionals received newistic validation. Their efforts to serve the target populations were relatively visible and, in the context of innovation, were seen as effective. So in place of concrete validation, their effectiveness was validated by the newistic phenomenon; if it is new, it must be good. Such validation drew upon the uniqueness of the situation, since no real solutions had been generated by the professionals working on poverty, illness, delinquency, and other problems. Since nothing else was seen as effective, an atmosphere of innovation promoted the idea that paraprofessionals were worth employing. As Eaton suggests, the status quo is evaluated negatively, and novelty is presumed to indicate validity.

The experiment also became an antidote to organizational ritualism. It became more difficult for persons to defend vested interests from the demand that alternate ways of getting the job done be considered. The introduction of a new manpower pool encouraged organizational flexibility, which is antithetical to the predisposition in any group, and particularly in bureaucratic organization, which tries to stabilize traditional relationships. The paraprofessionals used lines of communication to convey grievances which differed from traditionally perceived patterns. By door-to-door canvassing, they surfaced many unmet client needs which had not come to the attention of existing agencies. Not only did they affect the procedures of their own agencies, they also affected the service delivery patterns of other agencies.[25]

Finally, the workings of a self-fulfilling prophecy also apply to this newistic example. The introduction of paraprofessionals involved an ideology which encouraged change. The concept of self-fulfilling prophecy, on the other hand, postulates that if an ideology is espoused almost totally, its propositions will in fact become true, or manifest themselves in actuality. Since a high proportion of the early workers in the War on Poverty, both professional and para-professional, evidenced "believing minds" rather than "scientific minds," the groundwork was laid for fulfillment of the newistic prophecy that paraprofessionals in service to their own kind could substantially alleviate the social problems plaguing one-fifth of our population. The "scientific minds" have shown that this prophecy is not necessarily true, and other unanticipated consequences have been documented.[26]

The concept of newism has significant implications for manpower planning. In the light of organizational and professional resistance to change and the strong attachment to tradition, it appears that approaches to manpower planning should take newism into account as a basic ingredient in any strategy for change.

Underlying the newism concept is the commitment to experiment and change which is highlighted in the federal study on social work manpower:

> Without concomitant and drastic overhauling of the social welfare structure, including systems of job classification and methods of administration and provisions of services, the manpower gap will not be closed. . . . New methods of administration and provision of services must be devised to utilize social work auxilliary and technical personnel as members of a team in order that the available social work manpower may be used to the greatest effect.[27]

MANPOWER PLANNING AND SOCIAL PLANNING

The "planning" component of manpower planning is the primary focus of this final section. Planning has different meanings for different people. The literature on general manpower planning emphasizes the need for highly rational, systematic approaches which rely heavily on adequate data collection. The literature on social welfare manpower planning, going beyond this quest for sound data, is more concerned with decision-making in regard to social welfare policy (governmental and private), administrative policy, professional policy, and educational policy.[28]

Basic to a discussion of manpower planning seems to be the trilogy of supply, demand, and need. The problems related to the extensive slippage that occurs in statements using these three concepts is noted by David:

> *Need* represents expressions of social aspirations of expectations; *demand* represents descriptions of labor-market situations; and *supply* represents requirements of manpower and other resources for satisfying needs at a given level under unspecified conditions.[29]

These definitions demonstrate the difficulty in truly understanding what constitutes a manpower shortage. However, the concept of need appears to be more relevant to nonprofit human service sectors than are the concepts of supply and demand. The human service sector is highly value-laden and is oriented toward professional judgment; the notion of need, though not a formalized concept is useful in understanding the roadblocks to manpower planning. Boulding notes that a man's *demand* for medical care is what he wants; his *need* for medical care is what the doctor thinks he ought to have.[30] While such distinctions are more easily made in the medical field than in socal work, the notion of need seems to have relevance for both administrative policy and the interests of the social work profession.

In dealing with the interests of a professional, one returns to the notion of "functional indispensability." In the context of planning, Kahn suggests that such a notion is a "strategic myth" requiring the special attention of manpower planners.[31] He notes that it is quite normal for professionals to have a perception of their own indispensability and implies that effective manpower planning requires one to selectively ignore such perceptions. Kahn also suggests that manpower planners need to be alert to the characteristics of professions and of their bureaucracies, alert to the relationship of specialization to efficiency in establishing staffing policies, and alert to service requirements, work rules, and union contracts.

The reason for stressing the role of the planner is to highlight both the importance of the planning *process* in manpower deployment and the assumption that "an imaginative manpower planning process may become a major force for change in a total field of service."[32] If these are not understood, manpower planning can easily go the route of other planning efforts, producing a carefully drawn plan which cannot be implemented.

This leads to a need for a clear understanding of the intentions cited for manpower planning. Planning can evolve (1) out of the special interests of a profession and its training institutions; (2) out of administrative expedients of organization; and (3) from a mandate from the legislative and governing bodies which set the social welfare policies and fund the resulting programs. One of these approaches or a combination of them will be required by the increased range and level of demand for services; "the population is, indeed, developing a higher standard of receiving."[33]

The established fields of nursing and medicine together have evolved manpower plans to meet growing medical needs and to respond to technological innovations. The growth rate in those fields is symptomatic of what may take place in such other human service professions as education and social work:

> In 1900, there was one health worker for each physician, or one for every 380 people. By 1964, the ratio was 13 health workers for each physician, or one for every 66 people. It has been predicted that the health industry, which is now the third largest in the nation, will in 1975 be the largest in the United States and at that time it is expected that there will be between 20 and 25 supportive health personnel for each physician.[34]

The possibility of adding one million workers to the human service fields requires extensive planning in the differential use of manpower.[35] The implications of this possibility for research and for educational policy makers will be noted in later chapters.

In the light of social work professionalization and the newistic introduction of paraprofessional personnel, it seems apparent that we have another example in the manpower field of the tendency to think and act in a piecemeal fashion. New programs have been started for particular groups, and temporary remedies developed at the expense of long-range manpower solutions. Manpower planning takes on additional significance as noted by Lester:

> We live in a job economy. Less than 15 per cent of the nation's work force are self-employed. The rest are job holders and job-seekers. Paid employment supplies most of their income and occupies most of their days. Hence preparing for work, securing employment, and moving up occupational ladders are matters of crucial importance to the American people.[36]

He notes the lack of coordinated planning at the federal level where there is little relationship between the development of employment policy—regarding demand—and of manpower policy—regarding supply. If one adopts the concept of "disjointed incrementalism," in which social policies evolve on a haphazard and additive basis, the general nature of manpower planning in this country becomes self-evident.[37]

It is clear that the manpower available to deliver social services has expanded significantly with the arrival of paraprofessionals. What is not clear is the extent to which increasing caseloads and the demand for services have neutralized the added benefit of paraprofessional manpower to service programs. Furthermore, we still lack empirical evidence of how paraprofessionals have improved the quality of services. But it is clearly the belief of many people that social services have improved as a result of paraprofessional involvement.

Chapter 3

PARAPROFESSIONALS:

FROM CLIENT TO COLLEAGUE

Paraprofessionals and professionals both contributed to and were engulfed by the service turmoil of the 1960s.[1] Each group was to have its own unique reaction. Paraprofessionals soon found themselves experiencing a type of psychic stretch. They were recruited, trained hurriedly, if at all, and told to help both the agencies and their clients unscramble the web of human needs and misery. They were selected on the basis of such characteristics as low income, race, and sex. They were expected to possess competence on the basis of their political connections and their knowledge of the low-income community and the agencies serving that community. Their return to their neighborhoods as salaried members of the establishment produced considerable personal strain. While they returned in roles which enabled them to help their neighbors, they also became suspect. The emotional strength and the specific skills necessary to handle unusually complicated human conditions were in short supply.

They were pulled both by the demands of the agency and the demands of the community. They were not professionally trained and soon began to suffer under the degrading title of "nonprofessionals." As project moneys began to disappear, they found that they were truly the last hired and the first fired. Out of all these tensions, job security and advancement became the flag to rally around. Whereas they were hired as their brothers' keepers, they soon found that the realities of organizational life required them to look out for themselves. As part of the phenomenon of being pulled in two different directions at the same time, paraprofessionals were being rewarded for their compliance with the norms of an agency at the same time that they were being rewarded for their deviance. In this case, deviance took the form of criticizing the agency, questioning various practices, and generally calling into question the goals and objectives of the services they were being asked to deliver.

THE IDENTITY CRISIS

While paraprofessionals were experiencing this psychic stretch, the trained social workers were experiencing an occupational stretch resulting in an analogous identity crisis.[3] Their professional competence was being openly questioned. As far as the paraprofessionals were concerned, they were performing functions similar to those of the professionals and were receiving less pay. This type of in-house attack upon professional competence was certainly a new experience for most trained social workers. Criticism of the social work profession was keen within the rank and file of the profession. Criticism—somewhat less intense—had emanated from other professions and sometimes from the public, but this was the first time that so many people in the same agencies with little or no training had questioned social work competence.

The on-the-job questioning of competence was complemented by similar questioning of the knowledge base of social work. Like the paraprofessionals, the professionals were forced to find new modes of accommodation. Many of the idealistic social workers who took part in the early days of paraprofessional involvement either left their jobs or were forced out. Others stayed on to weather the storm, and still others arrived on the scene after the major storms of disenchantment.

The experiences related to the impact of paraprofessionals upon the professional social workers had only received limited attention.[4] Several earlier studies focused primarily on the capacities and capabilities of the paraprofessional. The literature fails to address such questions as:

1. What is the nature of the interaction between professionals and paraprofessionals?
2. What kind of people are involved in this interaction?
3. How do they work together?
4. Under what organizational conditions do they work?
5. What is the paraprofessional looking for in his relationship with the professional?
6. Can it be assumed that competence in the practice of social work methods—for example, casework, group work, community work—is synonymous with competence in supervising paraprofessionals?

In addition to analyzing the professional-paraprofessional relationship as a social-psychological phenomenon in organizational life, it is equally important to place the relationship in a context larger than the particular organizations in which the interactions take place. Both professionals and paraprofessionals can be viewed as part of an emerging social movement that might, in a sense, be called a professional social movement in which the technologies used in human service delivery are under attack and are being slowly replaced through experimentation with new modes of service delivery.

The combined efforts of professionals and paraprofessionals resemble attributes of a social movement, as evidenced throughout the country by the almost religious fervor with which paraprofessionals were recruited. The momentum behind hiring paraprofessionals has led some to the simplistic perception that hiring paraprofessionals is good and not hiring them is bad. The result is two conflicting reactions to the use of paraprofessionals: "How could we ever have done without them," and "What are we to do with them?" Grosser has suggested that

> the new careers movement, as this phenomenon (the use of nonprofessional personnel) has been designated, has, in our view, inflated a useful and relevant, albeit limited, strategy to the grandiose status of a social movement.[5]

There are difficulties in defining the use of paraprofessionals as part of a social movement; however, the popularity of using paraprofessionals in social service agencies reflects rising expectations in both professionals and paraprofessionals about the improvement of services that would transform the traditional service workers in bureaucratic organizations into a social movement of persons who would provide relevant and necessary client services.

There were some distinct ideological strains that accounted for the readiness of agencies to welcome paraprofessionals. Many human services agencies had been staffed primarily by whites. The rise of black militancy and the demand that blacks be allowed to serve their own helped to open the door for blacks to assume staff jobs. Other minority groups benefited from this thrust. There developed an unspoken assumption that agencies needed workers who could identify more closely with the needs of clients and who had a working knowledge of low-income neighborhoods. This led to the emphasis on low-income status, race, and sex as the selection criteria.

The professionals did not react to this movement as labor unions might have done. At least overtly they accepted the idea without the feeling of competition. At the start, paraprofessionals simply wanted to enter the agency with the idea of serving their community. They did not overtly state an ideology that professionals are not needed to deliver human services. They simply said that if you want professionals working in the community rendering services, paraprofessionals must be employed as well. Since the professionals were often overworked and could use the extra hand, there was an accommodation.

THE EMERGING SOCIAL MOVEMENT

Though literature is extensive in the fields of religious and political social movements,[6] very limited application of social movement theory has been made to human service reform. Notable exceptions can be found in Eaton's work on correctional reform in California[7] and Moynihan's analysis of the Anti-Poverty program.[8] Both authors focus their discussions on the professionalization of reform. The image of social reform inspired by the Poverty Program underlies much of the literature on paraprofessionals and professionals as participants in a social movement. As Moynihan notes,

> The war on poverty was not declared at the behest of the poor: it was declared in their interests by persons confident of their own judgment in such matters.[9]

Concepts applied to the professional-paraprofessional relationship require specific definitions. First of all, the term "social movement" refers to the emergence of an ideology and an organization. It is ideology combined with an organization that produces the momentum behind a social movement.[10] The organizational aspects of professionals and paraprofessionals as partners in an emerging social movement prove to be crucial. It was through extensive federal funding that paraprofessionals were introduced to the human service sector—for example, Head Start, Day Care, Family Service, and Neighborhood Service. This infusion of money through local community action programs helped to spawn a loose network of programs employing paraprofessionals.

Imbedded in the notion of democratic social reform was the idea that the poor ought to be allowed to help themselves. This was given impetus when it was discovered in the early days of the poverty program that even those institutions that claimed to serve the poor were failing, and that many more institutions which should have been doing so were not. Consequently the rhetoric of anti-poverty community action was predicated on the assertion that the poor were capable of working in and changing the institutions which should have been serving them and were not doing so.

How does one assess the emergence of paraprofessionalism as a social movement? Eaton has suggested six phases through which a professional social movement tends to develop.[11] These include crisis, incubation period, initiation, institutionalization, formalism and decay, and reorganization.

With regard to paraprofessionals, the crisis developed around the rediscovery of poverty in America and the subsequent focus on the substandard delivery of human services.[12] It was assumed that paraprofessionals, among others, could improve the level of human services. It is important to note that the technology for improving human services had not yet been developed. As Eaton notes,

> In a scientific reform movement, the crisis always involves complex uncertainties about the state of knowledge. . . . Widespread recognition of the existence of a crisis mobilizes public support favorable to change.[13]

The uncertainties were manifested as serious questioning of the relevance of traditional social service knowledge in generating competent practice, uncertainty about real paraprofessional competence, and continuing questions from the society at large regarding the inability of human service workers to solve expanding social problems.

The incubation period of the Federal Poverty Program was marked by chaos, confusion, and determination. The chaos and confusion resulted from the problems of mounting a national program quickly and within the intentionally wide latitude for experimentation permitted by the legislation. This latitude stemmed from the enthusiastic desire of leadership in the Kennedy administration to attack the roots of poverty and promote institutional change. One of the major vehicles for change was the local Community Action Program; it was under its auspices that the paraprofessionals gained prominence.

The third, or initiation, phase of paraprofessionalism was accompanied by the hiring of paraprofessionals primarily in family service programs, neighborhood service programs, and preschool programs. Professionals in these programs generally viewed the addition of paraprofessionals with optimism. Eaton notes in this regard:

> While anything new implies that there is a possibility of making a significant discovery, there also is intellectual acceptance of the prospect that the innovative program may fail to accomplish its purpose. This intellectual awareness of the possibility of failure is not tantamount to its emotional acceptance. In every scientific social movement, the innovations which are proposed are characterized by a hope that they work.[14]

The fourth phase of an emerging social movement is a settling-in process. This phase involved the use of and adaptation to paraprofessionals, though, at different times, agencies throughout the country experienced this phase. Some programs began using paraprofessionals soon after Congress passed the 1964 Economic Opportunity Act. It is speculated that most agencies and programs with more than five years experience of employing paraprofessionals have reached the institutional phase, however the retrenchment of funding human service programs in the 1970s has threatened the jobs of many paraprofessionals.

THE BEGINNINGS OF INSTITUTIONALIZATION

It was not long after the passage of the 1964 Economic Opportunity Act that studies of the effectiveness of paraprofessional personnel began to appear.[15] Most of the research focused on the exceptional success with which paraprofessionals were able to function. Very little attention was devoted to the role of the professional.

As with other scientific social movements, research was undertaken "to displace newness with evidence of validity as the basis for continued acceptance of the idea" that paraprofessionals and professionals are evolving new relationships with clients and other agencies that meet human needs.[16] Later chapters reflect an effort to move beyond the newness phenomenon to point out implications for future manpower planning, professional and paraprofessional education, and areas of further research.

The last two phases of a scientific social movement, formalism-decay and reorganzation, cannot be developed in relation to this movement at this time for several reasons. First, the idea that the efforts of professionals and paraprofessionals to deliver human services represent something akin to a social movement has emerged only recently. There has not been sufficient time either for a state of formalism or decay to have been reached or to come to the conclusion that no movement ever really existed. While some programs involving professionals and paraprofessionals have become formalized as a result of being shifted from poverty project money to agency hard money, it would be premature to assume any widespread formalism; nor have we reached the historical perspective from which to document the features of a social movement.[17] Eaton states another reason:

> Formalism and decay are minimized in scientific reform movements because there is a commitment to weigh issues, at least in part, on the basis of scientific knowledge. The scientific credo that all knowledge is only approximate serves as an antidote to the entrenchment of a formalism in a scientific social movement.[18]

There are similar reasons for not devoting major attention to the reorganization phase. Reorganization is taking place all the time, making it difficult to assess accurately whether a true social movement has passed into history or has become a permanent feature of the human services.

Part II

BUILDING CAREER OPPORTUNITIES

Chapter 4

PARAPROFESSIONAL

UTILIZATION ISSUES

ROBERT J. TEARE

In preceding chapters we have traced some of the events and philosophies leading up to the increased use of paraprofessional workers in the United States. The underlying philosophy has changed in character since the early 1960s. For one thing, the use of paraprofessionals is no longer viewed as merely a stop-gap measure or a temporary evil in which the best is made of a bad situation. Many planners and educators seem finally to have abandoned the notion that someday all social and human service workers will have a traditional terminal degree. Furthermore, much has been said about indigenous workers and the positive contribution they can make   to   the human services by virtue of their unique background characteristics. Additional momentum has been given to the paraprofessional movement by the assertion that under certain conditions therapeutic benefits accrue to the worker by virtue of his being part of the helping process. Finally, as we have discussed earlier, thoughtful questions have been raised about the relevance of traditional professional training and education. Many of these questions have centered around the notions of professionalism, credentialism, and the relationship between education and employment effectiveness.[1]

MANPOWER UTILIZATION MOTIVES

The evolving character of paraprofessionalism has given rise to a confusing situation. The forces generated over the past decade have resulted in a potpourri of motives which purport to explain the use of paraprofessional workers. Because these motives have profound implications for the selection, training, placement, and evaluation of such workers, any confusion associated with them needs to be cleared up. Although the paraprofessional literature is extensive, few writers , with the exception of Grosser[2] and Katan[3], have focused directly on the objectives and motives underlying paraprofessional employment.

Solving the Manpower Shortage—Motive 1

After reviewing the literature on paraprofessionalism, one receives a strong impression that the impetus to use the paraprofessional stems from a desire on the part of various professions to solve the problems created by a severe shortage of skilled manpower in social work and in other branches of the human services. Earlier, we discussed the difficulties of truly understanding what constitutes a manpower shortage in the social welfare field. The general literature on paraprofessionalism is of little help in this regard, since it contains many inconsistencies regarding the nature and magnitude of the shortage. Chester[4] has asserted that a manpower shortage permeates the entire human services field. Illustrative summaries of manpower needs in the various professions can be found throughout the general literature. The details of these manpower estimates and the inconsistencies associated with them need not be recapitulated here, despite the fact that the topic of manpower shortage has probably had more space devoted to it than anything in the literature. An excellent treatment of this topic can be found in a summary by Katzell et al.[5] To explain paraprofessionalism in terms of the single motive of the desire to solve a manpower shortage would be a gross oversimplification.

Provision of Employment—Motive 2

Given the historical visibility of a manpower shortage in social work and the human services and the chronic unemployment in certain segments of society, a solution to the predicament seems obvious: use social work and other components of the human services to provide jobs for the poor and the chronically unemployed. This objective can be found as both an implicit and an explicit thrust behind much of the legislation discussed in various sections of this book. This objective seems simple, but it turns out to be extremely difficult to implement effectively as a manpower strategy. Ferman has done an excellent job of documenting the problems associated with this type of job development.[6] Even this simple concept of job development has been made more complex in recent years. Attached to the employment motive is the New Careers philosophy, which emphasizes continuous employment and advancement opportunities. Providing social and human services jobs to the unemployed is thus no longer a simple objective. Depending upon one's point of view, providing employment in the human services can be seen as an end in itself or as only a means for providing access to the occupational mainstream of society.

Increasing the Efficiency of Services—Motive 3

With such a legacy of concern over the shortage of skilled manpower, social work and other disciplines have long searched for an ideal strategy for utilizing professional personnel. This search has resembled the approaches taken by business and industrial organizations in that it has concentrated on the development of rationales for dividing the labor between professionals and paraprofessionals.

The motive behind better utilization strategies is a meaningful one; much of what professionals currently do might well be done by persons with less training and/or skill. The development of job assignments and staffing patterns that would free the professional to carry out appropriate activities would go a long way toward relieving the bottlenecks in service and making the service delivery system much more efficient. This theme is much in evidence in some of the earlier—1960-1965—paraprofessional literature in social work.[7]

Implementing this objective assumes that a meaningful and acceptable rationale has been found for allocating the work to be done in the field. At this writing, no single framework exists. Reviews of work on this topic indicate that much effort has been expended and several frameworks have been formulated.[8] At present, experimental evidence upon which one might make a choice is either inconclusive or nonexistent. There are some who claim that such differentiation is inherently impossible.[9] Suffice it to say that this motive—the efficient use of differentially skilled personnel—represents a third major thrust behind the movement to use paraprofessionals. Its successful implementation requires the solution of a host of formidable technical problems. Some of these will be discussed in subsequent chapters and highlighted in the case study in Part III of this book.

Increasing the Effectiveness of Services—Motive 4

The most heated rhetoric about the need for paraprofessionals has centered around arguments that there are many clients whose needs are no longer met by social services.[10] The explanations take a variety of forms. Some have contended that the process of extended education often brings about undesirable changes that impede an individual's ability to respond to client needs.[11] Some have stressed the barriers to class distance between helper and client.[12] Others have laid the problem at the doorstep of professional autonomy.[13] Still others have stressed the waste and inefficiencies of the service delivery systems.[14] Thus, it would seem, the lack of service effectiveness has many causes.

Whatever the causes may be, a frequent response to the situation has been a cry for relevance. A common theme of the various mechanisms put forward to achieve this greater relevance has been a call for increased client participation in both the planning and delivery of services. This, unlike the three motives discussed earlier, is based on the premise that all or many of the present social service delivery systems are incapable of meeting client needs. It is further assumed that neither insights into these deficiencies nor the means to overcome them can come from sources other than the client population. It is this motivation and these assumptions that resulted in the Economic Opportunities Act (EOA) of 1964 and the host of New Careers legislation that followed it.[15]

Provision of Therapeutic Work Experience—Motive 5

Having its origins in the fields of mental illness, drug abuse, and alcoholism, this paraprofessional employment motive draws heavily on the "helper therapy" principle elaborated by Riessman.[16] The principle has two basic assumptions: (1)

placing individuals with problems in helping roles will initially result in therapeutic benefits for them; and (2) as these
benefits are realized, they will become more effective workers and have a positive impact on the client. The evidence to
support this principle is quite limited and, for the most part,
impressionistic. Perhaps because of the limited data and the
lack of clearly analogous situations in the social service area,
this objective has not received attention comparable to that
of other motives for utilization.

BENEFICIARIES OF PARAPROFESSIONALISM

As we have just seen, the motives behind the movement to
develop paraprofessional workers in social work and in other
fields of the human services represent a blend of altruism,
pragmatics, social justice, and politics. All of these motives—
and perhaps others—are present in the movement, but they
are emphasized differently by the various groups responsible
for the shape and direction of paraprofessionalism. Persons
speaking from the viewpoint of various professional organizations seem to place an emphasis on altruism and social
justice. They focus on the shortage of traditionally trained
workers—professionals—and search for scientifically based
and clinically meaningful strategies for dividing the labor.
They wish to make full use of the capabilities of scarce
professional manpower resources.

An examination of the literature dealing with many of the
publicly funded work preparation programs—with the exception of the EOA legislation—reveals an emphasis on the
objectives implied by the second motive. Here the purpose
seems to be to open up the social service field whenever
possible as an area of employment for the poor and the
chronically unemployed. Finally, if one studies the writings
of those associated with the New Careers philosophy, it is
immediately apparent that they place an emphasis on the

fourth and fifth objectives. Their writings, more than any others, question the viability of the traditional social service methods and models and argue for the unique contributions that can be made by the indigenous worker toward improving the conditions of clients.[17] They question the current division of labor but not on the grounds of efficiency. They argue—with some justification—that current manpower schemes prevent certain roles from being carried out and are thus impediments to meeting client needs. They further contend that present utilization mechanisms tend to isolate lower level entry positions and prevent them from leading to viable career ladders because of credential barriers.

When these motives are separated from one another and viewed from the vantage points of their advocates, it becomes clear that they are intended by their very nature to be of differential benefit to the various parties who are affected by the nature of service delivery systems—the professions, agencies and organizations, paraprofessionals, clients, and the general public.

Katan analyzed paraprofessional manpower motives from the standpoint of their beneficiaries.[18] He examined the theoretical content of these motives and, using rational criteria, tried to assess who would gain most from their implementation. We have summarized the results of his most interesting analysis in Table 1.[19]

The table highlights an observation made in the preceding section. There seem to be three major patterns of beneficiaries: those who profit most from motives (1) and (3), those who benefit from (4) and (5), and those who stand to gain from motive (2).

We should thus find three major constituencies for paraprofessionalism. As we have already suggested, this is actually the case. One group is drawn from the discipline and professions which must train and staff the organizations charged with serving the clients. These are the constituents for whom motives (1) and (3) will have the most payoff and consequently the greatest appeal. As we stated earlier, historically much of the writing generated by these groups has emphasized the manpower shortage and the need to develop formal models of task differentiation designed to free the professional from duties for which his skills are not required. Most of these writings have emphasized the useful but subordinate role the paraprofessional would play.

Table 1   Paraprofessional Motives and Beneficiaries

Motives	Various Beneficiaries				
	Professions	Organizations	Paraprofessionals	Clients	Public
1. Deal with manpower shortage	xxx	xx		x	
2. Cope with unemployment by providing jobs		x		xx	xxx
3. Increase service efficiency	xx	xxx		x	
4. Increase service effectiveness			xx	xxx	x
5. Provide therapeutic work experiences		xx		xx	x

xxx Primary Beneficiary   xx Second Beneficiary
  x Tertiary Beneficiary

The second constituency is the public at large—the tax-payer. This group, unaware of the technical difficulties involved and concerned about the increasing tax burden of welfare and social service systems, is most receptive to motive (2). To them it offers the promise of a reduction in unemployment and a decrease in the number of people who are on welfare. When one looks at the wording of much of the legislation surrounding work preparation programs—for example, Manpower Development and Training Act, Work Incentive Program, and Public Service Career Program—the emphasis on this theme is obvious.

The third major constituency is the paraprofessional and the client groups from which they are drawn. Writings centered on motives (4) and (5), which are of major benefit to these groups, stress the need to change service systems through client-paraprofessional participation in order to make them more relevant and effective. As typified in the New Careers literature, emphasis is placed not just on the need to create entry jobs—as would be done with motive (2)—but on the need to modify personnel systems so that these entry jobs would lead to viable career ladders. It places emphasis on the autonomous role of the paraprofessional and the reduction of the psychic stretch in progressing from client to colleague.

If this analysis does little else, it should help to explain why paraprofessionalism has attained such momentum in recent years. When its beneficiaries are identified, it becomes abundantly clear that there's something in it for just about everyone. Yet the question remains why a movement with such a potentially broad base of appeal should have so much controversy associated with it. In a review of the motives and their associated beneficiaries, there seem to be at least six reasons for so many unresolved issues:

1. Such a mixture of motives and potential target groups is quite likely to generate a population of

paraprofessional workers that is diverse in background and, depending on job situations, oriented toward different and possibly conflicting employment expectations.

2. As one examines beneficiaries, the person least likely to benefit is the paraprofessional. Paraprofessionals benefit only when they are permitted the autonomy to make changes and are provided with career opportunities to truly become colleagues of the professional workers.

3. A good many technical problems need to be solved before viable models involving the differential utilization of staff can be developed. An illustration of this is the need to develop an acceptable rationale for the assignment of tasks to workers.

4. The various motives make different assumptions about the need to change the systems themselves before progress can be made. Whenever systems— organizational structure, types of services, curricula, merit classifications—are challenged, controversy results.

5. Given limited resources, not all objectives can be implemented at the same time. Whenever priorities must be assigned, some things are always done at the expense of others.

6. Implementing these various objectives requires the use of fundamentally different job and manpower development methods. These methods will generally result in different job patterns for paraprofessionals, and these differences inevitably lead to debate.

Many of these issues will receive further attention, particularly those involving job roles and expectations, paraprofessional and professional adjustments, and the administrative task of job definition, assignment, training, and career development. Before proceeding further, however, it is important that we become somewhat better acquainted with the paraprofessional worker.

CHARACTERISTICS OF PARAPROFESSIONAL WORKERS

There are paraprofessionals in many fields of the human services—for example, education, corrections, rehabilitation, mental health. In this analysis, primary attention is given to those workers in the general field of social work and the provision of social services. This includes the broader range of paraprofessional social welfare activities carried out under a variety of social welfare programs as described by Lynton.[20]

Definition of Terms

Because the motives behind the paraprofessional movement are mixed, the names given to paraprofessional workers are quite varied. Our examination of the literature has revealed a variety of such terms as "nonprofessional," "preprofessional," "subprofessional," "paraprofessional," "indigenous nonprofessional," "new careerist," "ubiquitous nonprofessional," and many others. The motives behind the choice of term seem to be mixed. A particular name may be selected in order to:

1. Highlight or emphasize the way in which such workers should be used
2. Match the terminology specified in a piece of legislation in order to become eligible for program support
3. Reflect an obscure meaning and thereby offend the fewest number of people

The term "paraprofessional" seems to be the most frequently used at the present time. For us, the term refers to any individual, male or female, who lacks the traditional credentials—of either education or experience—for social work and social welfare jobs. In the field of social work, the absence of traditional education credentials is defined as anyone with less than a baccalaureate degree.[21] As a population, we are focusing primarily on those persons who are employed in public and private agencies in which the delivery of social welfare services is an important but not always the primary mission of the organization.

Numbers of Paraprofessionals

Any attempt to make an accurate count of the number of paraprofessional workers existing at any point in time is a frustrating and largely unrewarding task. There are several reasons for this. First of all, there is the problem of terminology. As noted earlier, a wide array of terms has been used to denote paraprofessionals. No standard definition of the paraprofessional in the human services field has been agreed upon, and none seems to be in the offing. The absence of standardized language greatly impedes interpretation of the enumerations that are available because one is never sure of the criteria used in making the counts. Second, when figures are given, they are often cumulative totals of paraprofessionals who have gone through various training programs or who have been employed in various settings. This is like taking a census by counting all the people who have ever lived in a particular place. It is not that the numbers are inaccurate; they are just not very helpful in estimating the current size of a given population. Finally, the administrative machinery surrounding paraprofessionalism complicates the problem. As indicated in earlier chapters, the legislative impetus to paraprofessionalism achieved peak momentum in the middle to late 1960s. Since then, the movement has been influenced by one hundred separate grant-in-aid programs authorized under thirty-five different Acts of Congress and administered by eight federal departments and agencies.[22] This apparatus understandably results in considerable fragmentation of available information.

Despite these difficulties, it is possible to make some rough estimates of the number of paraprofessionals at work in the social service field. At the present time, paraprofessionals are likely to be entering social service work under one of the following primary legislative mechanisms:

1. The Harris Amendment to the Social Security Act, which requires public welfare agencies to include in their state plans provisions for the employment of former clients as paraprofessional workers

2. The War on Poverty legislative program (the 1964 Economic Opportunities Act and the subsequent— 1966, 1967, 1969—amendments)

3. One of a number of other legislative programs—for example, in housing, education, and corrections— which create social service positions in a variety of organizational settings.

Estimates of paraprofessional participation in each of these areas have varied widely over time. Survey data about paraprofessionals hired under the Harris Amendment were gathered in 1970.[23] These data indicated that 10,547 paraprofessionals were employed by public welfare agencies as of March, 1970. No more recent data are available at this writing. At the height of the New Careers movement (1968-1970), estimates were given that over 250,000 paraprofessionals had found employment through the EOA Title V work experience programs.[24] Later data published by the University Research Corporation tempered these figures somewhat.[25] It is estimated that between 1967 and 1970, 20,000 trainees had gone through 115 New Careers projects funded under the Scheuer Amendment to the Economic Opportunities Act. Of these, about 10 percent—or 2,000 people—were classified as being in social services training programs. Accurate data on other programs and mechanisms—for example, in housing, corrections—simply do not exist. Since these mechanisms are diffuse and the OEO apparatus has been considerably altered, it is quite probable that these secondary—non-OEO—sources may constitute a far larger entry pipeline into paraprofessional social services in the 1970s than it did in the 1960s.

As can be seen, data on numbers of paraprofessionals are hard to come by. Based on projections from past data, we estimate that we are talking about a population ranging in numbers somewhere between 15,000 and 40,000 people. These are paraprofessionals who deliver social services to people despite the absence of traditional training and preparation. It should be remembered that this group is but a small segment of workers within a larger network of human services. The total population of paraprofessionals, though not accurately known at this time, is obviously much larger. In focusing on the problems and adjustments of those who are working within the social services framework, some of our observations can be generalized, especially regarding the occupational and organizational forces that surround the larger population of paraprofessionals.

General Characteristics of Paraprofessionals

While estimates of the numbers of paraprofessionals are difficult to find, studies that contain information about demographic characteristics of paraprofessionals are in somewhat better supply.[26] Based on a sample of twenty-two studies written between 1966 and 1970 covering a population of 19,570 paraprofessional workers and trainees, a number of accurate statements about general population characteristics can be made.[27]

It is abundantly clear from the data that the paraprofessional worker in social services is predominately female. Three explanations seem to account for this. First of all, most of the legislation propelling the paraprofessional movement was directed toward disadvantaged, low-income people. A good number of these are former public assistance recipients. Since many paraprofessional programs draw from AFDC rolls, for example, there is a greater likelihood of making initial contact with female heads of households than with males. Second, as we have discussed in the earlier chapters of this book, the social welfare field has historically been entered more frequently by women than by men. Finally, the limited data available on dropouts from paraprofessional programs suggest that males may be more likely to leave paraprofessional training programs than females.[28]

It is also clear that the paraprofessional is most likely to be a member of a racial or ethnic minority group. This results primarily from the fact that paraprofessionalism has largely been an urban phenomenon meeting the interests of the disadvantaged person with a limited range of employment opportunities. Blacks predominate, but it is not an exclusively black movement. Preliminary data from the studies surveyed indicate that geographic differences in racial and ethnic composition are already clearly evident. Paraprofessional entry appears, therefore, to be more a matter of economics than of race. Other clear demographic patterns of relatively low socioeconomic status and limited educational opportunities are evident.

Conclusion

As we look back on the antecedents of the paraprofessional movement, we see an exotic blend of deep commitment, technical and administrative ineptness, and opportunism. The motives are mixed and the problems are many, but despite the illusion, much about what we have viewed is not really new. We are dealing with an emerging social service labor force that is largely female. These persons are entering the social service field because they are a part of a class that has been forced out of an economic process which has been changing the country from a predominantly industrial to a service society. At the moment, they are searching for a way to convert their experiences into a knowledge base. The parallels with topics discussed in Part I—for example, the roots of social work practice, the role of women, and the early stages of professionalization—are quite striking. Para-professionals are certainly not the Lady Bountifuls of the late 1880s, but they do have more in common with that group than meets the eye.

Chapter 5

PARAPROFESSIONAL
JOB ACTIVITIES

ROBERT J. TEARE

In the previous chapter, we focused on the ways in which the motives and objectives for paraprofessional utilization were different from one another. One fundamental difference is that their implementation requires basically different methods of job construction. Many of the paraprofessional jobs we will illustrate in this chapter result from two basic job construction methods that we will discuss in some detail.

JOB FACTORING

If one is concerned about the need for provisional services and the shortage of people to provide them, emphasis must be placed on manpower strategies that are quickly implemented and have immediate payoff. These same strategies are necessary for quick relief from the pressures of unemployment in various sectors of society. The objectives of solving the manpower shortage and providing employment place a premium on job construction techniques that will produce more jobs quickly. Given this need for quick results, a typical response has been to use job factoring as described by Fine[1] and elaborated upon by Teare and McPheeters.[2] Job factoring has been a traditional way of constructing jobs in the industrial and business sector of the economy. It owes its origins in the United States to the concept of scientific management, as it evolved in the early 1900s.

Job factoring starts with a base of tasks as they are currently divided among various jobs. Its objective is to take those tasks, break them up or factor them into homogeneous clusters, and create jobs from the various clusters.[3] In service fields—for example, social work—it is assumed that the lower level or less difficult tasks can be assigned to less skillful workers and serve as the basis for paraprofessional positions. From the professionals' point of view, this method of job construction provides "task relief."[4] It relieves them of tasks for which their specific, high-level training is not required. Insofar as task relief is achieved, this method can also increase service efficiency.

From this discussion, it is clear that the method has some real advantages. On the positive side:

1. Jobs can be quickly and logically developed.
2. Specific standards of performance can be easily defined.
3. Since the jobs are homogeneous, training times can be shortened appreciably.
4. The procedure does not usually result in jobs that cut across traditional boundaries and is therefore not particularly threatening to those professionals who may wish to preserve established areas of expertise.

In short, job factoring is a useful technique that can quickly relieve shortages, deal with unemployment, and, potentially, result in considerable operational efficiency. Since it generally increases specialization, it has all the advantages that have historically been ascribed to that phenomenon. As we have stated, it has been the method most talked about by those who speak from the perspective of the disciplines and professions in the social welfare field.

Lest it be seen as a panacea, its disadvantages need to be looked at as well. On the negative side:

1. Given the homogeneity of the resulting jobs, there is a tendency for the tasks to be repetitious and, in all likelihood, boring and monotonous.
2. The procedure can aggravate status differences between jobs and widen rather than narrow the gap between professionals and paraprofessionals.
3. Without opportunities for staff development—for example, in-service training, academic leave—the jobs that are constructed can quickly become low-status, dead end positions.

It is to these real weaknesses of job factoring that the advocates of the New Careers approach have turned their attention. As Gartner has correctly pointed out, paraprofessional workers initially require a range of supportive services and will eventually require access to adequate training and educational credentials.[5] Without these, the job-factoring method as a long-range paraprofessional manpower strategy leaves a great deal to be desired.

THE DEVELOPMENTAL METHOD

Perhaps the most fundamental shortcoming of job factoring is that it does not deal with the objective of increasing the relevance and effectiveness of services, the fourth manpower motive we described earlier. In job factoring, jobs are constructed from an existing array of tasks. Thus it would be rare that new services would emerge from the process. Consequently, if client needs are not being met by the existing service system, the jobs constructed by factoring are no more likely to be relevant to the needs of clients. In fact, the resulting specialization and fractionalization may actually reduce the likelihood that the needs of the client will be served.

An alternative approach, the developmental method addresses itself more to these questions. This method, when applied to the social services field, looks first at the needs of the public to be served, making two basic assumptions as described by Fine:

1. Jobs in the professions come into being in response either to the needs of the public or to the problems of the profession.
2. Public needs are usually broader than the purview of professions that attempt to respond to them, and periodically the match between needs and coverage should be evaluated.[6]

The developmental method focuses initially on needs and problems rather than on existing jobs. Once these needs have been defined and categorized, the next step is to infer those tasks that are most likely to meet those needs or solve those problems. Existing tasks that are linked to obsolete needs are deleted, and only tasks perceived as still relevant are retained. It is basic to the developmental method to be little concerned initially with traditional boundaries between jobs, particularly with respect to professional and paraprofessional activities. Once an array of tasks, old and new, has been defined, they are grouped into clusters of activity around which jobs for both professionals and paraprofessionals can be constructed.

Various rationales for clustering tasks and making work assignments will be discussed in later sections of this chapter.

The most important asset of the developmental method is its emphasis on relevance and effectiveness. Since this process assumes that existing tasks may not be meeting present needs, it is far more likely to produce new kinds of jobs or services than is job factoring. Conversely, if existing activities no longer seem relevant, they may be deleted from the purview of the professions. Since activities are not initially reviewed within the framework of existing jobs, the tasks derived by this method have no inherent organization which relates to existing divisions of labor. Consequently, if job boundaries need to be expanded or contracted, if services need to be reallocated, or if structural changes need to be made in organizations, job development has potentially greater flexibility. It can be quickly seen that this method has a much greater likelihood than job factoring of achieving motive (4), the desire to increase service effectiveness. Also, since tasks can be combined with considerable flexibility, it is possible to construct jobs with tasks which will have therapeutic benefits for their incumbents. This is an essential feature for achieving motive (5), the desire to provide therapeutic work experiences.

The developmental method is no panacea either. It is more complicated than job factoring to carry out. This makes it more time-consuming and its products less immediately available. Furthermore, it assumes the participation of several levels of organizational personnel as well as clients in identifying needs and problems. Candid interactions of this kind are difficult to achieve and, when attained, are not likely to be placid. Finally, as we shall show in other sections of this book—particularly in Part III—the introduction of paraprofessionals into an organization requires a process of mutual adaptation. A method which permits free traffic across professional-paraprofessional job boundaries will be threatening to anyone, professional or paraprofessional, who wishes to protect his or her terrain.

In the discussion above we have related the major paraprofessional utilization motives to two job construction methods—job factoring and job development. These are the basic methods by which one can develop the content of jobs that will be carried out by paraprofessional workers. These methods are quite different in their assumptions and approaches.

Job factoring is best suited where the objectives for political or technical reasons are short-range results and an increase in the number of jobs that can be made available. It has some built-in efficiencies which, in the long run, can turn into impediments. The method protects professional boundaries and makes few, if any, assumptions about the relevance and effectiveness of present services. It has great appeal for decision-makers who view problems from the standpoint of the professions and the existing service delivery systems.

Job development is a far more difficult and cumbersome technique. It is not designed to increase the number of jobs. It is more concerned with the alignment of jobs to service needs. It places greatest emphasis on new job content and new service functions. It unfreezes traditional job boundaries by systematically ignoring them, and when applied with maximum vigor can be used to change the very structure of the service delivery system. In various forms, it has had great appeal for policy makers who view problems from the perspective of the clients and the paraprofessionals.

METHODS OF ASSIGNING JOBS TO WORKERS

The job construction methods described above are rarely referred to by name in the literature. They seem to be seldom recognized as explicit tactics for implementing paraprofessional manpower utilization strategies. As we have seen, however, the use of one or the other may have profound effects on how jobs and tasks are assigned to workers. To understand paraprofessional utilization it is essential to know the process of job construction, the theories and the methods by which the labor is now divided in the social welfare field. Let us turn to a discussion of that process.

Any discussion of frameworks for making work assignments on a differential basis ought to begin by describing the device which is probably used most frequently, the simple procedure of "underfilling" positions. Its use in the social welfare field has been described by Denham and Shatz.[7] This is not really a work assignment or placement strategy in a technical sense. No theory underlies it. In a situation where the need for highly trained personnel far exceeds the supply, underfilling is simply the pragmatic response of filling positions with persons who may not have the requisite skills at the time the tasks are assigned to them. In the paraprofessional field this usually means filling "professional" positions with paraprofessional workers. More often than not, one simply hopes for the best and provides whatever on-the-job training can be made available. In a good many instances, the new workers perform surprisingly well. Because of the random nature of the procedure, success is very difficult to duplicate and build into a permanent personnel utilization scheme. It is worth mentioning, however, because it is used so frequently. Furthermore, as we examine the inherent complexities of alternative frameworks, the simplicity of underfill will take on a certain seductive appeal.

The comments that follow include a discussion of the frameworks described in the social welfare literature drawing heavily on the work of Barker and Briggs. Both their earlier writings,[8] which resulted in an excellent evaluative review of the literature, and their later work[9] were done in association with the planning of staffing patterns in a hospital setting.

CASE UNIT METHOD OF DIFFERENTIATION.   This rationale, described by Finestone,[10] focuses on the "case"—or client—as the basic unit for making assignments. The caseload of an agency is reviewed in terms of individual cases. The severity and the difficulty of each case are evaluated and assignments are made to staff members on the basis of this evaluation. Clients with severe problems are assigned to a fully trained professional worker who performs all the tasks necessary to meet the needs of the client. Clients with less severe problems are assigned to less than fully trained personnel—paraprofessionals—who are also responsible for performing all necessary tasks.

The implicit assumption behind such a strategy is that all the activities involved in working with clients with severe problems requires a professional's skills and knowledge while none of those skills are required in tasks associated with clients whose problems are less severe. Since many cases involve multi-problem clients, such a clear differentiation of skill requirements is usually not feasible. While it has the advantage of giving the client a single worker to whom he can relate, the method usually ends up underutilizing the professional and overutilizing the paraprofessional. This under- and overutilization can usually be reduced somewhat by factoring conceptually different tasks—for example, clerical activities—out of the case activities and differentiating problem severity only with respect to the clinical aspects of cases. This is a modified version of job factoring, usually applied to clerical, eligibility, and administrative tasks, and is a fairly common practice among large public social service agencies which have enough staff to permit specialization by problem area.

TASK UNIT METHOD OF DIFFERENTIATION.   This method, also described by Finestone,[11] focuses on tasks as the basis for making personnel assignments. As a first step, the services rendered by an agency are evaluated for the complexity of the tasks associated with them.[12] Clients seeking services are then evaluated to determine which tasks must be performed to meet their needs. Complex tasks requiring a high measure of skill or training are assigned to a fully trained professional. Less complex tasks requiring less training are assigned to other workers—for example, paraprofessionals. This technique is, of course, simply job factoring under a different name. In addition to task differentiation, however, it requires that workers be differentiated on the basis of their abilities. This requires a fairly precise knowledge of the skills of all staff members—a virtual impossibility in large agencies. Furthermore, tasks tend to cluster together, and sometimes the range of complexity in these clusters is fairly broad. Thus, unless task differentiation takes the form of minute specialization, its effect will be that professionals will still be underutilized at times and paraprofessionals will occasionally be taxed beyond their skills.

VULNERABILITY/AUTONOMY.   Richan has proposed another approach, one based on the notions of client vulnerability and worker autonomy.[13] Vulnerability refers to the degree to which a client is susceptible to harm resulting from the fact that the worker may not have built-in social work values, knowledges, and skills. Worker autonomy relates to the degree to which a worker is able to function independent of supervision. Richan would blend these two notions into a strategy of task assignment. Clients who are judged to be highly vulnerable are assigned to fully trained professionals. Clients with low vulnerability would be assigned to less highly trained personnel—for example, paraprofessionals. Where services can be delivered according to specific guides—manuals, checklists—the paraprofessional would also be assigned.

Of course, this method begs the question of how client vulnerability will be determined. In many other respects, it really is a strategy involving the case unit of differentiation and has the inherent difficulties noted earlier.

THE EPISODE OF SERVICE.   Barker and Briggs[14] formally advocate a strategy of work assignments which they call the "episode of service." In their method, one begins by formulating typologies for groups of clients. Agency goals for each group of clients are determined, then evaluated according to the (1) range of methods needed to deliver the appropriate services, (2) ability of the agency staff to perform these methods, and (3) needs of the clients. Teams of staff members are formed to carry out units of activities or "episodes of service" that may or may not cut across a number of client groups. The fulfillment of agency goals depends on each group successfully completing its episode of service.

This strategy attempts to achieve more flexibility in assignments by focusing on clusters of activity and utilizing a team of workers with different skills. There is still the familiar problem of developing typologies of clients who have similar problems or needs. It does, however, make a formalized attempt to develop a staffing pattern based in part on the needs of the client. In this regard, it incorporates some aspects of the developmental method. The Barker and Briggs strategy was formulated in a hospital setting; it reflects the flavor of the medical tradition of "staffing" a patient. When this procedure is transferred to a social service setting, it carries with it problems of determining team leadership and of coordinating the teams' relationship to the client. In addition, it seems to conjure up an institutional setting where a fair degree of control can be maintained over the flow of clients and the range of services offered. Such is typically not the case in most decentralized social service settings.

OTHER STRATEGIES.   Anderson and Dockhorn also focus on assignment of work to paraprofessionals on the basis of tasks.[15] They specify the criteria by which tasks could be assigned by indicating that appropriate tasks for paraprofessionals are those that (1) can be screened first by professionals, (2) are within a range of skills that can be taught in a short in-service training program, (3) are repetitive in terms of approach, and (4) lend themselves to a prescription of method before action begins.

Teare and McPheeters,[16] in developing a set of roles and functions for social welfare paraprofessionals, indicate that tasks can be grouped and work assigned on the bases of the (1) the client being served (the case); (2) the objectives or purposes of the activities; (3) the skill level of the workers; (4) the task similarities (task differentiation); and (5) the logistics of the work setting. In essence, they simply reflect an awareness that each of these aspects at one time or another may need to be used as a basis for staffing assignments. They give primary emphasis to the blend of task similarities and objectives and through various clusters of roles they defined a range of jobs that paraprofessionals might assume.[17]

It can be seen from this overview that a fair amount of thought has been given to formulating methods of developing paraprofessional work assignments. As we stated in the preceding chapter, the technical criteria by which to choose an optimum staffing pattern are far from being well established. Much of what has been proposed up to now has been based on rational rather than empirical criteria. Highly specific research on task definitions, client risks, task complexity, and worker skill requirements is required before definitive guidelines can be given to agency decision makers. The beginnings of such research, illustrated with case material, are discussed in subsequent chapters.

The methods for dividing the labor have been mainly reductionistic in approach in that they have taken existing services and tasks and broken them up into smaller units. As such, they rarely go beyond the range of existing agency services—or the capacity of the agency to deliver them—and they have an implicit emphasis on job factoring. The usual result is that work is assigned to paraprofessionals so as to provide task relief to professionals and to lighten the burdens and stresses of social service organizational life.

THE NATURE OF PARAPROFESSIONAL ACTIVITIES

Much of the early writing dealing with the duties and tasks of social welfare paraprofessionals has a cautious and conservative flavor. In the early 1960s paraprofessionalism was a new and not quite legitimate effort designed to deal with the emerging problems of expanding services and staff shortages in the field. As the movement gained legitimacy, the flavor of the writing changed. As the decade progressed, the expressed scope of the paraprofessionals' responsiblities were expanded, and published material became more specific about the nature of their duties. It must be stated, however, that most of what is contained in the published literature of that period dealt more with the need for such workers than with specific formulations of their tasks. As we summarize the limited material dealing specifically with the paraprofessional utilization, we will concern ourselves with the few frameworks that have been proposed for describing the roles and tasks that paraprofessionals can carry out.

In 1962 a subcommittee of the National Association of Social Workers published a monograph about the use of paraprofessionals. Focusing on the concept of a case aide, it stated that (1) the primary purpose of an aide is to relieve· professional staff of responsibilities that do not require their skill; (2) an aide should be used only in conjunction with trained staff; and (3) it is dangerous to generalize about what case aides should do since clients' needs must be examined individually.[18] Another section of the document advocated the idea that approaches to using paraprofessionals should isolate the task as the key variable for formulating jobs and give less importance to the nature of the clientele and the agency situation.

In 1965, the Department of Health, Education, and Welfare (HEW) published guidelines for planning jobs and careers for auxiliary staff in public welfare. The principal purpose of such staff was to augment the ongoing work of the agency. The focus of such work was to be on specialized tasks. These guidelines, however, expanded on the somewhat narrower "task relief" philosophy implied by the earlier NASW document. Four functional levels were recommended:

1. *Administrative Aide*—a group of related tasks that are essentially administrative and clerical in nature but are parts of the social worker's job. The major function of personnel is to provide direct services to the social work staff.

2. *Research and Statistical Assistant*—an administrative assistant position that requires a higher type of responsibility and judgment.

3. *Household Helper and Homemaker*—tasks involving service to clients in their own home so as to facilitate the client's movements about the community. These are routine, time-limited tasks performed under the client's supervision.

4. *Neighborhood Worker*—a group of tasks that are designed to help individuals and families make use of public welfare services through the use of informal contacts in neighborhoods.

These recommended functions incorporated the traditional "task relief" dimensions in the descriptions of the first two functional levels. They did, however, include a second stream of activities to be performed outside of the agency setting that would be far less subordinated to the activities of professionals. The last two roles began to resemble—or perhaps reflect—the thinking that was associated with the New Careers philosophy as it existed at that time.

The most articulate spokesman for New Careers, Reiff and Riessman, characterized two major roles for paraprofessionals.[19] One role extended the influence of the professional worker and thereby made use of the "task relief" principle. The functions associated with this role reduced the burden on the professional and reflected agency values, attitudes, and objectives. The second role, which was to become the more visible of the two, was conceived as an extension of the client and the community. In this role, the activities of the workers and their personal characteristics become inseparable. These people, the indigenous worker,[20] did what they did because of who they were. Their essential value was their capacity to act as a bridge between the agency and the client group. Implicit in the bridge concept was the proposition that their indigenousness would give them a unique ability to communicate across class lines. Reiff and Riessman envisioned a strategy that would be "a created unity between the skilled specialist from the helping professions and trained workers from the groups being helped."[21]

It was the spirit behind this grassroots involvement of people that made it so compatible with the Economic Opportunities legislation and its subsequent amendments. Partly by design and partly due to timing, the New Careers philosophy became the manpower utilization strategy of the War on Poverty. It was to be the vehicle by which client participation, community action, and system change were to take place. This philosophy had a profound impact on the shape and direction of new careerist activities until the late 1960s.

Through the influence of the anti poverty legislation, new careerists and indigenous workers became closely associated with community action agencies and other soft money programs. New careerists became the link between the agency and the clients. They served as interpreters of client needs. They were asked to develop and deliver new services. In short, they began to function in fairly autonomous capacities.

Subsequent frameworks for utilization reflected some of this diversity. In 1965, Otis[22] defined three major modes of use for auxiliary personnel. They were the:

1. *Nonprofessional*—involves the performance of clerical, mechanical, maintenance, and generally routine tasks. These functions make it possible for the professional to have more time for his professional duties.

2. *Subprofessional*—involves functioning as an assistant to the professional and performing tasks that are a reallocation of the professional role. These tasks involve help in filling out forms, determination of simple eligibility requirements, carrying cases in a supportive manner, and the provision of simple, well-defined services. These activities increase the delivery of the simpler functions traditionally assigned to professionals.

3. *New Careerist*—involves carrying out functions which have not been performed or have been poorly performed by the professional staff because of their "middle-class" background. These functions capitalize on the "lower-class" status of the individual worker.

This framework again reflects a dual stream of paraprofessional utilization. One mode is subordinated to the professionals and is designed to relieve them from the burden of unrelated—for example, clerical—or simple service responsibilities. The other mode, more autonomous than the first, is obviously in line with the Reiff and Riessman framework.

The later work in the New Careers area began to reflect concern over the fact that role descriptions for indigenous paraprofessionals were not enough. It was recognized that even though the workers were permitted to carry out the functions for which their backgrounds were ideally suited, further adjustments had to be made in personnel systems. Elston's work typified this approach.[23] She called for a basic realignment of staffing patterns. Her general strategy advocated:

1. New kinds of workers (indigenous) carrying out new kinds of services (the job development thrust).

2. An examination and restructuring of professional assignments.

3. The use of professional-paraprofessional teams rather than a staffing pattern predicated on rigid hierarchical structures.

4. A range of supportive services to help new workers adjust and develop adaptive skills to the world of work.

5. Greater opportunities and incentives (education, training) for upward and horizontal mobility.[24]

Larson, et al.[25] provided a framework for expanded New Careerist functions that still holds as a fairly good current depiction of this type of utilization pattern. They talked about three major functional objectives for paraprofessionals. These involved: (1) influencing points of view, (2) therapeutic activities, and (3) service roles.

Under "influencing point of view" they placed the activities associated with orienting clients and serving as a bridge. "Orienting" refers to the worker's attempts to increase the client's awareness of issues and problems confronting him in the community. The bridge functions involve a variety of linkage activities. Of central importance is the agency's attitude toward letting the worker interpret the needs of the community for the agency. It was hoped that professionals would listen to ideas about activities and services that should be carried out by the agency.

Under "therapeutic activities" are included the notions of support, helping, and intervention. The "supportive role" involves listening to clients' problems, accompanying them to job interviews to provide moral support, and generally providing friendship in times of stress. The "helping role" requires more specific knowledge on the part of the worker, who provides advice on such matters as comparative shopping, legal rights, and eligibility for services and financial assistance. The "interventive role" is the most complex of the therapeutic functions. This involves establishing a relationship with a client or his family for the purpose of assisting the professional in counseling. It was felt that the paraprofessional would have an easier time gaining rapport with the client and would be more sensitive to his reactions to counseling.

The "service functions" include the role of expediter, outreach worker, and developer. The expediter performs routine clerical, mechanical, and personal duties when these are part of a necessary team effort. Outreach personnel are charged with going out into the community to seek the "hard core" or "delinquent-prone" who are not likely to come to the agencies on their own. These workers recruit for employment programs and work with teen gangs on the streets. The developer is primarily concerned with attempting to secure employement for clients. He or she represents the agency in conversations with firms and organizations which need personnel. In many instances, actual job placement and follow up are seen as part of the role.

In 1970, Teare and McPheeters published a monograph outlining roles that paraprofessionals in social welfare might play.[26] The monograph, based on a series of symposia using the developmental method, was an attempt to broaden even further the "bandwidth" of paraprofessional utilization. The authors recommended twelve roles: outreach, brokerage, advocating, evaluating, teaching, behavior changing, mobilizing, consulting, community planning, care giving, data managing, and administration. The monograph suggested that these roles not be viewed as rigid components but as elements from which various jobs might be constructed. The authors presented a set of guidelines for the development of paraprofessional positions based on various blends of these roles. In later chapters of this book, we will examine the model and the utility of these roles in suggesting curricular and staffing approaches.

In this chapter, we have focused on the literature that deals with the utilization and work activities of social welfare paraprofessionals. A variety of frameworks have been proposed for utilization. They contain a range of terms and roles, but it is possible to detect some similarities. Two themes run through them and reflect the evolution of paraprofessional utilization. The first is a notion of task relief, which frees the professional for duties suited to his training. This is historically the older theme and reflects the early emphasis on manpower shortages and the convenience of job factoring as a job construction technique. This mode emphasizes a high degree of prescription and close supervision by professionals.

The second theme, which emerged later, reflects the input of the New Careers philosophy. Stressing the uniqueness of paraprofessionals and using job development as its major method of job construction, it emphasizes autonomy and relatively high discretion in paraprofessional activity. It relates most closely to the need to make services more relevant and effective. These two themes characterize the major thrusts of utilization at the present time. How these varying themes of paraprofessionalism have impact on training, integration into agency structure, and career development is a major concern in the remaining chapters of this book.

Chapter 6

PARAPROFESSIONALS

AS ADULT LEARNERS

There has been relatively little systematic research on the impact of paraprofessionals and professionals on each other and the process by which professionals and paraprofessionals make accommodations to each other in organizational settings. Some have suggested that the professional-paraprofessional relationship represents an "approach-avoidance" situation in which there may be both advantages and disadvantages to maintaining a work relationship.[1]

Early and somewhat contradictory impressions of this relationship led to the belief that (1) paraprofessionals enhanced the superior status of professionals; (2) paraprofessionals sought guidance from professionals, who responded anxiously with doubts that the paraprofessional's expectations could be met; (3) paraprofessionals were urged to assume as much responsibility as possible in order to relieve professionals; (4) paraprofessionals' independence narrowed the gap in status between themselves and professionals leading to the reluctance of professionals to give up accustomed duties; and (5) paraprofessionals' frustrations increased as they began to act like "professionals," but their status and salary remained unchanged. While many of these issues are addressed in Part III, it is necessary first to take an organizational view of the professional-paraprofessional relationship and the implications for staff development.

The unique aspects of the professional-paraprofessional relationship represents a departure from the traditional supervisor-supervisee relationship. The traditional view includes managerial control and downward communication on the part of the supervisor, and subservience, passivity, and compliance on the part of the supervisee. This traditional relationship was seriously threatened and, as a result, modified by the dynamic and fluid nature of programs carried out under the War on Poverty. New relationships between staff and consumers required new accommodations to the traditional supervisor-supervisee relationship. It was· replaced, in part, by a new colleague relationship.

While traditional communication patterns continued to operate, the professional, as supervisor conveying organizational demands downward to the paraprofessional as supervisee, was confronted by paraprofessionals who began to send messages back up from the chain of command. These messages included a desire for a different supervior-supervisee relationship, increased autonomy based on the paraprofessionals' community expertise, a greater recognition of life experiences in contrast to traditional credentials, and a role in the policy formulation process which affected agency operations. One of the more significant results of the pressure generated by paraprofessionals was a redefinition of their training needs and a new approach to them as adult learners. Similarly, as will be noted in the next chapter, professionals began to recognize their own needs as adult learners.

As paraprofessionals received increasing legitimation, the social services were faced with growing demands for career mobility and effective staff development programs. It has frequently been suggested that "if the 'paraprofessional' revolution is to create more than jobs, if it is to develop genuine careers for the poor, moving them up the ladder, step by step, authentic training is the key."[2] Traditionally, staff development programs for both the entry level worker and paraprofessionals focus on orienting the worker to a specific job function. Relatively few attempts have been made to provide comprehensive training programs that will move beyond initial orientation of the worker to the agency. There have been few efforts directed toward developing generic training that would provide the worker with skills and knowledge basic to effective work in a variety of human service fields. Thus, if the entry level worker is ever to achieve the goal of a "genuine career," training at this level will require considerable attention.[3]

Although the paraprofessional is a relatively recent addition to the social services, the literature is replete with suggestions and recommendations for specialized content that should be included in paraprofessional training programs. Though training paraprofessionals has probably received the most attention from various New Careers organizations, community colleges and various federal and state governmental agencies are also responding to their training needs.

A selective review of training programs conducted in health, education, and welfare agencies reveals that most of these agencies emphasize orienting the paraprofessional to the employing agency and developing knowledge and skills that will allow the worker to function efficiently in that agency. With few exceptions, training programs do not attempt to develop skills and knowledge that will be transferable to a variety of human service fields. For a variety of reasons, many of the programs that have recently emerged at the community college level also tend to offer specialized curricula, with the result that their graduates are only qualified to work in a limited sector of the human services—for example, mental health technology, corrections, and child care.

Yet there is a recent trend toward providing generic training at the entry level including the knowledge and skills that have been found common to effective work in all human service fields. The University Research Corporation has suggested that training at the entry level should progress from generic training in the human services to specialized training in the fields of health, social services, and other related fields, and finally to specialized job training. A training manual prepared for beginning workers in Social and Rehabilitation Services of HEW also advocates training in generic content areas for all beginning workers prior to specialized job training. The California community college system has developed an associate degree in the social services based on a generic approach to establish learning experiences that will prepare the student both for immediate employment in a variety of fields and for continuing education opportunities. Finally, many of the Public Service Careers training programs are beginning to provide a core of common learning experiences for the entry level human service worker.[4]

However, at the present time, most training for the entry level worker stresses the development of agency-specific knowledge and skills. More often than not, the content of this training reflects the service approach of a particular specialized sector of the human services, with relatively little attention being given to relating this training to the rest of the human services. A new training model is needed that will meet the demands of workers for career mobility and effective staff development programs. Before discussing such a model, it is important to identify some of the assumptions about the paraprofessional as an adult learner as well as the assumptions inherent in the design of training programs.

THE MEANING OF ANDRAGOGY

Adult trainees can be approached from a different theoretical perspective than that usually taken with children. Theories of pedagogy, from the Greek meaning "child leading," are quite different from theories of *andragogy*, meaning "man leading." Training adult human service workers thus requires a full understanding of the factors relating to adult learning theory. In many situations paraprofessional human service workers with high school diplomas or less are likely to have had poor learning experiences with traditional school and classroom situations.

Knowles has indicated that there are some crucial characteristics of adult learners that render them significantly different from child learners. These are:

1. *Mature Self-concept:* The adult is an independent personalality who is self-directing.

2. E*xperience:* The adult, by virtue of having lived longer, has had greater and more varied experiences that can serve his learning frame of reference.

3. *Readiness to Learn:* Unlike a child in a compulsory learning environment, the adult has specific role needs which may serve to motivate his learning.

4. *Orientation to Learning:* Adults are concerned with problem-solving. Learning must have practical application in meeting immediate needs rather than learning for more abstract purposes or for its own sake.[5]

These characteristics are of increasing importance in the actual learning environment. The distinctions are evident in comparing the child learner environment to the adult learner environment. The dominant teacher and the dependent learner are replaced by an interdependence and self-directing atmosphere between the teacher and learners, so that it becomes a helping rather than a directing relationship. The traditional grade and class grouping is reduced to grouping learners according to their needs and interests. The knowledge and skills are acquired for solving today's problems rather than knowledge stored away for some possible future use.

In focusing on the paraprofessionals as adult learners, it is important to take into account their work experience, their needs as determined by an assessment of their background, their prior life experience, and the abilities that they bring to the training situation. Training paraprofessionals requires an understanding of the relationship between agency objectives and the learner's needs, goals, and occupational identity. The worth of each paraprofessional is crucially linked to the broader view of the worth and utilization of paraprofessionals as a whole.

The need for certain skills in and knowledge about interviewing, reporting, problem-solving, referrals, program information, and related areas is common to paraprofessional workers in a variety of the human services. The need to understand these generic activities serves as a basis for the development of a training model which includes both the process and the content required for upgrading paraprofessionals.

Development of effective training programs and materials appears to rest on the application of adult learning theory to the roles commonly performed by paraprofessionals. Training is most effective if it occurs within a planned framework using training materials which adheres to some predetermined instructional design.

Let us examine two models in order to highlight the process approach to training paraprofessionals. The first, a training model developed by Lynton and Pareek, divides the training sequence into three phases: (1) the pretraining phase

—initial expectation and readiness, training specifications, and selection of participants; (2) the training phase—exposure to material, reinforcement, retrial, internalization of knowledge; and (3) the post-training phase—performance on the job, continuing education, additional on-the-job training.[6]

The pretraining phase calls for initial clarification of needs of both the worker and the agency. An understanding of workers' backgrounds, education, and prior experiences gives some assessment of the skills and competencies that they will bring to the training situation. The agency's objectives should be clearly reflected in the training objectives. The training phase establishes an appropriate climate and surroundings for an effective training session, including scheduling and agenda procedures. It is in this stage that the important relationship of trainer and trainee solidifies, the group development process begins, and material and concepts are internalized. The post-training phase encompasses support and evaluative procedures. Here review and revision of program materials is completed along with an assessment of trainee performances. More training, education, and consultation may be needed. This step of the model includes an overall evaluation of the program and how well its training objectives were met, contrasted with evaluations of the participants and their increased competencies.

Another training model emphasizes the instructional procedure for curriculum design and the related sequence of procedures. The model developed by Briggs to clarify the ingredients of the instructional design process includes: (1) stating objectives and performance standards; (2) preparing tests based on the objectives; (3) analyzing objectives for structure and sequence; (4) identifying assumed entering competencies; (5) preparing pre-tests and remedial instruction, or planning an adaptive program, or screening students or accepting dropouts planning a dual-track program; (6) selecting media and write prescriptions; (7) developing first-draft materials; (8) small group tryouts and revisions; (9) classroom tryouts and revisions; and (10) final revisions and performance evaluation.[7]

The combination of these models provides the elements for a framework within which to conduct the adult learning process of paraprofessional training. Table 2 provides an overall framework for the design of a training process. The nature of paraprofessional training content beyond agency orientation programming is as important to the training of paraprofessionals as is the structure of the training experience.

Table 2

A Model for Training and Instruction

Training Model	Instructional Design Model
Pre-Training Phase	Steps 1-5, involving readiness training specifications, identify assumed entering competencies, selection of participants.
Training Phase	Steps 6-9, exposure to material, reinforcement, retrial, internalization of knowledge.
Post-Training Phase	Step 10, performance evaluation, improvement on the job, continuing training and education.

DESIGNING TRAINING CURRICULA

Traditional approaches to agency staff development have emphasized the uniqueness of each of their agency functions and seem to have precluded their developing a generic approach to the teaching of human service knowledge and skills. The irrationality of this approach has been effectively illustrated by the experiences of paraprofessional workers who have been recruited with no human service experience and have functioned effectively in specialized fields with some orientation and very little formal training. For example, paraprofessionals working in the community could be trained to help rehabilitate people who have been institutionalized regardless of the reason for their commitment, whether they were retarded or had committed a criminal offense. The emerging trend toward comprehensive, unified human services for the poor, mentally ill, retarded, delinquent, and disabled has brought to the surface most dramatically the need to reconceptualize traditional approaches to staff development and training in the human services.

Any curriculum design process rests on a set of basic assumptions regarding the learner, the training process, the training method, and the training content. In traditional approaches to training and staff development, curricula have been designed with little regard for the needs of the trainee and without emphasis on job ladders, lattices, and hierarchies. They have been based on assumptions that do not recognize the unique learning/teaching transaction that occurs when the learner is an adult worker. Thus, any attempt to develop an innovative design for paraprofessional training must be based on a set of new assumptions that form the basis for designing flexible curricula.

The first set of assumptions is related to the objectives of training. Button has outlined the objectives of training that have served as reference points for designing an integrated framework for paraprofessional training. He states:

> First, not because it is most important but rather because it is most obvious and concrete, there is a body of knowledge and theoretical concepts upon which practice is based . . . . Second, there will be a series of skills underlying successful practice . . . . Third, beneath the surface of personal skills lie the attitides and outlook of the people seeking to exercise those skills . . . . Fourth, one of the reasons that attitudes can be so resistant to change is that they are rarely held singly but as part of a whole complex of attitudes, which in turn may be embedded in deeper personality factors.

These training objectives provide the basis for a generic approach to paraprofessional training which may be stated as follows:

1. There is a body of knowledge and theoretical concepts upon which human service practice is based.

2. There are skills which can be identified as forming the basis for successful work in the human services.

3. Services can be improved when paraprofessional staff acquire an integrated and generic body of human service knowledge and skills.

Innovative training designs rest upon a recognition that the paraprofessional worker is an adult learner whose training needs will be met most efficiently through programs based on the andragogical process—as opposed to the pedagogical process. Ingalls has succinctly outlined the needs of adult learners and defines the andragogy process as follows:

1. It is a way to learn directly from experience.

2. It is a process of reeducation that can reduce social conflicts through interpersonal activity in learning groups.

3. It is a process of self-directed learning from which the adult can continually reassess his own learning needs as they emerge from the demands of the changing situation.[9]

Thus, the paraprofessional human service worker should be viewed as an adult with unique characteristics that dictate how training should be designed and implemented. Since traditional training methods are based on a pedagogical approach to learning, the tendency has been to transmit knowledge and skills primarily through a directive, didactic relationship in which the learner is passive and dependent on the dominant teacher. Given a recognition of the andragogical process, this traditional approach can no longer be accepted as a viable means of attaining current training objectives.

Therefore, training methods for paraprofessional human service workers will be most effective when:

1. The learner is given the opportunity to learn by doing and by practicing.

2. The goal of the method is identified as the acquisition of problem solving skills—that is, learning must be problem centered.

3. The method provides the learner with constant knowledge of his progress.

4. The method provides a measure by which results can be evaluated through objective and observable criteria.

Since the training of paraprofessionals should reflect their prior work experience, their needs in the agency, and the special abilitiies they bring to the training situation, training techniques that are individualized will offer distinct advantages to this population. For the worker, individualized instruciton provides the potential for increased job satisfaction, increased identification with an occupation, and a transferability of skills to different or higher level jobs. For the organization, individualized instruction standardizes the training materials and presentation, provides a means for realizing an increased competency in job performance, and serves as a means for determining work performance improvement among a differential work force. A review of paraprofessional training materials in the various human service settings indicated that although the content of these training materials was written with specific reference to a particular human service setting, there was, in fact, a core of common knowledge and skills that could be identified.

A recent study of paraprofessional utilization and the development of a conceptual framework of social welfare manpower utilization provides a new perspective for training

programs. Although there have been several studies conducted on paraprofessional utilization, the study done by
Katan has provided some empirical evidence to support the
notion that paraprofessionals in a variety of human service
settings perform a core of common activities, regardless of
the setting.[11] Katan surveyed paraprofessionals in seven
human service settings and found that their activities could
be organized into three groupings: those dealing with finding
out about clients and their needs, those dealing with the
creation of links between the clients, the organizations, and
the delivery of material resources, and those directly involved
in helping the clients—that is, teaching and personal counseling.

Finally, the factors above can be viewed in light of the
theoretical framework for social welfare work activities developed by Teare and McPheeters.[12] This model projects
nine primary objectives or "centers of gravity" of social
welfare and twelve roles or "clusters of alternative activities"
that are performed in order to meet the nine objectives.
These twelve roles represent theoretically the total range of
worker activity that occurs in any social welfare organization,
and are not viewed as individual jobs but as activities that can
be grouped or clustered into jobs (see Table 3).

Viewed totally, the findings of Katan and Teare and Mc-
Pheeters lead to the potential development of an integrated
framework of human service knowledge and skills for paraprofessional training. Since the roles of paraprofessionals that
Katan identified were strikingly similar to those projected by
Teare and McPheeters, and since the content generic to the
human services derived from review of the paraprofessional
training literature was also closely related to the roles, it
became apparent that a specialized curriculum could be
structured around the twelve roles.

Table 3

Generalist Worker Roles

1. *Outreach*

Implies an active reaching out into the community to detect people with problems and help them to find help, and to follow up to assure that they continue toward as full as possible a fulfillment of their needs.

2. *Brokerage*

Involves helping a person or family get to the needed services. It includes assessing the situation, knowing the alternative resources, preparing and counseling the person, contacting the appropriate serve, and assuring that the client gets to it and is served.

3. *Advocacy*

This has two major aspects:
a. Pleading and fighting for services for a single client whom the service system would otherwise reject—regulations, policies, practices, etc.
b. Pleading or fighting for changes in laws, rules, regulations, policies, practices, etc., for all clients who would otherwise be rejected.

4. *Evaluating*

Involves gathering information, assessing client or community problems, weighing alternatives and priorities, and making decisions for action.

5. *Teaching*

Includes a range of teaching from simple teaching—how to dress, how to plan a meal—to teaching courses in budget or home management and teaching in staff development programs; teaching aims to increase peoples' knowledge and skills.

6. *Behavior Changing*

Includes a range of activities directed to changing peoples' behavior rather precisely.

	Among them are simple coaching, counseling, behavior modification, and psychotherapy.
7. *Mobilizing*	Involves working to develop new facilities, resources, and programs, or to make them available to persons who are not being served.
8. *Consulting*	Involves working with other persons or agencies to help them increase their skills and to help them in solving their clients' social welfare problems.
9. *Community Planning*	Involves participating and assisting in planning of neighborhood groups, agencies, community agents, or governments in the development of community programs to assure that the human service needs of the community are represented and met to the greatest extent feasible.
10. *Care Giving*	Involves giving supportive services to people who are not able to resolve their problems fully and to meet their own needs, such as supportive counseling, fiscal support, protective services, day care, and 24-hour care.
11. *Data Managing*	Includes all kinds of data gathering, tabulating, analysis, and synthesis for making decisions and taking action. It ranges from simple case data gathering, through preparing statistical reports of program activities, to evaluation and sophisticated research.
12. *Administering*	Includes all of the activities directed toward planning and carrying out a program such as planning, personnel, budgeting and fiscal operation, supervising, directing, and controlling.

CONCEPTUALIZING A TRAINING CURRICULUM

The twelve-role model of manpower utilization could be used as a reference for developing an integrated curriculum of human service knowledge and skills, but some characteristics limit its usefulness in designing training materials for the paraprofessional. First, the degree to which some roles overlap makes it difficult to define specific training content for the overlapping roles—for example, outreach and broker, community planner and mobilizer, teacher and care giver. Second, it is necessary to redefine some of the present role descriptions in terms of the knowledge and skills that are needed for paraprofessional human service work—for example, evaluator, data manager, advocate, administrator. Third, the distinctions between some roles are arbitrary and do not accurately reflect actual activities in the human service fields—for example, care giver, teacher, and behavior changer. Fourth, there is no overriding organizational framework within which the roles could be clustered. It is necessary to reconceptualize the roles in terms of some rational framework that will reflect the generic activities of paraprofessionals in the human services. Fifth, the activity of controlling patients, inmates, residents, or clients that is performed in many human service settings on an on-going basis could not be accounted for in the original model.

Given these constraints and weaknesses, modifications of the model can be made to develop training materials for paraprofessionals. Four primary areas requiring specialized skills can be identified in training content for paraprofessionals: (1) working in the human services; (2) getting services to people in need; (3) counseling and treating human service consumers; and (4) working with consumers and other workers to manage services. The first area serves as an orientation to the world of human service work, while the remaining three areas are seen as the primary groupings of work activity in the human services from which service roles and activities are derived (see Figure 1). The client, patient, inmate, or resident who receives human services is referred to as a "consumer," a less stigmatizing label for people in need of human services and for whom human service agencies exist. The components in Figure 1 require further elaboration:

1. *Working in the Human Services:* Paraprofessionals in the human services need to build their skills upon a broad understanding of what it means to work in a human service agency. This includes a working knowledge of the primary elements of a comprehensive human service agency—which might include programs related to public welfare, mental health, corrections, vocational rehabilitation, public health, and mental retardation. It requires a knowledge of the variety of consumers who seek assistance from such agencies, the range of their unmet needs, some familiarity with the kinds of situations in which human service agencies intervene. Paraprofessionals need to understand the various kinds of human service communities—for example, institutions, neighborhoods, consumer groups, wards, agencies—and the characteristics that are common to them all. They need to understand the world of work in the context of human services—that is, the work setting, basic work principles and values, and the nature of human service work. These elements provide an understanding of the varied settings of human service work and its general nature.

2. *Getting Services to People in Need:* At the outset, paraprofessionals need to understand those human service work activities which relate to individuals who need services, how to give information on services, how to connect consumers with the appropriate sources of help, how to follow up on referrals, how to negotiate the delivery system for the consumer when necessary, how to defend consumer rights, how to identify unmet community needs, and how to mobilize resources in the community. These activities can be grouped into the following three roles, and training content can be structured around the primary activities in each of these roles: (1) *brokering,* which relates to identifying resources in the community, giving information and referring, and reaching out to individuals in the community; (2) *consumer advocating,* which relates to understanding advocacy, learning some techniques of advocacy, and understanding the

basic rights of human service consumers; and (3) *mobilizing*, which relates to learning how to identify unmet community needs and learning the techniques of mobilizing in a community.

Figure 1

An Integrated Framework for Paraprofessional Skill Training

1. WORKING IN THE HUMAN SERVICES

Overview of a Comprehensive Service Agency	The World of Human Service Work
1. The human service delivery system	1. Nature of Work
2. Human service consumers	2. Worker and work principles
3. Human service communities	3. Work setting

2. GETTING SERVICES TO PEOPLE IN NEED

Brokering	Consumer Advocating	Mobilizing
1. Community resources	1. Advocating techniques	1. Unmet community needs
2. Giving information and referring	2. Rights of human service consumers	2. How to mobilize
3. Reaching out in the community		

ACQUISITION OF
GENERIC KNOWLEDGE
& PROBLEM-SOLVING
SKILLS

3. COUNSELING AND TREATING HUMAN SERVICE CONSUMERS

Counseling	Behavior Changing	Consulting

1. Helping skills	1. What is behavior changing?	1. The consulting process
2. Building helping relationships	2. Behavior changing techniques	2. Asking other workers for help
3. Coaching & teaching skills		3. Giving other workers help
4. Counseling groups		

4. WORKING WITH CONSUMERS AND OTHER WORKERS TO MANAGE SERVICES

Information Collecting	Information Managing	Supervising
1. Collecting information	1. Recording	1. Staff communicating
2. Updating information	2. Reporting	2. Using supervision
	3. The case conference	3. Giving supervision

3. *Counseling and Treating Human Service Consumers:* Another important area concerns those activities connected with short term coaching, counseling, teaching, and consulting, with activities relating to longer term, disability-focused support, therapy, or control on an ongoing basis. Related paraprofessional activities can be grouped into the following three roles: (1) *counseling,* which relates to developing helping skills, building helping relationships, coaching and teaching human service consumers, and advising groups of human service consumers; (2) *behavior changing*, which relates to understanding the meaning of behavior changing and having some knowledge of the varied treatment techniques and control methods that are used to change behavior, for example, parenting, reality therapy, and behavior modification; and (3) *consulting*, which relates to understanding the com-

ponents of the consulting process, learning how to ask other workers for help with consumer-related problems, and learning how to give other workers help with consumer related problems.

4. *Working with Consumers and Other Workers to Manage Services:* Finally, paraprofessionals need an understanding of the organizational demands for accountability related to activities concerned with data collection and information processing within the organization. Here paraprofessional activities can be grouped into three roles: (1) *information collecting*, which relates to collecting consumer information and updating consumer information; (2) *information managing,* which relates to learning the skills of recording, reporting, and understanding some of the mechanisms that are used to manage and share information—for example, the case conference—and (3) *supervising,* which relates to developing skills in staff communication, using supervision, and giving supervision.[13]

These four areas can be used to describe and define the generic activities, knowledge, and skills that can serve as a basis for an integrated framework for paraprofessional training. Such a framework relates training to the skills that are required to perform at the paraprofessional level in the human services. Finally, this framework can serve as a foundation for developing more specific knowledge and skills that may be unique to special program areas in various human service settings.

While the emphasis in this chapter has been on a more comprehensive approach to the training of paraprofessionals, similar attention is needed in the area of preparing professionals for the new supervisory requirements of managing paraprofessional personnel. These issues will be addressed in the next chapter.

Chapter 7

PROFESSIONALS

AS ADULT LEARNERS

Recent interest in increasing the accountability of social agencies and programs has renewed discussion of the role of staff supervision in agency management. Efficiency-minded administrators have raised an important issue in the debate over service delivery: Is supervision an administrative process designed to supervise people or to supervise services? The supervisory process has always included elements of both, but in the literature, which has reflected considerable preoccupation with managing people, it is only recently that issues of service management have surfaced.

The issues related to the supervision of paraprofessionals are quite similar to the recurring debate over the management of untrained personnel in human service agencies. However, two new elements have developed to complicate the issue of supervising paraprofessionals. First, paraprofessionals were hired in part on the basis of their specialized knowledge of the client community. Such specialized knowledge had rarely been a factor in the past for hiring untrained workers for welfare departments, prisons, or mental hospitals. As a result, supervisors of paraprofessionals were forced to recognize unique competencies which made paraprofessionals different from the traditionally untrained workers. Second, the increasing alienation of the American workforce resulting from ever-increasing technological change has led to a new interest in and pressure for development of workers' self-management capabilities. In this context, the existence of paraprofessionals has raised serious questions about traditional approaches to the supervision of workers. The post-industrial era reflects increased interest in the needs of workers and their ability to develop and maintain greater control over their work sites and ultimately their destinies. Before discussing these new issues it is important to review briefly the supervisory issues as they are reflected in the social services.

SUPERVISION REVISITED

The supervisory relationship has traditionally carried overtones of the parent-child relationship and may even reactivate in workers some of the inner conflicts characteristic of childhood. It may encourage dependency, and rivalry may arise among those supervised. Kadushin notes that threats to personal integrity and sense of adequacy may be involved, since the possibility of error or ignorance, however limited, and a certain sense of vulnerability are implicit in the relationship.[1] Shame, criticism, disapproval, or rejection may be feared. Even without these elements, supervisees are commonly required to accomplish change of one sort or another in their behavior, work, or even to some degree their personality. They are asked to do the unfamiliar rather than the familiar. The result often is anxiety and discomfort with new patterns of behavior. The simple act of accepting direction from others is often extraordinarily difficult, as is submitting to the authority of the supervisor.[2]

Supervision in social work has historically included many tasks and had many purposes which depend upon changing social contexts of service and differing views of social work. The redefinition of student supervision from the days of the charity organization society and its apprentice system to contemporary university-based graduate professional education has been significant. Central to this process of redefinition has been the debate between the administrative function and the teaching function of quality supervision.[3]

The administrative aspect of supervision includes such managerial responsibilities as procedures for employment, promotions and terminations, staff orientation and training, periodic evaluation, and caseload control. The teaching component of supervision has traditionally included enabling the worker to develop skill and knowledge through the use of in-service training sessions and opportunities to attend workshops and conferences. In the past, however, great stress was placed on the one-to-one relationship between supervisor and worker in which the worker was viewed primarily as a learner. The supervisor often tended to be overprotective or contolling. Thus, as Aptekar notes, while in social work in general we have moved rapidly into areas of social science thought, in supervision we have held on to a psychiatric or individualistic view of supervision to a degree quite out of keeping with a social science orientation.[4]

Aptekar sees supervision in systems terms in which the supervisor-supervisee relationship is a part of the agency as a system and therefore the total learning situation must be taken into account. Responsibility must be divided up and seen in organizational or systemic rather than personal terms. Supervision becomes a partial rather than a total experience, and its significance to workers depends upon the goals they set for themselves, their willingness to share responsibility, and their view of work in terms of an overall systems framework.[5]

What is the worker's perception of supervision and of the position in which he or she is placed in the agency? Wasserman found that only a small minority of his sample of workers felt their supervisors to be competent; the rest saw supervision primarily as a bureaucratic control device having little to do with social work values and skills. The supervisor functioned mainly as a mediator for the organization and was viewed as insecure and frightened, unsure of his authority and power, conforming, and more interested in organizational demands and needs than in those of the clients.[6] Davis pinpointed the problems inherent in the traditional view of supervision, noting that (1) the assimilation of knowledge and the worker's internalization of standards are weakened by an emphasis on extreme controls, (2) the worker's professional contacts within the agency are too limited, (3) assignment of the teaching and administrative functions tend toward a concentration of power in one person, and (4) this dual function leads to an overly complex assignment for the supervisor.[7]

In the light of these problems, Lucille Austin and others have suggested that the administrative and teaching functions should be divided and performed by two different staff persons to mitigate the inherent strains and conflicts of the supervisory relationship and to facilitate the independent function and professional growth of the practitioner.[8] The traditional primary technique of individual supervisory conferences would be supplemented or replaced by peer group supervision, team supervision, consultation, and other such devices. Fizdale contends that the traditional reliance of agency workers on their supervisors can be eliminated through peer group supervision in which several persons of equal caliber each carrying their own service responsibilities work together providing mutual support and advice in meeting the clients' needs.[9]

Scherz provides another perspective from which the teaching and managerial aspects of supervision are seen as essentially administrative in character. In this view, teaching can be done in the process of fulfilling administrative functions through the supervisor's leadership responsibilities. The worker decides what particular concepts or techniques are best suited to each case; the supervisor decides when to offer assistance and when to suggest the use of other agency resources in the interests of a case. Accountability of workers for their work is stressed, while the supervisor is no longer seen as responsible for what happens with each client.[10]

An adaptation to Scherz's ideas on supervision can be found in the policy statements by HEW's Social and Rehabilitative Services (SRS) on the new Operational Planning System (OPS).[11] The OPS is conceived of as one of several elements in an overall management system designed to provide for rational, sequential, and integrated planning and evaluating procedures with accountability and effectiveness measurements built in. The OPS is a short-range management tool which converts long-term goals of a program and financial plan into specific objectives for a current fiscal year. It is oriented toward results, defining objectives, and surfacing problems in order to facilitate cooperation among different agencies. In the application of OPS to supervision, objectives are used to evaluate performance of subordinates and to serve as a basis for output appraisal, career counseling, and identification of training needs.

Under the OPS approach, the job responsibilities of an individual are closely tied to the objectives of the particular service component in the organization. The advantage of such a structure is that it becomes possible to measure the performance of an individual by the contribution his work makes to the achievement of a particular organizational objective. Although the results of this system are still uncertain, it is relatively simple to implement and applicable to either a large or small agency.

A key concept in the OPS approach is that a large part of the responsibility for supervision is shifted to the employee. Thus in the planning phase of OPS, the employees review the nature of their activities and determine the key results they expect to achieve in the year ahead. These are considered their job responsibilities. In a conference, the employee and supervisor then review and negotiate those objectives seen as attainable, so that an agreement is reached between them. At the end of the year, during the review phase, the individual's performance is appraised by the supervisor on the basis of work results and their impact on the achievement of agency objectives. The worker's actual achievements are evaluated in terms of accountability and effectiveness in explicit and measurable ways, and compared with the job responsibilities set forth at the beginning of the year. On the basis of the year's performance the employee and the supervisor jointly draft another, modified set of job responsibilities for the next year.[12]

While the new OPS approach holds much promise for increasing agency accountability, it has been conceived in context of clearly defined and mandated services. In such a case, policy and program decisions are still made by top level administrators, and therefore both workers and supervisors continue to operate within the constraints of their agency programs. The accountability issue tends to emphasize the needs of the agency and to apply only indirectly to the needs of the clients. The needs of the staff, both supervisors and workers, receive even less attention. As a result, there has been renewed interest in the training component of supervision, emphasizing the needs of both workers and clients.

SUPERVISING PARAPROFESSIONALS

It is difficult to argue that the basic principles of good supervision are different when applied to paraprofessionals than to other types of workers. There are, however, certain considerations which take on importance in the supervision of paraprofessionals. Supervisors of paraprofessionals experience a psychic stretch similar to that, previously described, which affects paraprofessionals. Other supervisors who have no responsibilities for paraprofessionals often have difficulty understanding the paraprofessional's particular expertise. This has led to a limited acceptance of paraprofessionals, much confusion, and some defensiveness. Supervisors obviously must recognize the potential psychic stretch in which they are pulled by the needs of their supervisees on the one hand, and the doubts and fears of their colleagues on the other. In addition, it is not clear whether supervisors have dealt successfully with their feelings about supervising personnel with different cultural backgrounds. Extensive self-awareness and cultural awareness is basic to an effective supervisory relationship with paraprofessionals.

The supervisory process for paraprofessionals includes the basic components of diagnosis of staff capabilities, utilization of supervision time, identification with agency function, and use of supervision.[13] As in all good supervisory relationships, the supervisor assumes a shared responsibility for assessing the worker's productivity, his current strengths and weaknesses, his progress toward the mastery of old and new tasks, and his potential for continued growth and development.[14] What is new in this process is the desire of paraprofessionals to participate actively in it so that new criteria related to such areas as life experience enters into the assessment process. For example, an organization of paraprofessionals was able to convince a university president to exempt paraprofessionals from the freshman year on the basis of their life and work experience. Supervisors of paraprofessionals need to recognize that some of the old worker subservience found in traditional supervisory relationships is giving way to a new atmosphere of shared worker assessment and participatory management of workload.

There will be a continuing need for supervisors to help paraprofessionals with caseload management. Paraprofessionals, like many workers before them, will benefit from gaining new perspectives on such common problems as overidentifying with client, closing a case, or imposing one's own values upon a client. Supervisors will be called upon to help paraprofessionals manage their dual responsibility to the agency and to the client. Such assistance lends itself both to individual supervisory conferences and to group supervision with other paraprofessionals who may be experiencing similar tensions. Leon summarizes some of the more sensitive aspects of the professional-paraprofessional supervisory relationship in the following way:

> The professional should be aware that the paraprofessional may see and use the supervisory process differently. He may be more apt to use direct methods of confrontation. The supervisor must develop skills to work with this comfortably. The paraprofessional often does not see the sharing of weakness with the supervisor as particularly appropriate or growth-producing. . . . He may be unable to admit a problem because he was hired as an "expert." He recognizes that he has some expertise but may feel that he is putting his job in jeopardy by admitting weaknesses. The supervisor must create a climate in which the paraprofessional feels free to risk and to share.[15]

SUPERVISOR AS TRAINER

While the literature on supervision has reflected a concern with the administrative and teaching functions of supervision, very little attention has been given to the trainer functions as part of the repertoire of a supervisor. While some have suggested that training workers should be separated from the supervisory process by establishing staff development programs, it is suggested here that supervisors have considerably more contact with workers than do staff development personnel, tend to be more knowledgeable about worker needs, and are far more numerous than the usually limited number of personnel in staff development programs. This line of thinking in no way negates the importance of staff development; it merely suggests that the expansion of the supervisor's training functions represents an untapped resource for upgrading and educating paraprofessionals.

Recent research in adult education provides some new insights into the training functions of a supervisor. As noted in the previous chapter, Knowles's work on andragogy has implications for supervisors interested in expanding the teaching functions of the supervisory role.[16] In supervising paraprofessionals, an old adage of Confucius takes on even more meaning when one recalls the difficulties many people experience in our public school educational system where there are few opportunities to learn by doing:

> I hear and I forget
> I see and I remember
> I do and I understand.

Both adults and children can identify with the observations of Confucius. Since living itself is an educational experience, paraprofessionals have repeatedly reminded professionals that we must look at all of life as a learning experience.

Supervisors also need to be aware of the process of unlearning. With the rapid expansion of new knowledge, it becomes increasingly necessary to unlearn old ways and engage in a continuous process of reeducation. This process also contributes to a reduction of conflict in our agencies between the young and the old, the top and the bottom, and the blacks and the whites.

Related to reeducation is the need to master the process of learning itself. The pressures of daily life rarely allow professionals and paraprofessionals to engage in formal educational experiences. There are at least four important concepts which underlie the learning process for an adult.[17] First, the adult self-concept of autonomy and self-direction is reaffirmed as the relationship between the supervisor (teacher) and paraprofessional (learner) shifts from one of domination to one of reciprocity and assistance between two mature adults. Second, life experience is a crucial ingredient in the process of learning. In this case, one way teacher-to-learner communication is replaced by shared two or three way communication, emphasizing a community of teachers and learners where everyone's experience is valued. A third concept relates to the readiness of adults to learn, in which learners group themselves according to their interests and the supervisor serves as a facilitator, helping learners diagnose their learning needs. The supervisor serves more as a resource person than as a planner of predetermined curricula.

The fourth and final concept relates to replacing the traditional educational time perspective of preparing for the future—storing up information with a new orientation to learning by working on today's problems today. Andragogy emphasizes problem-centered learning, in contrast to subject-centered learning, in which supervisors help paraprofessionals expand their problem-solving capabilities on the job. The problem-centered approach does not replace the subject-centered approach; it merely highlights the motivation of adults to reach for new knowledge and skills when they have a need to know arising from their ongoing work situation.

On the basis of these four concepts, Ingalls summarizes the process of learning in the following seven steps:

1. Setting a climate for learning
2. Establishing a structure for mutual planning

3. Assessing interests, needs, and values

4. Formulating objectives

5. Designing learning activities

6. Implementing learning activities

7. Sharing evaluation of results (reassessing needs, interests, and values)[18]

These steps can be employed by a supervisor of paraprofessionals with the knowledge that andragogy is primarily a process where the participants serve as the major source of content related to needs and interests. Andragogy, then, is a way to learn directly from one's own experiences, a process of reeducation, and an approach to self-directed learning where learning needs can be reassessed continuously depending on the demands of changing work situations.

Throughout this chapter it should have been increasingly apparent that professionals must pay more attention to their roles as adult learners and to the process of lifelong learning. Insufficient attention has been paid to the continuing education needs of professionals. In the decades ahead the public will demand considerable accountability in all professions. Licensing regulations in the medical, legal, and dental professions have required periodic refresher courses. In many states, teachers must register for college courses in order to maintain their certifications. These mechanisms for encouraging continuing education have not yet been emulated in most human service occupations and professions. However, it appears that the expansion of continuing education and in-service training programs for the human services is on the horizon.

Emphasis on the process of supervision must be balanced with equal attention given to the output of good supervision. The accountability issue in social service management relates primarily to output; not necessarily how a worker accomplished something, but what was actually accomplished. The ability to define the output of social services is based upon a clear understanding of social service work. Analyzing social service work is the subject of the next section.

SUPERVISOR AS JOB ANALYST

One of the many consequences of the employment of para-professionals is increased attention to analyzing the nature of work in a social service agency as well as the effectiveness of the services themselves. Over the past several years much has been written about new methods of manpower utilization, new technologies for assessing manpower need, and new conceptualizations of manpower planning and service delivery.[19] It is clear that the future functioning of professionals and paraprofessionals relates to a larger problem, namely the careful determination of agency goals and objectives as a precursor to clearly defined role functions for social service personnel.

While increased attention has been given to finding ways to recruit, educate, employ, and effectively utilize social service manpower with less than a college degree to work in the social services, discussion has shifted away from describing personnel merely on the basis of credentials and has moved toward analyzing what workers do, predicting what they can do, and finally deciding what they should be doing. "Current developments indicate a trend both to increased personnel specialization on the one hand, and the emergence of new 'generalist' roles on the other."[20]

Research by Teare and McPheeters has led to increased understanding of the generalist concept as reflected in the twelve role model noted in Chapter 6. As noted in Chapter 5, this model is based on a developmental approach to manpower utilization in which jobs in an organization are developed through an analytical process which begins with an identification of client and system needs. When agency functions or objectives have been derived by the developmental process, it is possible to infer a set of worker roles such as outreaching, advocating, evaluating, teaching, behavior changing, mobilizing, consulting, community planning, care giving, administering, and data managing.[21] These eleven roles can be grouped or clustered into centers of worker activity or jobs. The criteria for role clustering rest with the organization and its definition of need. The role model provides a new way to conceptualize the nature of service delivery systems and how jobs are developed within a social service organization. As one attempts to analyze and document manpower need, it is critical to understand and evaluate all components of the service delivery system rather than simply assess the nature of the work presently being performed.

While the issues of task definition await further research, beginning efforts have been made to test the role model in the area of university curriculum development and reorganization.[22] In an effort to organize a wide variety of opinion on worker roles, Table 4 was developed to indicate the way in which the roles might be clustered at different levels of worker background. The generic title of "assistant" is utilized by a wide variety of workers and includes the entry level paraprofessional with a high school diploma or less. The title "technician" has been used widely to designate the two-year community college graduate. Social workers, for years confused by the general public with untrained workers. are those at the B.S.W., and M.S.W., and D.S.W./ Ph.D. levels of social work practice. It is suggested that workers who possess less than a baccalaureate degree are involved in the delivery of social services primarily in the context of pre-social work practice. This does not question the quality of their work, nor the contributions to service that they make. It simply indicates that a worker at a pre-baccalaureate level may choose from a variety of career tracks. As a result, all levels of practice above the baccalaur-

Table 4.   Role Clustering for Social Service Career Lattices

Generic Title	Paraprofessional Assistant	Paraprofessional Technician	Professional Social Worker	Professional Social Worker	Professional Social Worker
Background	*Academic:* High School or Less *Experiential:* Life Experiences and/or Prior Work Experiences	*Academic:* Community College(a) *Experiential:* Specialized Field Experience and/or Prior Work Experience	*Academic:* University-BA or BSW, Social Work Major with Liberal Arts(b) *Experiential:* Supervised Field Work and/or Prior Work Experience	*Academic:* University-MSW, Direct Services and Indirect Services(c) *Experiential:* Supervised Field Work and/or Prior Work Experience	*Academic:* University, Ph.D., Methods & Content Areas (d) *Experiential:* Supervised Research & Teaching and/or Prior Work Experience
Role Clusters	*Care Giving *Outreaching	*Brokering *Behavior Changing Care Giving Outreaching	*Mobilizing *Advocating *Evaluating *Data Managing Brokering Behavior Changing	*Consulting *Teaching *Planning *Administering Mobilizing Advocating Evaluating Data Managing	*Policy Consulting *Program Administering *Researching Role Teaching Role Planning

*Primary roles which are clustered for job development with role overlap taking place with next level worker

a. For example: Mental Health, Mental Retardation, Child Care, Corrections

b. For example: Direct services including casework, group work, and community organization

c. For example: Advanced direct services including casework, group work, and community organization or Indirect services including supervision, consultation, staff development, planning and administration

d. For example: Practice and research methods along with knowledge of specific fields of practice and social problem areas

eate degree are regarded as professional social work practice. In an effort to identify the backgrounds of workers at each level, distinctions have been made between academic and experiential backgrounds. In addition the roles of workers at each level are identified in terms of the twelve role model. The distinction between generalist and specialist is not considered in this figure; we need only note that each level of practice is essentially a specialized area in which workers could be competent to perform a certain specified cluster of roles, with an awareness of roles performed by other levels of workers.

There has been increased concern expressed in the literature about the overlap between workers at different levels.[23] When roles are clustered at each level it is important to recognize that they represent the competencies of the worker at that level. However, as one progresses up a career ladder, he can be expected to assume and gain competencies in additional roles. As a result there will be obvious overlap between role competencies at one level that are built upon those at another level. Therefore, role overlap exists only in the knowledge and skill base of the worker, and does not constitute duplication of function with other workers.

In Table 5 it is suggested that the various roles are learned by workers at each level with competencies defined primarily by a certain set of roles. Thus at the assistant level, the worker performs primarily in the care-giving and outreach roles. At the technician level the worker may perform primarily in brokering and behavior-changing roles though he is competent in care-giving and outreach. At the B.A. social work level, the worker may perform primarily in roles in data managing, client evaluating, advocacy, and mobilization. And at the M.S.W. level, the worker may perform primarily roles that include administering, planning, teaching, and consulting. At the social work doctoral level, the worker may perform primarily in program consulting and administrative and research roles. The doctoral level worker might also be in-

Table 5.   Role Specificity and Role Overlap on Social Service Career Lattice

	Assistant or Aide (Diploma)	Technician (A.A.)	Social Worker (B.A.)	Social Worker (M.S.W.)	Social Worker (Ph.D.)
Administrator				Administrator	Policy Consultant & Administrator
Planner				Planner	Researcher
Teacher				Teacher	Role Teacher & Planner
Consultant				Consultant	
Data Manager			Data Manager		
Evaluator			Evaluator		
Advocate			Advocate		
Mobilizer			Mobilizer		
Broker		Broker			
Behavior Changer		Behavior Changer			
Care Giver	Care Giver				
Outreach	Outreach				
		(Role Overlap)	(Role Overlap)	(Role Overlap)	(Role Overlap)

Advancement Through In-Service Training and/or Higher Education volved in role teaching and role planning for the entire set of roles. As one can see, there is overlap at each level, which is seen as functional in that, at every level, workers are aware of other roles performed by workers at other levels. It is important to stress that workers at each level need to be aware of the fact that their primary competencies are recognized in terms of certain role clusters.[24]

It is also important to note that career mobility should not be defined simply by academic degrees or credentials. Therefore agencies must plan for career mobility through staff development and in-service training. It should be possible for an entry level worker at the high school level to advance through the hierarchy of an agency simply by accumulating experience and specialized in-service training. This idea has yet to receive wide acceptance, both because credentials have played a major role in defining worker functions in our social services agencies, and because agencies tend to view staff development programs as luxuries that serve only specialized functions, such as intensive short-term training for special program orientation and reorientation.

The ideas presented in Figure 1 and Table 4 are still highly tentative. They reflect the growing interest in differential staffing and the tremendously difficult task of organizing social service according to worker competence and client needs. However, staffing patterns must ultimately relate to the purpose, goals, and objectives of the agency.

As services and staffing patterns in social service organizations are redesigned, personnel systems are being reevaluated. Increasingly, personnel managers are recognizing that personnel systems ultimately must be based upon a careful analysis of the service delivery system. Jobs must be restructured to provide the flexibility in personnel administration necessary to accomplish new service objectives. As a result, personnel systems must be restructured. This is being viewed from two perspectives: redefining jobs to arrive at more functional definitions and redefining jobs in such a manner as to reflect the concept of the career lattice. Let us highlight some of the major concepts of functional job analysis in order to identify one approach to analyzing jobs.[25] Functional job analysis can be useful as (1) a conceptual system for defining dimensions of work activity, and thus a way of conceiving the world of work; (2) an observational method for looking at worker activity; and (3) a method of analysis to evaluate the design of work and its performance.

As a systems approach, functional job analysis helps to delineate what work must be done and what workers must do in an organization to define explicitly its purpose, mid-range goals, and short-range objectives. It is assumed that within an organization (system) all interrelated components (subsystems) and their activities are coordinated in some logical fashion according to a master purpose, and that the inputs of the subsystems are converted into outputs of the total system. As the organization identifies its purpose, goals, and objectives, component parts of the organization can convert organizational objectives into subsystem goals, which are in turn converted into subsystem objectives. For example, a state juvenile corrections agency (system) may have set an objective to reduce the number of juveniles held in detention by 50 percent. A bureau charged with responsibility for juvenile foster homes (subsystem) may take this objective as a bureau goal. One of the bureau objectives derived from this goal may be to establish 200 foster homes across the state within one year.

Each subsystem objective is analyzed in relation to what work must be done and what workers must do in order to accomplish that objective. This process is referred to as "task analysis." A series of task statements can be developed for each subsystem objective. These task statements contain information about performance standards, training content, and the relationship of tasks to cognitive, interpersonal, and physical phenomena. The application of functional job analysis allows the analyst to make decisions about an organization's manpower needs without being bound by the existing system of personnel deployment. This allows the organization to redesign jobs and reallocate personnel in the manner that accomplishes their objectives most efficiently and effectively.

The application of a systems approach to planning in an organization assists its staff in (1) measuring progress towards specified ends, (2) organizing resources—money, time, manpower, technology, and (3) making internal changes in accordance with changing needs and conditions as it pursues its purpose. "Systems purpose" refers to the ultimate end result desired by the organization. A set of intermediate results referred to as "system goals" are derived from the purpose of the system. In turn, "system objectives" are derived as a set of immediate or short range results from the goals of the system. As "system objectives" are defined they become "subsystem goals" leading to a further refinement of objectives. See Figure 2 for a scheme that shows graphically the relationship between system purposes, goals, and objectives.

Figure 2.

A Systems Approach to Job Analysis

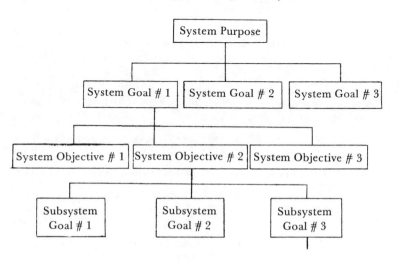

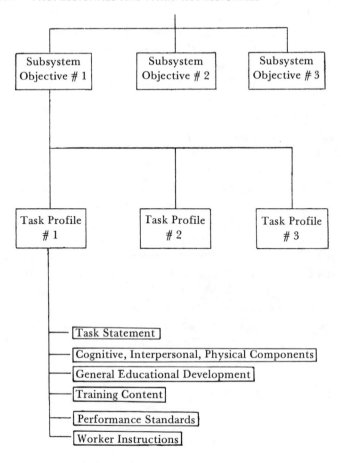

In the social services, "systems" may be defined as agencies, departments, or branches of government depending upon the degree of specificity desired in system definition. For example, a small private family service agency could be considered a system in order to define purpose, goals, and objectives, including such organizational units as intake, information and referral, and counseling. The operating divisions within a large agency would be considered subsystems, and in turn their bureaus could be considered subsystems. Subsystems are considered to be blocks of work that clearly allow for the division and allocation of resources.

As an example of how purposes, goals, and objectives are developed, let us examine a state agency charged with the administration of programs for the mentally retarded. The process of task analysis begins at the point where subsystem objectives are identified.

> *System:* State agency of mental retardation
>
> Purpose: To achieve the highest degree of well-being possible for all mentally retarded children and their families within the state.
>
> Goal # 1: To place in approved foster homes X percent of all parentless children presently residing in state institutions within two years.
>
> Objective # 1: To establish X number of approved foster homes in the state within one year.
>
> *Subsystem*: Foster home placement bureau
>
> Goal # 1: To establish X number of approved foster homes in the state within one year.
>
> Objective # 1: To complete within three months a survey of all potentially suitable foster homes within the state.[26]

In order to identify the specific steps necessary to accomplish objectives, special attention must be given to the identification of tasks. In task analysis, task refers to the smallest unit of activity that makes an immediate contribution to the subsystem objective. A series of task profiles can be developed for each subsystem objective. The task profile in a functional job analysis system contains the following information. An entire technology has been developed which includes special scales:

> 1. *Task Statement:* The task statement contains information about *what work must get done* (refers to the subsystem objective) and *what workers do* (refers to worker functions). A good task statement contains the following information: who—performs what action (input)—to whom

or what—to produce or achieve what (output)—using what work aids—upon what instructions.

2. *Cognitive Interpersonal and Physical Components:* This refers to the relationship of the task to three properties—data, people, and things.

3. *General Educational Development:* This refers to the language, quantitative, and reasoning skills necessary to perform the task.

4. *Performance Standards:* This refers to the criteria against which actual results of the task are compared. Performance standards consist of: (1) qualitative or descriptive statements about qualities of behavior such as speed and tact; (2) quantitative or numerical standards which refer to objective performance criteria which require no interpretation, such as how many interviews can be conducted in an hour.

5. *Training Content:* Training content is developed in two categories that reflect the various components of the task statement: (1) general training (functional skills) refers to those competencies that relate to data, people, and things. This training often takes place in the context of the academic setting; (2) Specific training refers to those competencies that enable an individual to perform a specific task according to the standards required to satisfy the agency and client.

6. *Worker Instructions:* This refers to the degree of prescription or discretion implicit in the task and the amount of supervisory direction that may be needed.[27]

The premise of functional job analysis is that jobs are created by grouping a number of tasks which have been described in a task profile. A job, then, is a grouping or clustering of task statements. This clustering can be done in a variety of ways. Homogeneous clustering can be developed based on worker functions. Homogeneous clusters can also be developed on general educational development or even the level of worker instruction necessary to carry out a job. Another alternative is the heterogeneous cluster approach, which insures a mixture of tasks related to different worker functions, general educational development, and the level of worker instruction.

Homogeneous clusters are obviously less complex and more systematic, but there are critical limitations. Such clusters can easily lead to a job factoring approach where tasks are grouped on the basis of their complexity. The least complex tasks are usually assigned to workers with less education. This is the basis for strong reaction by paraprofessionals to the routine, nonchallenging aspects of their jobs. Heterogeneous groupings, on the other hand, provide for more job diversity and recognize the responsibility of the system to arrange jobs to reflect both the needs of the service clientele and the capabilities of the worker.

These approaches raise critical questions for supervisors. Do you tailor jobs to workers or fit workers to jobs? While functional job analysis is a useful technology for redesigning jobs, it does not represent a total solution for integrating the needs of the field—client, worker, and organization—with the personnel system. This situation calls for a more comprehensive approach to career planning and career management, which will be discussed in the next chapter.

Chapter 8

PLANNING FOR

CAREER MOBILITY

It is becoming increasingly apparent that as a result of the rapid technological changes of the post World War II period, we are moving toward a service economy. As more and more worker functions are assumed by machinery, greater attention is being directed to the expansion of services to meet our many human needs. At the same time, there has been an expansion of the job market in government. Today over one-sixth of the entire national work force is employed by a governmental agency at either the national, state, or local level. A growing segment of this work force is assuming job responsibilities in the area of human service.

A careful analysis of this service economy indicates that a new human service industry with many sectors is developing. As heavy industry includes steel, oil, and automotive industries, the human service industry includes mental health, public welfare, corrections, health care, and education, to name just a few. As these various sectors have come to be seen as components of a larger industry, there has been a growing recognition that the human service industry as a whole must have greater understanding of the needs of its work force. In the industrial arena, these needs surfaced through the unionization of workers. To date, this form of employee organization has played only a minor role in the human service industry. As a result, administrators and workers must pay a great deal more attention to personnel planning, service planning, and staff development planning. An industry that prides itself on meeting the needs of clients must also meet the expectations of workers in the areas of job clarity, job mobility, and job upgrading.

To meet the needs of human service workers today, it is proposed that career planning strategies be developed that include three components: staff deployment for effective service delivery, personnel planning related to classification examinations and performance standards, and staff development planning related to the continuing education needs of workers to improve service delivery and upgrade worker capability. Such a planning strategy is the primary focus of this chapter.

Basic to such career planning is the process of institutionalizing career lattices. Much attention has been given in recent years to expanding opportunities for workers to move up the ladder of job opportunity, performing more job functions, and assuming greater responsibility. Though it has been much discussed, there is certainly no agreement on how career lattices should be built. There is a growing understanding that the career lattice implies worker mobility in both horizontal and vertical directions. The horizontal direction includes expanding opportunity across agency programs as well as between agencies for workers at all levels. The vertical notion implies career opportunity for advancement both in job function and salary.

The career lattice notion takes into account the need to expand equal employment opportunity for workers at all levels, from the high school graduate or less through graduate-level human service personnel. The design of such a career lattice requires careful analysis of existing job classification schemes, classification examinations, and performance standards. It also requires a careful review of existing in-service training or staff development programs to determine the extent to which workers are receiving agency-based training that will lead to career advancement. It is also crucial to assess the service delivery system which is being used to provide services to clients. Here we direct special attention toward the needs of community-based service programs as opposed to institution-based programs for, as noted earlier, the job demands and opportunities for paraprofessionals are different in community and institutional programs.

CREATING CAREER SYSTEMS

Although career mobility has only recently surfaced as an issue in human service organizations, it has received considerable attention from various research organizations and governmental agencies. The early studies of career mobility programs for paraprofessionals and New Careerists have centered further attention on the dynamics of career mobility for the entire system of the human services.

In 1969, the National Committee on Employment of Youth conducted a study of a small sample of those agencies employing their graduates. The major objective of this study was to determine those factors that had an impact on the career mobility of a selected group of paraprofessionals. Generally, the study showed that:

1. The paraprofessionals had proved beyond a doubt that they were more than capable of performing a wide variety of generalist tasks in the human services, performing them in many cases better than the professionals.

2. The employing agencies generally rewarded the para-professionals with sizable raises, much higher than many had expected.

3. The paraprofessionals rewarded the agencies in turn by being extremely stable employees, although this limited movement to other jobs was probably significantly influenced by the lack of better opportunities elsewhere.

4. Opportunities for genuine career advancement for paraprofessionals were either severely limited or completely nonexistent. The obstacles to career advancement were many, including civil service requirements, professional standards, lack of supplementary training and education; but one obstacle dominated them all: the insistence in all but one agency on baccalaureate degrees for eligibility to higher level jobs.[1]

The study also showed a serious absence of career lattices planned for the paraprofessionals. There were virtually no standards establishing equivalency for experience in para-professional jobs among different agencies in the human services. Thus, the employing agencies and the employment counselors had difficulty directing paraprofessionals to alternative job opportunities. On the basis of these findings it was recommended that Congress and those agencies which fund paraprofessional programs issue a national declaration guaranteeing not only equal employment opportunity but also equal opportunity for advancement. It was suggested that this policy be implemented by the development of measures designed to help paraprofessionals advance within the existing framework of agency hiring policies and job structures, by development of measures designed to assist agencies in changing that framework to accommodate para-professional advancement, and by the design of measures to help agencies evaluate the total framework of their services and their use of manpower.

A statement supporting the development of career mobility programs was recently prepared by the National Association of Social Workers.[2] This document provides guidelines for job roles, functions, and training that apply to a series of job levels for personnel providing social services. In regard to career mobility programs, it suggests that manpower development and utilization in the social services should have a planned career system that will provide a sufficient number of job levels to establish a continuum of logical steps from one level to another and offer opportunities for vertical and horizontal mobility. It suggests that job descriptions should be structured to provide a career lattice with different entry levels, opportunities for multiple careers, and horizontal and vertical mobility. Career mobility programs should also provide for a continuing program of career development for all social service personnel, through advanced education in educational institutions, pre-service and in-service training, and continuing education program.

While the policy statements of the National Association of Social Workers provides evidence of signficant progress in the human services, relatively few human service organizations have been able to implement its guidelines. One notable exception has been a human service career system planning effort in the state of Illinois.[3] The Human Services Manpower Career Center in Illinois has assisted in developing three career systems: one in mental health, one in connection with the Adult Division of Corrections, and the third in the area of children and family services. The primary goal of all three efforts was, within a given human service delivery system, to maximize the possibilities for all employees to advance themselves in increased responsibility, earnings, and personal growth and job satisfaction, while at the same time fulfilling broad management goals and expectations.[4] Generally, efforts in all three systems focused on structuring job descriptions so that vertical and horizontal mobility was provided for all employees. Formal educational requirements were minimal; career development and skill training provided by the various departments became the primary basis for upward mobility.

One of the most comprehensive conceptual studies of career mobility in the human services was recently completed by the Social and Rehabilitation Service of HEW.[5] This study was designed to review what is known about worker job mobility, especially in the human services, and to organize this knowledge into a valid and meaningful conceptual framework. The study made suggestions for improving the management and career design of workers in the human services. Based on a review of the literature, it was suggested that factors that influence career mobility include the initial entry of a worker into a job or occupation, employee turnover, and internal mobility. This conceptual framework provided the basis for recommendations designed to improve the structure of career mobility in the human services. Two recommendations were that career mobility programs should provide job opportunities for a broad range of personnel, especially those who do not possess the traditional academic degrees, and that human service agencies must recognize their increased responsibility for providing training programs for all workers to facilitate their professional growth, development, and advancement into supervisory and administrative positions.

This selective review of recent literature supports the conclusion that there has been a serious lack of career mobility planning in the human services, especially for indigenous and paraprofessional workers. However, it also indicates that the situation is changing. Since many professional organizations and human service agencies are now recognizing the importance of creating more job opportunities for personnel at all levels, more attention must be directed to planning and implementing career mobility in the human services.

Many professional associations and organizations are becoming increasingly aware of the need to redesign job classifications in order to create more job opportunities for personnel at all levels. The American Medical Association is working on the acceptance of the new medical assistant. The National Association of Social Workers in 1970 admitted the trained baccalaureate-level practitioner into the profession. Some of the most dramatic progress, however, can be seen in a recent policy statement of the American Hospital Association on its career mobility programs. It emphasizes the need for employees to have opportunities to advance in responsibility and income and in turn to affect the quality of patient care. The policy statement indicates the following major goals:

1. Reducing the manpower shortage in the skilled and semi-skilled occupations by training current personnel for positions in the shortage areas

2. Reducing the rate of turnover by opening opportunity for employees through training by advancement, thereby providing a more stable staff for the institutions

3. Breaking down some of the barriers to job advancement in health occupations by:
   (a) Developing occupational ladders that would define job pathways built on job activities performed at lower levels, but related in terms of skills and knowledge
   (b) Developing educational ladders that would define sequential levels of education and experience and permit individuals to progress upward through these levels without duplicating previously required training
   (c) Developing released time courses of studies as well as support activities such as counseling that would enable individuals to meet the requirements of upward mobility while retaining their regular employment

4. Using many of the established techniques for job upgrading and combining them into a coordinated program

> that will offer employees genuine advancement to meet
> the manpower needs of health care institutions, and im-
> prove health care in the communities they service[6]

It is important to note in this policy statement that emphasis is placed both on occupational ladders which relate
specifically to the job classification scheme and on educational ladders which relate directly to in-service training and staff
developing. This further points up the need for collaborative planning between the service sector and the educational
sector. The need to build career lattices must be accompanied
by policy statements which indicate the directions of organizational change. The American Hospital Association has
spelled out the directions in which career mobility programs
can improve patient care while at the same time more effectively utilize existing manpower.

JOB MARKET CONSIDERATIONS

It is a well known fact that in many cases career opportunities are controlled administratively, if not legally, by arbitrary restrictions at the point of entry and at the transfer
points in the job hierarchy. For example, there is an in-group
phenomenon in which the good job becomes available only
to those personnel who are in the agency or have personal
knowledge of a vacancy. This means that women and blacks
and other minority group members are usually frozen out of
these opportunities. As one student of the labor market
observes:

> The labor market behaves quite differently in periods of
> expansions and contractions. In years of rapid growth, the
> opportunity for workers to advance into better jobs (i.e.,
> to be upgraded) is much greater than when ouput and em-
> ployment are stable or declining. In a recession, the oppo-
> site of upgrading often occurs: workers with more skills and
> more seniority bump workers with lesser skills. Many work-

ers remain employed in a period of recession only by accepting a job for which they are overqualified and which pays less than the one they previously held. This phenomenon of downgrading during periods of slack activity decreases the amount of upgrading required when business improves. Many workers already have the skills required to move into more demanding assignments.

It is unquestionable that a human service industry is very much affected by the total economy, especially in periods of recession when many out-of-work employees from the industrial sector apply for employment in the public service sector. The influx of former aerospace employees into city, county, and state government jobs is a case in point.

Educational opportunity plays a major role in facilitating the upgrading of human service personnel. Though high school programs have generally failed to give human service personnel an edge in the job market, community colleges through their technician programs have provided human service workers with a definite edge in obtaining skilled jobs. Nonetheless, adult vocational training must be broadened and deepened in order to expand career opportunities. For example, there is a shortage of part-time training opportunities under public auspices for workers to add to their skills through late afternoon, evening, or weekend training programs.

The recent pressure for job upgrading and design of career lattices has come primarily from the lower levels of personnel in the human service industry. In particular, the new community workers hired through the poverty programs and other New Careers programs have identified the need for expanding job opportunity through upgrading and advancement. However, as Ginzberg has noted:

> The advocates of the new careers approach have not taken adequate account of the head-on conflicts that will arise from their efforts to increase promotional opportunity for the less skilled with the limited number of good jobs that

exist, the larger number of competitors for these jobs, and the difficulties of removing the legal, administrative, and organizational impediments that currently control access to these jobs.[8]

While competition may be keen at the entry level, there is growing interest in the contributions made by techician-level workers trained at community colleges, though there are continuing problems at this level in the areas of certification and licensure. Needless to say, there is a need to reverse the trend toward specific educational and program requirements for licensure of professional recognition. As Brecher notes in his study of the health service worker:

> The guarantee of quality and consumer protection for which licensure is designed might be achieved equally as well by open examinations. This would give recognition to skills acquired in a variety of settings not limited only to formal programs approved by professional associations. To assure that examinations tested for the skills needed to perform a given job, and neither more nor less, the statutes should be enforced by representatives of the consuming public as well as the particular practitioners and other professionals.[9]

SERVICE DELIVERY ISSUES

The career lattice concept is based both on increasing the quality of service and providing opportunity for upgrading the salaries, responsibilities, and morale of personnel. It is important, however, to understand the service delivery implications of career lattices. An underlying assumption of the career lattice approach is that services to clients will be increased and improved. While it is fairly obvious that reducing a teacher-pupil or nurse-patient ratio will improve the quality of service, it still remains to be seen whether society is willing to pay the increased price for whatever additional benefits accrue. This raises questions about societal priorities related to overall governmental spending and to a domestic policy which is committed to meeting the needs of all people through services provided in a public human service industry.

Federal agencies responsible for human service programs are under increasing pressure from Congress to account for service dollars. Federal service planning has moved dramatically in the direction of service impact evaluation by identifying the following major program goals for families and children receiving services under the Title XX provisions of the Social Security Act:

1. Self-support: To achieve and maintain the maximum feasible level of employment and economic self-sufficiency

2. Self-care or family-care: To achieve and maintain maximum personal independence, self-determination and security in the home, including, for children, the achievement of maximum potential for eventual independent living

3. Community-based care: To secure and maintain community-based care which approximates a home environment when living at home is not feasible and institutional care is inappropriate

4. Institutional care: To secure appropriate institutional care when other forms of care are not feasible.[10]

Service delivery will be redefined in terms of removing barriers to these goals through new or existing services. This process is based on measurable objectives with such criteria as the number of clients screened, referred, placed, and counseled. This will require individual service plans to be developed by human service personnel with special emphasis on moving clients through and ultimately out of the service system.

As we proceed to redesign our human service agencies by shifting our emphasis from institutional care to community-based care, the human service industry will be more visible to the total society. There will also be a strong push to co-ordinate community-based services to avoid duplication and to increase service effectiveness. With this thrust in mind, it becomes apparent that altering career mobility within the entire industry will also require more attention to the employment of such traditionally excluded groups as women and minority group members. This will raise questions about the value of job equity in relationship to job efficiency.

Those administrators responsible for delivering quality human services must also take into account the increasing need for programs to upgrade workers, programs which can be designed to meet one or more of the following policy objectives:

> Altering occupational structures so as to provide a greater proportion of upper level jobs; increasing the proportion of better jobs filled internally; rationalizing the criterion used to select those who are to be advanced; enlarging the pool of manpower eligible for advancement; and increasing the job satisfaction of employed workers.[11]

While the primary emphasis of human service programs is the delivery of quality services to clients, more attention must now be given to upgrading human service personnel.

In addition to the issue of quality services, there is an increasing need for continuous assessment of how services are delivered. The use of differentially staffed human service teams has received attention in selected agencies around the country. Though they are only preliminary, research findings show the team form of work group organization proving more effective than simply reducing the caseloads of traditional human service workers.[12] There also appear to be early indications that the cost of delivering services may be reduced by using a team approach as opposed to the individual worker serving hundreds of clients.

Finally it is important to note that very little attention has been paid to worker morale in the human service industry. Serving the complex needs of institutionalized clients or managing caseloads in the community can tax the knowledge, skills, and altruism of any normal person. To what extent have jobs been evaluated in terms of the variety of activities performed by workers? Human service workers can suffer as much as assembly line workers from unbroken routine and boredom. Career planning must take worker morale into account in the context of service restructuring, job classification revision, and staff development programming.

Comprehensive career planning begins with an assessment of the service delivery system and its components. Service delivery systems must be thoroughly analyzed before manpower needs can be documented. An identification of the competence of workers and of the most effective and efficient methods of deploying staff flows from analysis of what services are to be delivered, how they are to be delivered, to whom, and for what purpose.

As decisions are made about work distribution and the creation of new jobs, attention must be directed at the personnel administration system. Job classifications, qualifying examinations, and performance standards must be evaluated and redesigned as service delivery systems are redesigned and new types of workers utilized. Attention should be directed to making functional definitions of the jobs that emerge from an analysis of service delivery systems. Human service organizations have responsibilities to both clients and workers. A sound system of personnel administration should not only select and utilize workers so as to provide the best possible services to clients, but also to accommodate the career aspirations of workers.

With these changes, new training materials must be created to prepare workers to perform at the highest possible levels of competence consonant with their job functions and to provide a mechanism for career mobility. The career concept adds a new facet to agency staff development, as training is related both to job performance and career advancement. The process of career planning is complex. It requires a commitment both to the concept of career mobility and to acquiring the technical skills required to assess manpower utilization in a changing service delivery system. Until there is major occupational restructuring, there will be few opportunities for upgrading human service personnel. The shift from institution-based services to community-based services is one of the significant changes of the 1970s in the human service industry. As a result, future organizational changes may be even more important than technological changes in reshaping the occupational structure of the human service industry.

In an effort to develop an understanding of the ingredients of the relationship between professionals and paraprofessionals in order to reshape the occupational structure of human service delivery, a pilot study was conducted. The study of professionals and paraprofessionals in community-based services is described in the following chapters. Particular attention is given to the process of organizational role-taking in order to determine the functions performed by professional and paraprofessional workers and the organizational factors associated with a collaborative working relationship.

Part III

A STUDY IN PARAPROFESSIONALISM

Chapter 9

STUDYING THE PROFESSIONAL -
PARAPROFESSIONAL RELATIONSHIP

As noted earlier, the body of experience in the utilization of paraprofessional personnel has been growing since the enactment of the federal antipoverty legislation. There has developed an expanding list of observations about the response of professionals to the use of paraprofessionals. The following are highlights of these reactions: (1) Professionals' perceptions of their own expertise are threatened. (2) There is resistance among them to the use of paraprofessionals. (3) There is anxiety among them about role blurring and the loss of identity. (4) There is a presumption that the limited competence of paraprofessionals will lead to a lowering of standards. Other ideological observations have been made, to be sure, suggesting that it is democratic to employ paraprofessionals, that they are as good as anybody else, and they may even be better.

Are these emotional responses on the part of the professionals? Or is there an empirical base for either the positive or negative responses? The study that follows has developed a data base concerning the nature and extent of the professional-paraprofessional relationship in the light of personal and organizational characteristics. All personnel included in this six-city study were employed primarily by antipoverty agencies in the cities of Pittsburgh, Cleveland, Baltimore, Cincinnati, Philadelphia, and Atlanta.

The institutional phase of paraprofessionalism as an emerging social movement serves as an organizing theme for this study. Within this framework, we will focus in detail on the organizational role-taking experienced by the professionals and paraprofessionals. By analysis of this institutionalization process it will be possible to shed some light on the changing nature of our human service delivery system as well as on the changing face of professionalism. It will be noted also that a mutual co-optation is taking place as the professional social worker interests the paraprofessional in the principles of social work and the paraprofessional interests the professional in reorganizing the priorities of practice.

This study explores the impact of the professional upon the successful inclusion of the paraprofessional into the work force of the social services. If it is true that the professional plays a major role in determining the nature of the relationship, it seems reasonable to assume that the professionals are in large part the gatekeepers of the destiny of the paraprofessionals. If this is true, then the nature of the professional-paraprofessional relationship documented in this study has implications for professionals, paraprofessionals, agency administrators, and trainers.

The professional's view of paraprofessional job effectiveness also has important implication for service delivery issues. Do paraprofessionals actually increase or decrease the quality of service? How do they affect standards of social work practice? When the paraprofessional is seen as an important asset to an agency in its attempts to provide better services, then the quality of service issue takes on increased significance. If the paraprofessionals are seen as window dressing, serving the purposes of agency public relations with the poor, this finding will also have an affect on the use of paraprofessionals in delivering services.

This study adds another dimension to understanding the ingredients of an effective professional-paraprofessional team effort. The readiness of the professional to differentiate between professional and paraprofessional tasks, as well as to tolerate the similarities of these tasks, has implications for effective agency operations. In particular, it will be possible to assess the professional's "effective use of self" not just in terms of affecting clients relations, but also in terms of the paraprofessional. The readiness of professionals to teach and trust paraprofessionals relates directly to effective service delivery. Whether the professionals can or cannot do this has implications for the future training of professionals.

THEORETICAL CONSIDERATIONS

The wide range of literature on organization theory makes it imperative merely to highlight its parameters and then focus on organizational behavior and role-taking. Organization theory relies heavily on Weber's late nineteenth century analysis of formal organizations in which organizations were viewed as highly planned, rational, efficient, stable, and stratified by a hierarchy of workers.[1] Much of the theory building in recent years still draws heavily from Weber's work. However the post World War II era, stimulated by Barnard's work in the 1930s,[2] saw the rise of much study of the informal aspects of formal organizations.[3] It is only very recently that attempts have been made to theoretically merge the notions of formal and informal organizations.[4]

Presthus, in his work, *The Organizational Society*, notes that organizations are large, fairly permanent social systems designed to achieve limited objectives through the coordinated activities of their members. In similar fashion, Scott depicts organizations as collectivities that have been est-ablished for the pursuit of relatively specific objectives on a more or less continuous basis.[5] Scott then goes on to charac-terize the formal and informal aspects of organizations as having (1) the relatively fixed boundaries, (2) a normative order, (3) authority ranks, (4) a communication system, and (5) an incentive system.

Organizations have also been defined as any group of per-sons which includes a system of roles defining their inter-action with one another.[6] Still others view organizations as the products of the interaction between cultural and tech-nological systems, resulting in a social structure which is based upon cultural values and equipped with specific tech-niques to achieve certain goals.[7]

It is important to note that the foundation of organ-izations is the division of labor. There are many ways in which the organization's division of labor can be analyzed. Scott suggests three general levels of analysis: (1) the be-havior of its members, (2) the functioning of a particular aspect of organizational structure, and (3) the interrelation-ship of organization.[8] It is to that first level of analysis, the behavior of the organization's members, that this study is directed.

It is important to understand the organization's influence upon the individual. Merton mentions Veblen's concern over "trained incapacity," in which one's abilities function as inadequacies or blind spots; Dewey's "occupational psycho-sis," in which routines lead to preferences and discrimina-tions; and Warnotte's "professional deformation," in which the individual is remade in the image of the organization.[9] These negative aspects of bureaucracy are contrasted with the bureaucracy's need for a high degree of reliable behavior in terms of conformity, discipline, prescribed patterns of

action, and the infusion of appropriate attitudes and sentiments.[10]

Merton applies these observations to the problems of the
intellectual in bureaucracy.[11] He focuses upon the nature of
the intellectual's clientele—the policy makers, the general
public, and the technical scientific community. In the first
case, the intellectual serves as an advisory role. In the second
case, serving the general public, the intellectual remains
detached from the bureaucracy. In the third case, the intellectual serves in a technical role, worrying about means
and not ends which can manifest itself in serving the interests of science and methodology, or serving the general
ambitions of the intellectual in seeking advancement in the
bureaucracy.[12] This issue of the intellectual's clientele
poses the same type of questions for the paraprofessional.
Whom does the paraprofessional serve: the agency, the
community, or himself?

Etzioni approaches the issue of the clientele in the context of compliance in which an individual serves as a "lower
participant" affected by the power of the organization.[13]
As a result, the individual develops different types of involvement, which Etzioni refers to as (1) alienative, (2) calculative,
and (3) moral. While the first type refers to persons who
operate primarily in total bureaucracies or institutions, such
as the military, prisons, or mental hospitals, the calculative
and moral types of involvement more closely approximate
the description of those serving science and those serving the
public, respectively.[14]

In addition to a typology of involvement, it is important
to mention the nature of conflict faced by individuals in
organizations. Scott notes four main areas of conflict experienced by professionals in bureaucracies: (1) the resistance to
bureaucratic rules, (2) the rejection of bureaucratic stan-

dards, (3) the resistance to bureaucratic supervision, and (4) the conditional loyalty to bureaucracy.[15] He notes that as a result, a professional tends to participate in two systems: his profession and the organization. He emphasizes the distinction to make the point that it is important to examine the profession and the bureaucracy as separate institutions as well as to examine the relationship between the individual and his organization.

Taking the public school as an example of professionals in a bureaucracy, Corwin notes the important distinction between the institution of the school and the institution of the teaching profession.[16] In describing the organizational behavior of a professional employee and a bureaucratic employee, he found that on a "continuum of standardization" the bureaucratic employee seeks to stress the uniformity of all clients' problems in contrast to the professional, who stresses the uniqueness of each client's problems.[17] The organizational climate of the public school probably produces a great deal of overlap between the bureaucratic and professional orientation of teachers. Further evidence is needed to explain the predisposition of professionals to identify particularly with individuals who have unique or special problems which are seen as interesting and requiring the use of professional skills. When clients are treated differentially, does the professional orientation or the list of rules of the organization become the main instrument of action?

In assessing the impact of the organization upon the individual, additional research questions can be posed. To what extent do the professionals conform to Corwin's "continuum of standarization"? Do paraprofessionals demonstrate the bureaucratic employee traits in stressing the uniformity of client problems? Or do professionals tend to demonstrate such traits more often than do paraprofessionals? According to this continuum, then, how professional are professionals?

Organizational Constraints

For paraprofessionals, there are significant organizational constraints which depend upon their base of operation. If they are outside the network of direct service agencies—for example, a new position in local government, a position in a demonstration project, or a position in a religious organization—they derive their strength from their position in another peripheral organizational structure. As a part of a complex of services, paraprofessionals may function in one agency to influence a variety of other agencies in the community.

The source of paraprofessionals' organizational strength is a major determinant in achieving change. This strength includes the power of their own personalities, their human relations skills and contacts, and their inside knowledge of agency functioning which are crucial when they work for agencies (e.g. new neighborhood service centers) outside the network of traditional direct service agencies (e.g. welfare department). On the other hand, if paraprofessionals operate from within an agency, they assume an intra-agency role. As they attempt to facilitate service among various departments and offices, their presence is often seen as the agency's overt commitment to serve low-income clients and as a recognition of the intrinsic difficulty of agencies in serving this function.[18] Their presence may also reflect the covert aims of the agency to hire paraprofessionals as window dressing, which will be elaborated on later. What is even more difficult for the agency to envision is the paraprofessionals' need for independent power and authority within the agency so that their function may not be subverted by other agency needs.

If paraprofessionals are granted such power and authority, they may play a major role in improving agency functioning and efficiency. Here authority is seen as the mixture of suggestion and persuasion, limited in effectiveness by the degree to which the superior responds to, accepts, and understands the subordinate. This represents a shift in the traditional authority pattern.[19] As a result of this shift, paraprofessionals become buffers and two-way facilitators, absorbing the strains from both clients and superiors. They intervene in the vicious cycle of misunderstanding, mutual rejection, and despair that can so easily build up between overworked agencies and overburdened clients.[20] By sanctioning the paraprofessional's intervention on behalf of the clients, the agency may provide itself with a form of quality control—that is, clarifying old policies and establishing new policies—as it attempts to insure against the dangers of overly institutionalized practice and procedures.

Another organizational consideration focuses on the function of the paraprofessional. What might be learned from Sills's study of volunteers is that the ambiguity of agency program and operation for the "untrained" facilitates the "process of selective perception" developed by the volunteer and similarly by the paraprofessional, and is based on their own values and past experiences.[21] As a result, they see the agency as they want to and as they have come to understand its function. This important perspective might provide the paraprofessional with the material evidence necessary to bring about program and procedural change, provided that the paraprofessional is not totally co-opted and acculturated into the service system. As an ideal, the process of training new paraprofessionals can be designed not to come up with "junior" professionals but to recognize that the paraprofessional possesses different kinds of skills from the professional.

An analysis of organizational theory and organizational constraints should also include an understanding of the influence of the individual upon the organization. Role theory provides a body of knowledge which helps to identify the social-psychological aspects of organizational role-taking.

ROLE THEORY

A study of the literature on role theory leads directly to problems surrounding the multidisciplinary use of the concept "role." The psychology-oriented writers view role theory in the context of the personality ingredients of a given role. The sociology-oriented authors utilize role theory in terms of the structural factors of demands upon the roles which people assume. In addition, those authors with a social-psychological orientation stress the importance of how roles are perceived and ultimately performed as the key focus of role theory. Each of these approaches is taken into account in seeking an understanding of the connection between the individual and the complex organization.

At the outset, it is important to highlight the many definitions of "role." Gross and his co-authors provide an excellent overview of the concept of role in their introduction to the study of school superintendents.[22] They trace the origins of role theory back to the anthropologists and the early explications of role in cultural terms. In this context, role took on the meaning of "normative cultural patterns" in which societies ascribed roles to individuals, thereby assigning status. The combination of status and role are defined in terms of attitudes, values, and behavior prevalent in the society.

Gross further notes that role can be defined in a social-psychological context as an individual's definition of his situation with reference to his and other social positions. Related to this definition is a further refinement of role in more structural terms, as the behavior of actors occupying social positions. These approaches to the general definition of role can be integrated into a single frame of reference as suggested by Gross:

> Three basic ideas which appear in most of the conceptual-
> izations considered, if not in the definitions of role them-
> selves, are that individuals: (1) in social locations (2) behave
> (3) with reference to expectations.[23]

In his analysis Gross develops a definition of role in which he
stresses its "relational" and "situational" manifestations and
states that roles are sets of evaluative standards applied to an
incumbent of a particular position; in essence, sets of expectations.

Other writers, such as Gerth and Mills, stress the recur-
rence of units of conduct and, in stressing the dynamism of
ongoing behavior, cite the recurrent interactions forming
patterns of mutually oriented conduct as the essence of
role.[24] In addition to the continuing dynamism of interaction, the longitudinal approach to role is noted in emphasizing birth, maturing experience, evolvement of self
image, and seeking continuous approval leading to the kind
of person one becomes. This approach to role can be somewhat simplistically summarized as follows:

> Everyone is three persons: what he thinks he is, what
> others think is he, and what he thinks others think he is.
> The fourth—what he really is—is unknown, perhaps it
> doesn't exist.[25]

In a similar manner Brown stresses the dynamism of the
concept role and notes that roles are fixed but that people
pass through them—for example, student, apprentice, jour-
neyman.[26] While he admits that there is a certain amount of
creative interpretation allowable in given roles, he states that
roles are sets of norms and that norms are prescriptions for
behavior. Noting that roles are units of a social system and
that personalities are enduring traits and motives linked to
a human organism, he observes that social role is merely the
convergence of prescription, expencancy, and performance.
In the context of passing through roles the psychological
phenomena affecting individual personalities can be catego-

rized in terms of "intra-role conflicts" involving a number of complementary roles—for example, being a father as well as a sailor at sea—and "inter-role conflict" derived from the kinds of roles that conflict—for example, being a judge and a prosecutor simultaneously.

The concept of passing through various roles and the resulting conflicts leads to some hypotheses about the professional and the paraprofessional. To what extent do professionals experience "inter-role" conflict as a result of being trained as caseworkers in contrast to supervising paraprofessional personnel for which they have received very little training? And to what extent do paraprofessionals experience "intra-role" conflict as a result of serving the needs of their employers and serving the needs of the community which they presumably represent?

While other references could be noted for further refinement of the definition of role, it seems more advantageous for this study to cite the eclectic view of Levenson, who successfully integrates the major aspects of the concept "role" in the context of the organizational setting.[27] Levenson combines the structural (sociological), the interpersonal (social psychological), and the personal (psychological) aspects of the concept. In doing so, he stresses the interrelationship of (1) given role demands and role opportunities, (2) the role perceptions and performances, and (3) the personality in its role related aspects. Role is then defined as an aspect of organizational physiology, involving function, adaptation, and process.

In this study it was important to note that roles exist not only in value systems and professional traditions but also become institutionalized in job descriptions. The use of job descriptions provides organizations with opportunities to make role performance more predictable. However, such descriptions also invite the possibility of deviations, in the sense that people sometimes fail to live up to certain role expectations or, in other cases, actually perform roles that are not in their job descriptions. A review of a sample of paraprofessional job descriptions, for example, revealed an extremely broad definition of role and function. Assessment of such descriptions in terms of organizational role predictability leads to two possible interpretations: (1) that a broad description was based on the fact that no one could predict paraprofessional job performance; or (2) that paraprofessionals could function best if given the widest latitude. Role demands, role performance, and the unique personality in role-related functions were significant unknowns for both the professional and paraprofessional.

While job descriptions indicate the formal role expectations, the informal aspects are more difficult to define and therefore appear less frequently in the literature. When the informal division of labor conflicts with the formal division of labor, discrepancies arise that may result in certain compromises between persons of different status, such as the professional and paraprofessional. Taking organizational roles provides a context for understanding such discrepancies.

ORGANIZATIONAL ROLE CONFLICT

To be overly client oriented and to transmit the client's demands upward has been traditionally a relatively unrewarding experience in many organizations. What is under certain conditions a great strength, namely the paraprofessional's ability to identify closely with the low income individual's problems and feelings, can under other circumstances promote difficulty if the identification remains too narrow.[28] With paraprofessionals playing a buffer role between the agency professionals and the client group, and with the limited training paraprofessionals have for handling such a role, there is a high probability that they will be co-opted. The strong tendency for co-optation to the side of the agency professional can lead to what Etzioni calls "simulated co-optation."[29] This suggests that the communication problem between the agency and the client has been solved with the creation of the buffer role, whereas in actuality it only conceals the need for real communication and influence.

The result of such co-optation can lead to the paraprofessionals' loss of touch with the community. In addition, their new status can lead to feelings of superiority over poor people as paraprofessionals themselves soon aspire to middle class status. Such feelings of superiority will militate against their effectiveness as the paraprofessional may fall into the trap of blaming the victim such as poor people for their poverty condition. Not only do the paraprofessionals become upwardly mobile as a result of their salaried positions and prestige, but they also tend to become upwardly conforming to the strong pull towards middle-class status.

As an example of co-optation, community organization aides in antipoverty progams were concerned about the rationale for being hired. It seemed to them that the so-called low income leaders who were stirring up problems for the housing authorities, city halls, and city councils were suddenly hired by the antipoverty programs. As a result, they found it difficult to continue their local fights when restricted by the limitations of their new staff positions. As Pearl and Reissman again point out:

> The main danger here is that indigenous low-income workers may be utilized to forestall, reduce, or deflect the militancy of the community they represent . . . . They can be employed with a one-way communication focus to subtly and effectively convey the wishes of their employer—whether in the school, the social agency, the city administration, or the welfare department. To put it crudely, they become a new kind of indigenous stool-pigeon.[30]

Another area of difficulty concerns the issue of authority. Many paraprofessionals have problems handling authority, possessing it, or responding to it, because of their personal experiences and class standing. Since they have had little opportunity to exercise authority in their own lives beyond their families, it becomes a new phenomenon which requires some adjustment. On the other hand, they have usually had poor experiences of reponding to authority—housing authority and power of eviction, police departments and problems of brutality, welfare departments and power to withhold checks. So paraprofessionals must also learn to adjust to the authority—rules and regulations—of the agency for which they work. As a result, the new job positions for the paraprofessional require a specific set of sanctions from the agency regarding the enforcement of responsibility and the specialization of decision-making which serve as the primary factors in establishing the authority of the paraprofessional.[31]

All of these dilemmas culminate in the relationship of the paraprofessional to the professional. Agency adminstrative personnel tend to have difficulty defining the roles and abilities, tasks and competencies of the professional staff, especially around the notion of the flexibility needed to appreciate and understand the paraprofessional.[32] Such flexibility takes the form of permitting the reorganization of job classifications and accepting paraprofessionals into a team structure. To complicate this picture, the members of the social work profession to serve as team members in many problem-solving situations. However, like the paraprofessionals, they too have had to learn new roles. In particular, they have found it necessary to shift from a team member role or supervisor role to the role of team leader.

Within this same problem area, additional precautions are necessary with respect to reverse alienation in which professionals tend to be devalued by emphasizing the past difficulties of professionals in reaching and truly communicating with the poor. It has been difficult for professionals to adjust to the fact that the employment of indigenous paraprofessionals produces new roles for the professionals as consultants, supervisors, teachers, coordinators, and team leaders, thereby creating new role expectations to complement the role of the new paraprofessional.

While change in social institutions is quite slow and, therefore, perhaps difficult to predict, it is clear that many new jobs have been created for the low-income, indigenous persons as paraprofessionals. However, the crucial issue centers around the ultimate utilization of paraprofessionals and the institutionalizing of paraprofessional job positions into career patterns, whereby the paraprofessional can advance. The issue of career patterns boils down to one basic question:

> Whether new careers are going to develop into a movement of the poor for the poor, serve as a basic approach to poverty and to the reorganization and derigidification of the professions, or simply be an expansion of the paraprofessional job market.[33]

The addition of the paraprofessional to the agency staff can be strategic in influencing a more flexible role definition for the professional. At the same time there is danger that the paraprofessional will be molded into the human service system more often than the paraprofessional will be able to alter the role definition of the professional.

However, it is also necessary to highlight the dangers inherent in romanticizing the role of the paraprofessional. Such dangers have been concisely itemized by Hubert Jones of the Roxbury Multi-Service Center:

1. Polarization between professional and paraprofessional results in severe problems in providing team approach to the delivery of services.
2. Faulty assumptions are made when the competence of paraprofessionals is assessed only in terms of ghetto living experience. There is a great need for in-service training.
3. Problems of agency self-aggrandisement as experienced when paraprofessionals are hired as "window

dressing" with little attention given to specific service problems and jobs.

4. Failure syndrome results when paraprofessionals are
    not involved in true service delivery or in the de-
    cision-making aspects of changing agency programs.
5. Paraprofessionals tend to be as frightened and con-
    fused as professionals in a new service delivery
    agency and are sometimes more withdrawn.
6. A myth has been created that only paraprofessionals
    teach professionals when in actuality it is a two-way
    street.[34]

Despite these problems, paraprofessionals have made significant contributions in: (1) recognizing and pointing out
some of the inhibiting elements found in the roles assumed
by professionals by forcing professionals to distinguish between social distance and objectivity; (2) helping to point
out tasks which can be carried out by paraprofessionals; and
(3) helping professionals become advocates for the clients
and more strategy-oriented in the problem-solving process.
And in turn, the professionals' contribution has included
demonstrating: (1) how action proceeds from knowledge
about a situation; (2) that on-going learning is crucial to
improving job performance; and (3) that in the day-to-day
job performance, professional values of confidentiality,
self-determination, and job dignity of the indivdual have
relevance.

Chapter 10

ORGANIZATIONAL ROLE-TAKING

Both role theory and organization theory provide an important knowledge base for this study in that they contribute to an understanding of the interaction between two different status groups as they perform similar and overlapping tasks. The new organizational roles developed by professionals and paraprofessionals influence the behavior of both. They affect the development of deviations from such professional norms as "only a trained social worker can do that" and the way these deviations are sanctioned because of new values that are incorporated by both professionals and paraprofessionals (such as, "We both can do that").

The analysis of organizational roles also leads to increased recognition of how importantly belief systems affect interpersonal behavior. Actually there is a good deal of role differentiation between professionals and paraprofessionals. However, these real differences—for example, status and salary—are modified by the adoption of a belief system in which the high-status people indicate to the low-status people that it is theoretically possible for their role differences to be reduced or even for their roles to merge. This modification of beliefs can be achieved through education, experience, and a cultural sensitizing to organizational and professional norms. The implication is that the routes are open for paraprofessionals to achieve professional status.

A THEORETICAL MODEL

The concept of organizational role-taking serves as the key element in the theoretical model utilized in this case study. Katz and Kahn observe that each individual responds to his organization in terms of his perception of it, a perception which may differ in various ways from the actual organization.[1] Therefore, they suggest that in order to study organizational roles one should identify the relevant social system or subsystem, locate the recurring events which fit together, and ascertain the role expectations of a given set of related offices. By focusing on an individual's self-concept and the fact that a role consists of one or more recurrent activities, Katz and Kahn suggest the concept of role episode. This episode consists of role-sending—expectations and information—and role-receiving—perceptions and behavior. The role episode is influenced by three additional phenomena: organizational factors, interpersonal factors, and attributes of the persons involved. All factors appear in Figure 3, which highlights the theoretical model and the dynamics of organizational role-taking.[2]

Since the Katz and Kahn model implies that organizational role-taking occurs primarily within the confines of a formal organization, another question is posed for this case study. To what extent does the focal person—that is, paraprofessional—in both formal and less formal organizations also have role expectations which result in role messages being sent back to the role sender—that is, professionals? In this case the

Figure 3.

Katz and Kahn Model for Organizational Role-Taking

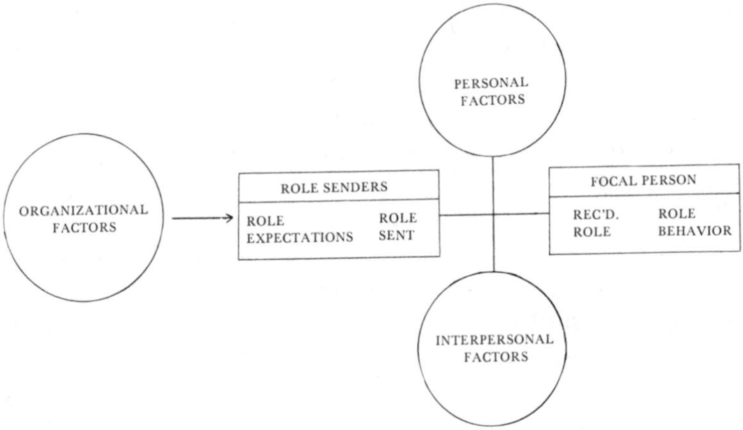

professionals receive role messages which in turn affect their own role behavior. This feedback effect in the model serves as the theoretical focal point of this study.

The Katz and Kahn model served as the organizing framework for the study and data was collected on the personal, interpersonal, and organizational factors influencing the professional-paraprofessional relationship. An analysis of common tasks was used to make partial assessment of the degree of congruence between the role expectations of the professionals and the role behavior of the paraprofessionals.

A modification of the model, noted later in the chapter, helps to clarify the manner in which paraprofessionals have influenced the expectations of the professionals. It is possible, then, to assess the paraprofessionals' higher-than-expected job performance and their generally smooth transition into organizational life in terms of their role-sending potential. For the professional, did the process of organizational role-taking involve a shift from an emphasis on supervisory control to the development of a consultative role based on autonomy for the subordinate? For the paraprofessional, did the organizational role-taking involve a transition from the subservience of a client role to the autonomy of a colleague role? These questions require further refinement in order to research the professional-paraprofessional relationship to determine the nature of role expectations and resulting behavior. While the process of consultation among colleagues represents a respect for each other's roles and functions, it will be noted in the next few chapters that the relationship is influenced significantly by organizational, personal, and interpersonal factors.

THE CENTRAL QUESTIONS

The central questions concern the nature and extent of discrepancies and similarities between the divison of labor between professionals and paraprofessionals and their beliefs about what should be professional and paraprofessional tasks and functions in social services. This problem is characteristic of complex organizations and of the traditional status hierarchy among workers.

It is important to point out that the differences between professionals and paraprofessionals is not easily noted by the outsider. In a hospital, physicians wear white coats and stethoscopes. In the agencies under study, employees are not distinguished by any symbol whatever. They can wear similar clothing. Indeed, in some cases the paraprofessional may be better dressed than the professional. In other words, the client would not know who is who. The same might be said for the executive of a large agency. The status difference is known only to the insiders. It is based on the size of their paychecks, the kinds of questions they can answer or that are likely to be put to them, and the kinds of tasks that they are assigned. These facts make the blurring of status and roles very complicated. As a result, they are most interesting to analyze and study. Both the compatability of the work relationship and the conflict rising from confusion over roles and functions provide focal points for the central questions.

From preliminary observations made in several agencies, certain problem areas related to the nature of the professional-paraprofessional relationship could be identified. The study began with several hypotheses in mind:

1. *Professionals will consistenly perceive the capabilities of paraprofessionals regarding client problem-solving more narrowly than will paraprofessionals.* In this situation, the supervising social worker operates on the assumption that the paraprofessional can perform very few meaningful tasks. While they might be considered able to gather information, very few paraprofessionals are perceived as having the capability of formulating plans of action to better the situation of a client. In essence Mrs. Smith, who is poorly educated, black, and has a low income, is considered capable of very little other than relating the agency's program to the client population. Paraprofessionals, on the other hand, perceive a much broader role for themselves and assume functions formerly carried out by professionals.

2. *Professionals, because of their higher status and training, will perceive significantly more work flexibility for themselves than will paraprofessionals.* The social worker is socialized through professional training to assume different roles according to client needs. The training assumes that flexibility in client relations carries over into work role flexibility and that seeking new solutions for the problems of the family on welfare carries over into seeking new ways to improve the functioning and service delivery of the agency.

While professionals may assume such flexibility for themselves, they will not perceive the same for paraprofessionals, whom they see as needing a great deal of structure—keeping schedules and attending to details—based, in part, on the presumption that paraprofessionals are incapable of changing their plans to help a client in the midst of an undertaking. In essence, professionals expect very little from paraprofessionals in relation to the creative use of self.

3. *The nature of the agency-based social work profession predisposes the professionals toward perceiving the need for stronger supervisory control of paraprofessionals than paraprofessionals deem necessary.* Linked to the social worker's perception that Mrs. Smith, the paraprofessional, needs a highly structured job is the notion that she will require strong supervision. Conditioned to seek and provide on-the-job supervision, professionals will perceive similar needs on the part of paraprofessionals in order to be accountable to the agency. Mrs. Smith, for her part, will comply with this common agency expectation but will perceive professionals as preoccupied with establishing a supervisory relationship. "Leave me alone and let me do it my way," will be the reaction to the social worker's predisposition towards strong supervisory control.

THE RESEARCH FRAMEWORK

A conceptual model adapted from the work of Katz and Kahn was used as a tool to map out the ongoing relationship between professionals and paraprofessionals (Figure 4). It proved to be helpful in charting the dynamics of the relationship. It represents an adaptation of the original model, since the professional-paraprofessional relationship was hypothesized as different from the traditional supervisor-

Figure 4.

Conceptual Model of Organizational Role-Taking

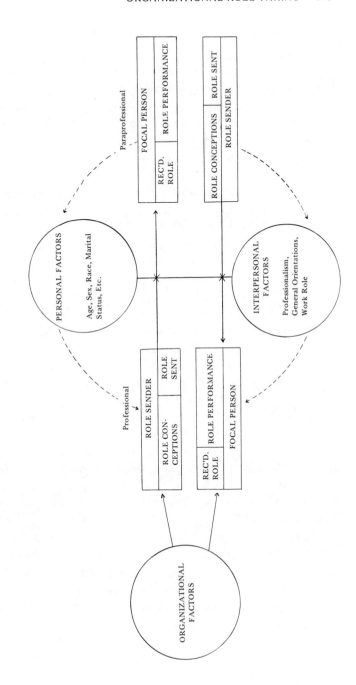

supervisee relationship in which authority flows primarily downward.

The model explores the logical alternatives that exist when professionals and paraprofessionals interact in regard to specific functions. It allows for the possibilities that professionals will accord paraprofessionals the same as, lower, or in certain respects higher status than themselves. Organizational factors, personal characteristics, and the elements of the ongoing relationship provided the framework for analysis.

The organizational influences of agency leadership, communication, program location, organizational differentiation, tradition, and community relatedness were considered important contextual variables which were assessed for the role demands which they made upon the professional-paraprofessional relationship. Second, personal characteristics—such as age, sex, race—of the professionals and paraprofessionals were viewed as important independent variables affecting the relationship. It was also important to assess interpersonal factors through attitudes related to values about professionalism, attitudes about the work role, and general orientation to the notions of trust, self-confidence, responsibility, and idea conformity. Third, it was necessary to delimit the nature and extent of the relationship itself. In doing so both the role perceptions—How do you view your supervisor? How well has the paraprofessional adapted?—and role performances—How are tasks assigned? How often do you meet with your supervisor?—were assessed from the perspective of the professional as well as from that of the paraprofessional.

The components of the conceptual model represent an attempt to order the complex web of human interactions. Under such complex conditions, how is labor divided? Who should be the one to discuss child-rearing practices with a client, the professional or the paraprofessional? Both? Under what conditions? Similar questions can be raised about many of the wide range of tasks which constitute the core of the worker-client relationship.

The analysis of tasks leads to the phenomenon of role-blurring in which the professional and paraprofessional share similar tasks and contribute different levels of understanding. Where the paraprofessional can relate most effectively to the emergency nature of the client problem, the professional might relate more effectively to the precipitating causes and long range consequences of the problem. Each response complements the other. Both responses overlap. As a result, role-blurring becomes most effective when there exists some degree of role differentiation.

This case study, then, seeks to gain a further understanding of the following issues:

1. Does *role-blurring* mean lack of role clarity? If so, does a lack of *role clarity* impair the ability of the professional or paraprofessional to adapt to new situations? If not, what does role-blurring mean?

2. How important is the distinction that the *equality* of professionals and paraprofessionals which derives from providing equally important agency functions does not necessarily mean *equivalence* in the area of knowledge and skills?

3. And finally, how pervasive is the attitude that *different* roles in delivering social services implies that there are inferior roles in which staff members, for example, associate menial tasks with lower status levels in the hierarchy of the agency?

The organizational nature of human service programs lends itself to competition for recognition. The new paraprofessionals were seen as answers to the problems of delivering services to the poverty areas of our cities. As their numbers grew, their desires for recognition also increased. Pruger and Specht observed:

> In the case of organizationally based professions, the forces that insure organizational discipline complement the pressures that induce professional reliability. And, because much of the professional's self-image rests on this perception of his dearly bought competence, competitors arriving on the scene through non-traditional routes must almost certainly be considered impudent upstarts, if not conscious usurpers.[3]

Who are these competitors? Who are the professionals who are presumably threatened by these alleged upstarts? As with any case study, it is important to gain a profile of the participants as background material for understanding relationships. It is then possible to assess the degree of competition presumably provided by paraprofessionals as well as the degree of resistance displayed by professionals.

CHARACTERISTICS OF SAMPLE POPULATION

The differences between professionals and paraprofessionals in this study were not simply a matter of education although this is the manifest basis of the distinction. Because education is linked to so many other factors, there were significant status and social experience differences. For example, 43 percent of the professional social workers as opposed to 76 percent of the paraprofessionals were black. The professionals were generally younger than the paraprofessionals. For many paraprofessionals, it was the first job in which satisfaction could be gained daily from helping those in need. For some, their jobs as health expediters or neighborhood aides represented the first step out of menial day labor. For others, it was a chance for fresh air outside the assembly line routine of the laundry plant. While the career lines varied, the upward movement from domestic work to factory work to human service employment was quite common. Paraprofessional employment meant dignity for the first time, and many feared to lose this newfound status if they questioned the dead end nature of their jobs.

As a result of the extensive research carried out on paraprofessionals, it is possible to assess the representativeness of the paraprofessional sample in this study in relation to other findings. (This is not the case with respect to the sample of professionals, in which, comparable research findings are most nonexistent.) Information in Table 6 is organized into the following categories: racial composition, marital status, educational status, age, sex, salary, and employment status prior to paraprofessional employment. When contrasted with national data on paraprofessionals, several interesting differences emerge.[4] Significant differences occurred in the categories of age, education, and prior employment status. The paraprofessional population in this study was substantially older—75 percent over forty years of age in contrast to approximately 25 percent in a national study—was better educated—51 percent with some college compared to 6 percent in the national study—and generally had been employed prior to paraprofessional employment— 77 percent compared to 11 percent in the national study. Other categories from the national study compared closely to the data in this study.

Table 6.   Select Profile of Paraprofessionals under Study in
Six Eastern Cities
(N = 323)

1.   AGE

39 or under	25%
40 or over	75%
Total	100%

2.   RACE

Black	76%
White	20%
Other	4%
Total	100%

3.   SEX

Male	13%
Female	87%
Total	100%

4.   MARITAL STATUS

Married	45%
Divorced, Separated, Widowed or Single	55%
Total	100%

5.   EDUCATION

Some College	51%
High School Diploma	33%
Without High School Diploma	16%
Total	100%

6.   SALARY

Over $6,000	14%
$4,000 to $6,000	50%
Less than $4,000	36%
Total	100%

7.   EMPLOYMENT STATUS (Prior to paraprofessional employment)

Unemployed	23%
Employed	77%
Total	100%

One finding which appears significant in the profile data is that just prior to their paraprofessional employment a large percentage—77 percent—of the paraprofessionals were employed in positions ranging from clerical and sales positions to cooks and domestic workers. This information contradicts the commonly held notion that paraprofessional jobs were filled by the unemployed. Quite to the contrary, these jobs seemed to have benefited the *working* poor.

The population of paraprofessionals under study also represented considerable experience beyond their immediately prior employment. Two-thirds of them—67 percent—had been working for more than two years as paraprofessionals immediately prior to their present job and 28 percent of this group had more than four years of paraprofessional experience. Their income levels tended to reflect this experience; over 13 percent earned more than $6,000 per year and the majority—51 percent—earned between $4,000 and $6,000. There was still a substantial proportion—36 percent—of paraprofessionals who earned less than $4,000 per year in 1970. In terms of the number of wage earners per family, a sizable proportion—58.5 percent—of the paraprofessionals represented the primary source of family income. The remaining 41.5 percent combined incomes with a spouse's or relative's salary to support the family.

When it came to organizational involvement, a large number of paraprofessionals—72 percent—did not belong to a paraprofessional association. This topic received a great deal of attention in the data collection discussion sessions. Many paraprofessionals expressed considerable fear about organizing into an association, fear based on suspected retaliation from their agencies. Only in Pittsburgh was there a strong commitment to a paraprofessional association, one which had already produced significant results by opening up educational opportunities at the local community college and university. For many paraprofessionals, it was the first time that organizing had been discussed so openly.

No data could be found on the number of professional social workers involved with paraprofessionals either nationally or regionally. Therefore this study represents the only known attempt to describe the population in six eastern cities. Since no other group of social workers was available to test the representativeness of this sample, this study places more emphasis on comparisons between the characteristics of the professionals and paraprofessionals. Table 7 represents a profile of professionals included in the study. It includes the same categories as those used with the paraprofessionals, with the addition of educational status and number of years' experience in supervising paraprofessionals. All the social workers held masters degrees. Over two-thirds of them —69 percent—had less than three years experience in supervising paraprofessionals; the remainder—31 percent—had more than three years experience.

Table 7.   Select Profile of Professionals under Study in
Six Eastern Cities
(N = 100)

1. AGE

39 or under	49%
40 or over	51%
Total	100%

2. RACE

Black	43%
White	56%
Other	1%
Total	100%

3. SEX

Male	31%
Female	69%
Total	100%

4. MARITAL STATUS

Married	58%
Separated, Widowed, Divorced or Single	42%
Total	100%

5. SALARY

Less than $8,000	4%
$8,000 to $12,000	55%
Over $12,000	41%
Total	100%

6. SUPERVISORY EXPERIENCE
    (Exclusively with Paraprofessionals)

Less than 3 years	69%
3 or more years	31%
Total	100%

There was a smaller proportion of black social workers—43 percent—than of black paraprofessionals—76 percent. The professionals—49 percent under the age thirty-nine—were significantly younger than paraprofessionals—25 percent under age thirty-nine. The sex distribution was somewhat similar: 69 percent female in the professional group and 87 percent female in the paraprofessional group. A larger proportion of professionals—58 percent—were married than of paraprofessionals—45 percent.

The salaries of professionals—55 percent earning $8,000 to $12,000 per year—were generally double the amount paid to paraprofessionals. A large proportion—41 percent of professionals earned over $12,000 per year. The income of 73 percent of the professionals was the primary family income. It was also noted that a large proportion of professionals—87 percent—belonged to one or more professional organizations and that 62 percent of them attended meetings ranging in frequency from monthly to semiannually.

Two additional categories can be used to assess differences between professionals and paraprofessionals. In seeking to learn with whom each group spent its off-the-job free time, it was found that the majority of professionals—70 percent—and of paraprofessionals—91 percent—spent their time with people in other lines of work, primarily neighbors and family members. It was suspected, but not found conclusively to be so, that a significantly higher proportion of professionals would fraternize with people in the same profession than might be the case with paraprofessionals who had yet to create a colleague subculture, as evidenced in part by the lack of paraprofessional associations.

In comparing data on the size of the community in which each population was raised before reaching sixteen years of age, it was suspected that professionals would come from more urban backgrounds and paraprofessionals from more rural origins. However, this category also yielded no significant differences, as both professionals—65 percent—and paraprofessionals—58 percent—came from urban backgrounds—a large city or suburb of over 100,000 population. In the light of the fact that the data was gathered only in large cities, this finding is not too surprising.

Data was also collected on the degree of professionalization demonstrated by the social workers. When asked about the relevance of their training for their current work with paraprofessionals, 76 percent of the professionals felt their training was only somewhat relevant, if at all. Reading professional journals was used as an indicator of interest in the profession; 82 percent of the professionals either read one journal regularly or several journals sporadically.

In response to inquiries about the nature of manpower shortage in the human services, one-half of the professionals—49 percent—felt that more professionals should be hired while the other half felt it was equally important to hire more paraprofessionals. On the topic of values, professionals felt that job satisfaction—91 percent—and freedom on the job —62 percent—were very important. Of less importance generally were financial security—69 percent "somewhat or rarely important"—and professional indentification—78 percent. These values are summarized in Table 8 and receive further attention later as they affect the professional-paraprofessional relationship.

Table 8.   Value Orientations of Professionals
(Percentages)

Values	Very Important	Somewhat Important	Rarely Important	Total
Job Satisfaction	91	9	0	100%
Freedom/Autonomy	62	29	9	100%
Financial Security	28	53	19	100%
Professional Identification	18	42	40	100%

To complement the demographic data for each group, information was also gathered on the general orientations of the professionals and paraprofessionals. Information on personal predispositions external to the work setting provided a broader description of each group. While complete personality information would require extensive psychological testing, it was decided to attempt a social profile of each respondent. This approach was based on Roger's theory of self, in which he suggests that a person is pretty much what he says he is.[5] Though he has been criticized for this common-sense viewpoint, his approach provided the rationale for the construction of a general orientations scale.

The scale was divided into four categories related to self-concept: trustfulness, self-confidence, accountability, and idea conformity. These categories were derived from a study of the relationships among social class, occupations, and personal values.[6] Data on trustfulness related to the beliefs of professionals and paraprofessionals as to what extent their fellow man could be trusted. It was found that the professionals—87 percent—were generally more trusting than the paraprofessionals—67 percent. The category of self-confidence was used to gain information on the degee to which the professionals and paraprofessionals were confident of their own capacities. The professionals—84 percent —and paraprofessionals—79 percent—both reflected a high degree of self-confidence.

The category of accountability was used to assess the degree to which both groups had a sense of being controlled by outside forces in contrast to a sense of having some control over their own fate. Here the two groups differed sharply. Professionals—81 percent—had a strong sense of organizational accountability and responsibility in contrast to the more fatalistic view of the paraprofessionals, only 33 percent of whom shared the perceptions of the professionals.

The fourth category, idea conformity, was incorporated in the scale to assess the degree to which professionals and paraprofessionals believed that their ideas mirrored those of the social groups to which they belonged. In this case, both professionals—45 percent—and paraprofessionals—49 percent—displayed similar perceptions of independent thinking, perceiving their ideas as differing from the ideas held by their respective social groups. The remainder of each group—55 percent of the professionals and 51 percent of the paraprofessionals—viewed their ideas as similar to the prevailing sentiments of their social groups. Table 9 represents a summary of these general orientation findings.

Table 9.   General Orientations

| | Professionals (N = 100) | | Paraprofessionals (N = 323) | |
	High (%)	Low (%)	High (%)	Low (%)
Trustfulness	87	13	67	33
Self-confidence	84	16	79	21
Accountability	81	19	33	67
Idea conformity	45	55	49	51

While there is a danger in placing too much confidence in generalizations about the characteristics of the two samples, several tendencies do emerge. The paraprofessionals represent an older, predominantly female, poorly paid population somewhat akin to the profile of the social work profession twenty years ago. The disproportionately high number of blacks and the absence of young male paraprofessionals might be explained in terms of the low salaries, somewhat precarious status, and the poorly defined functions of paraprofessional employment. On the other hand, an older and more experienced population of women who have shared the lifestyles of their clients and whose work requires much compassion, perseverance, and understanding might preclude the entrance of young, inexperienced males or whites.

The paraprofessionals represent a rather stable population with aspirations for advancement as reflected in their prior employment histories and rising educational level. Further evidence can be given to support the high degree of aspiration detected among the paraprofessionals. Given a hypothetical choice of careers and asked to assume that they had all the necessary qualifications, paraprofessionals—70 percent— overwhelmingly selected the social work profession.[7]

The high degree of self-confidence and reasonably high degree of trust in their fellow man among paraprofessionals reflect important ingredients for the emergence of a social movement, as does the high degree of job commitment despite poor personnel practices. The responses to the degree of idea conformity which divided the paraprofessional population in half symbolize the new ambivalence created when a lifetime influence of working-class ideas is confronted by the middle-class orientations of the professionals with whom they work. The low degree of accountability among paraprofessionals reflects, in part, the continuing feeling of fatalism which arises from the uncertain job security and a lack of opportunities for advancement. The problems related to advancement and career ladders have been noted earlier.

In contrast to the paraprofessionals, the professionals epitomize middle-class standing. With master's degrees, salaries which are twice those of paraprofessionals, and a general youthfulness in contrast to paraprofessionals, the professionals reflect the recent trends in the social work profession.[8] The increasing number of blacks—43 percent in this sample—as well as the rising proportion of men in the social work profession—31 percent in this sample—are an indication of renewed interest among professionals in the involvement of paraprofessionals in service change and service delivery.

Many professionals are new to the supervision of paraprofessionals. This can be accounted for in part by the brief history of major paraprofessional involvement in community services, dating only from the Economic Opportunity Act of 1964. Consistent with the aims of professional social work practice, this sample of professionals reflects a generally high degree of trustfulness, self-confidence, and accountability. These professionals appear to represent a special breed in the social work profession, a finding which will be supported with further evidence in the following chapters.

Chapter 11

WHO DOES WHAT?

Experimentation with new divisions of labor raises basic questions about what is a professional task and what is a paraprofessional task. Many paraprofessionals have assumed tasks that traditionally have been within the sphere of professional activity. In this study an ideological dimension of equal competence became apparent. With increasing experience, paraprofessionals have come to believe that they can perform tasks which have traditionally been reserved for trained social workers. This belief has gained support simply because some paraprofessionals have been extremely success- ful in developing beginning social work skills quickly. On the other hand, there are also professionals involved in this growing ideology who find themselves believing that para- professionals can perform traditionally professional tasks. For some professionals this raises serious questions about the nature of their own practice. For others, it is a welcome

opportunity to expand their skills into new areas of consultation, teaching, supervision, and administration. In any event,
the ideological component found in this emerging social
movement is significant.

In addition to the ideological component of equal competence, the study of a social movement must assess the context in which the movement developed, namely the agency.
Agencies have been involved in an experiment of planful
status manipulation. Low status persons, the paraprofessionals, have been introduced into professional agencies with a
mandate, rarely explicit, to experiment with the extent to
which status differences can be minimized. When such
differences persisted, it was implied that they should be
rationalized on the basis of some measurable standard of
what the professional and paraprofessional are capable of
performing. What happened in agencies which experienced
this planned change effort?

The evidence indicates that existing status differences
were not fully accepted, resulting in pressure from paraprofessionals for greater equality. Paraprofessionals began
to complain about poor salaries and the lack of career ladders
and began to question the agencies' motivation for their employment. These complaints arose despite the fact that
paraprofessionals came from occupations in which the career
opportunities were far more limited and the salaries much
lower. In other words, by being placed in a new system where
they were interacting in an overlapping fashion with people
of higher status, they began to adopt some of the standards
of the professionals. There was a very rapid increase in their
level of aspiration, reflected in part by their dissatisfaction.

However, evidence gathered for this study indicates that
the status differences are not of such a gross nature that they
lead to a clash or friction within the agency. There is a
remarkable degree of consensus on the roles and functions
of each level of employee in the agency. Indeed, the proportion of professionals and paraprofessionals who agree on

their respective roles and functions is much greater than those who differ. The data on the work relationship, job flexibility and performance, task differentiation and analysis, and work role rigidity provide some of the evidence which reflects the similarity of views.

DIMENSIONS OF THE WORK RELATIONSHIP

Data was collected in four categories in an effort to assess both groups' perceptions of the work situation. The categories included job effectiveness, job flexibility, job performance, and task differentiation. The paraprofessionals' activities were assessed through examination of the perceptions and attitudes of both professionals and paraprofessionals.

A key finding was the consistently strong similarity of perceptions regarding work roles shared by professionals and paraprofessionals irrespective of agency or city. In the area of job effectiveness, the professionals felt that the paraprofessionals had increased the program effectiveness of the agency. Since the early days of the War on Poverty, it has been assumed that effectiveness is based in large part on paraprofessionals serving their own neighborhoods. When asked to assess this assumption, one-third of the professionals felt that it was very important for paraprofessionals to serve their own neighborhoods, one-third felt that it was somewhat important, and the remaining third agreed with a majority of paraprofessionals—52 percent—that it was important that paraprofessionals serve any neighborhood. One inference which can be drawn from these responses is that the paraprofessional job relates more to individual skills and agency supports than it does to the type or location of the clientele.

Another dimension of paraprofessional job effectiveness was assessed through the differential perceptions of how agency acceptance was increased in the community as a result of employing paraprofessionals. Some professionals—29 percent—felt that the presence of paraprofessionals in the agency had greatly increased the acceptance of the agency. A majority of paraprofessionals—57 percent—felt that they had greatly increased agency acceptance in the community and therefore were effectively performing the jobs for which they were recruited. Other professionals—42 percent—felt that there had been only a limited increase in agency acceptance, a view held by only a minority of paraprofessionals. This differential perception highlighted the difficulty of finding measures of effectiveness which can be trusted with some degree of confidence. The degree of community acceptance was difficult to determine. It was clear, however, that the paraprofessionals found it more important to be positive about their impact than did the professionals, in order to support the ideology that there are specialized skills utilized by paraprofessionals in relating to the community.

JOB FLEXIBILITY

The diffuse nature of paraprofessional job descriptions made it difficult to assess performance accurately. As a result the data reflects attitudes about autonomy, flexibility, and performance. As a measure of paraprofessional job flexibility, professionals and paraprofessionals were asked to characterize the degree of paraprofessional autonomy as perceived in terms of freedom to function on the basis of one's own best judgment, either allowed or actively fostered by the agency. While 38 percent of professionals perceived paraprofessional autonomy to be high and 47 percent saw it as medium, a majority of paraprofessionals—55 percent—as noted in Table 4—perceived a high degree of autonomy on the job. Only a minority of paraprofessionals—30 percent—viewed their autonomy as medium. Despite the relative similarity of perceptions of paraprofessional autonomy held by both professionals and paraprofessionals, paraprofessionals continued to perceive their jobs as limited. The lack of job stability as seen in the repeated complaints about poor salaries and lack of career ladders appeared to be an important hindrance to the paraprofessionals' ability to derive any job satisfaction from their perceived high degree of autonomy on the job.

Table 10.   Differential Perceptions of Paraprofessionals' Autonomy (Percentages)

Autonomy for Paraprofessionals	High	Medium	Low	Don't Know	Total
Professionals' View (N = 100)	38	47	5	10	100%
Paraprofessionals' View (N = 323)	55	30	5	10	100%

Several approaches were used to assess the complexities of job performance. Both the professionals and paraprofessionals were asked to assess the degree to which paraprofessionals were given enough to do and were encouraged to strive to the extent of their capabilities. A large proportion of the professionals—77 percent—stated that paraprofessionals had enough to do and were encouraged to strive to the utmost of their capabilities. Among the paraprofessionals, 93 percent responded that they were given enough to do, and 82 percent felt that they were sufficiently encouraged.

The professionals were also asked to evaluate the extent to which the paraprofessionals had adapted to their jobs. A majority of professionals—78 percent—felt that paraprofessionals were involved in their jobs and were seeking self-improvement. Only 22 percent felt that there was some indifference toward the job or that employment was viewed as "just another job."

Despite the difficulties in gaining multiple assessments of job performance, data showed that professionals offered positive comments about the general excellence with which the paraprofessionals performed their jobs. Yet the lack of clearly defined job expectations made it difficult to know how performance could actually be measured. While there appeared to be some agreement between the professionals and paraprofessionals regarding job performance, questions related to task analysis yielded more definitive findings.

TASK DIFFERENTIATION

The primary souce of data on task differentiation was a task analysis scale. However, more general questions were also raised about the complexity of tasks and the professional component of task performance. Both sets of respondents were asked to categorize the types of paraprofessional tasks undertaken—routine as opposed to complicated. Fifty-nine percent of the professionals and 46 percent of the paraprofessionals perceived an equal balance between routine and complicated tasks assigned to and carried out by paraprofessionals. Of the remaining professionals 23 percent thought that the tasks were mostly routine; 17 percent considered them mostly complicated. Of the remaining paraprofessionals, 35 percent considered their tasks mostly routine; 15 percent considered them as mostly complicated, as noted in Table 11.

Table 11.   Complexity of Paraprofessional Task (Percentages)

	Mostly Complicated	Mostly Mixed	Mostly Routine	Do Not Know	Total
Professionals' View	17	59	23	1	100%
Paraprofessionals' View	15	46	35	4	100%

The professionals were asked if there was any difference between their tasks and those of an experienced paraprofessional. The professionals—78 percent—generally stated that there were differences and highlighted their diagnostic, treatment, supervisory, and administrative skills. It was interesting to note that 18 percent of the professionals felt that there were no significant distinctions between their tasks and those of the paraprofessionals. Such a response is an indication of the extent to which the ideology of equal competence is beginning to be accepted among professionals.

As noted in the last chapter, one of the central questions of the study concerned task management; it was hypothesized that professionals generally would define the scope of paraprofessional capability more narrowly than paraprofessionals, thereby reserving more potential paraprofessional tasks for themselves. No significant evidence was found to support this contention. This lack of evidence is significant, but it is important to cite the findings before reaching any conclusions.

In the development of a task analysis scale, specific tasks were organized around differentially complex problems with the level of difficulty and risk slanted toward the observed abilities of the paraprofessional.[1] The range of difficulty of task management was rated independently by several social work practitioners. On the scale in Table 12, both sets of respondents were asked to choose for each item who ought to carry out each of ten different tasks, ranging from the discussion of child-rearing practices with parents to reporting and following up housing code violations.

The major finding is the significant amount of task overlap indicated by both professionals and paraprofessionals. When the response patterns of both groups were contrasted, strong agreement between groups was found in seven out of ten tasks. Agreement in this case means that a majority in both groups felt that either the professional or the paraprofessional could carry out the task.[2] It also meant that a large pro-

Table 12.   Task Analysis Scale

	Professionals Always	Usually Professionals	Either	Usually Paraprofessionals	Paraprofessionals Always
1. Discuss child-rearing practices with parents	A	B	C	D	E
2. Form therapeutic relationship with a delinquent teenager	A	B	C	D	E
3. Assist older person with pre-retirement counseling	A	B	C	D	E
4. Represent the agency in community citizen's meetings	A	B	C	D	E
5. Follow up released state hospital mental patient	A	B	C	D	E
6. Help organize a group of mothers on welfare	A	B	C	D	E
7. Handle referrals to local agencies regarding a young unwed mother	A	B	C	D	E
8. Assist family in housing relocation caused by urban renewal	A	B	C	D	E
9. Accompany family to well-baby clinic	A	B	C	D	E
10. Report and follow up housing code violation	A	B	C	D	E

portion of the remaining respondents in each group chose similar directions for the task management—that is, usually professionals or usually paraprofessionals.

For purposes of analysis, the tasks were divided into three groups: professional type tasks, paraprofessional type tasks, and mixed tasks. The responses to the professional type tasks are noted in Table 13. Approximately half of each group agreed in each case that either professionals or paraprofessionals could perform these three tasks. The remainder of each group tended strongly to feel that professionals ought to carry out tasks related to more involved interpersonal relations whether in the area of child-rearing, delinquency, or aging—Tasks 1 through 3.

When it came to labeling tasks as "usually professional," the professionals were generally more willing to make such a distinction than paraprofessionals. However, it is interesting to note that paraprofessionals were more willing to label a task as "professional always" than were the professionals. The paraprofessionals were more confident about defining the professionals' domain than were the professionals.

In the mixed set of tasks there was also generally strong agreement that either the professional or the paraprofessional could carry out the tasks. The results are found in Table 14. The respondents tended to classify tasks as either professional or paraprofessional in about the same proportions. For example, Task 6, helping to organize a group of mothers on welfare, attracted approximately 21 percent of each group to the "usually paraprofessional" category.

There was a slightly greater tendency on the part of professionals to assign a task to the professionals' domains than there was for paraprofessionals to assign a task to a paraprofessionals' domains. It is conceivable that professionals respond in such a way because they perceive more ramifications to a task due to their training and experience. However, when tasks appear sufficiently ambiguous each group seems to claim the tasks for itself.

Table 13.   Task Analysis Overlap for Professional-Type Tasks
(Percentages)

	Professionals Always	Usually Professionals	Either	Usually Paraprofessionals	Paraprofessionals Always	Total
Task # 1	Discuss child-rearing practices with parents					
Professionals (N = 100)	5	30	51	7	7	100%
Paraprofessionals (N = 323)	12	17	51	12	8	100%
Task # 2	Form therapeutic relationship with a delinquent teenager					
Professionals	11	34	49	4	2	100%
Paraprofessionals	18	18	45	11	8	100%
Task # 3	Assist older person with preretirement counseling					
Professionals	6	27	59	6	2	100%
Paraprofessionals	10	20	49	11	10	100%

Table 14. Task Analysis Overlap for Mixed-Type Tasks
(Percentages)

	Professionals Always	Usually Professionals	Either	Usually Paraprofessionals	Paraprofessionals Always	Total
Task #4	Represent the agency in community citizens' meeting					
Professionals (N = 100)	10	7	75	6	2	100%
Paraprofessionals (N = 323)	8	7	63	12	10	100%
Task #5	Follow up released state hospital mental patient					
Professionals	9	38	39	12	2	100%
Paraprofessionals	17	20	43	11	9	100%
Task #6	Help organize a group of mothers on welfare					
Professionals	5	9	59	21	6	100%
Paraprofessionals	7	8	50	22	13	100%
Task #7	Handle referrals to local agencies regarding a young unwed mother					
Professionals	5	27	49	15	4	100%
Paraprofessionals	8	11	56	13	12	100%

The third group of tasks, making a total of ten, was made up of primarily paraprofessional-type tasks. These responses are noted in Table 15. While there is a strong tendency to define these tasks as in the domain of the paraprofessional, it is interesting to note that a substantial proportion in both groups felt that either the professional or the paraprofessional ought to be able to carry out these tasks. The ambivalent responses of professionals to this group of presumably paraprofessional tasks reflects the continuing difficulty in clearly recognizing and respecting the domain of paraprofessional tasks.

While there were several differences among professionals and paraprofessionals, in their perceptions of who can do what, the overriding theme was agreement. In essence, both groups displayed unusual consensus on the interchangeable nature of their functions as highlighted in the ten tasks. In only a few cases was it clear that either professionals or paraprofessionals were uniquely qualified to do certain tasks.

We have here further evidence of role blurring. Those professionals and paraprofessionals who identify with this emerging social movement have no difficulty accepting the overlap in job functions. Those wary of this movement find the lack of clearly defined job domains uncomfortable. Many silently worry about the role blurring, since a logical extension of such thinking calls into question the educational requirements from high school to graduate school which support the many distinctions in performing social service functions. It was found that this concern was not the kind of thing people were generally willing to talk about.

The high degree of agreement in the area of job overlap is significant and needs to be assessed in comparison to other professions in which professionals and paraprofessionals work together. Do nurses, aides and registered nurses or teacher aides and certified teachers exhibit similar kinds of mutually agreed upon role blurring or consensus regarding the extent to which they can do much of each other's work?

Table 15. Task Analysis Overlap for Paraprofessional-Type Tasks
(Percentages)

	Professionals Always	Usually Professionals	Either	Usually Paraprofessionals	Always Paraprofessionals	Total
Task # 8	Assist family in housing relocation caused by urban renewal					
Professionals (N = 100)	1	6	49	37	7	100%
Paraprofessionals (N = 323)	9	9	51	22	9	100%
Task # 9	Accompany family to well-baby clinic					
Professionals	0	2	20	57	21	100%
Paraprofessionals	3	3	41	35	18	100%
Task # 10	Report and follow up housing code violation					
Professionals	3	6	40	40	11	100%
Paraprofessionals	8	18	48	13	13	100%

Additional research is needed to assess the professional-paraprofessional relationship in other professions.

Since the category of mixed tasks seemed to elicit some of the more divergent responses, several factors were analyzed to explain this variation. Race appeared to be a significant factor in the group of professional respondents. A higher proportion of black than white professionals selected the "either" category after both of the professional and paraprofessional task categories had been combined.

White professionals—32 percent—tended to relinquish more tasks to paraprofessionals than did black professionals—16 percent—probably due to greater deference on the part of white professionals to the low-income, predominantly black paraprofessionals' relationship with the clientele.[3] Black professionals—81 percent—appeared to be more open to the interchangeability of professional-paraprofessional involvement in problem solving. In contrast, the tendency of whites to select distinctly professional and paraprofessional task domains indicates that they may have a fairly fixed sense of task management and that the blacks may have a more flexible approach.

The factor of race is also significant between generally white professionals and predominantly black paraprofessionals. The following comments of one of the respondents adds a certain sense of reality to this issue:

> I am white and my 4 co-workers are black. I feel very sensitive about this. We enjoy a relatively warm relationship and I think they trust me more than they do most whites, but I have ambivalent feelings and think that I am not able to be as aggressive or directive as I normally would be.

The level of self-confidence among all professionals irrespective of race was assessed in terms of the category of mixed tasks. As might be expected, a large proportion of professionals—84 percent—displayed a high degree of self-confidence.

Again several interpretations can be made. There is a possible contradiction in the fact that two-thirds of the professionals with a high degree of self-confidence opted for the task category indicating a high degree of overlap with paraprofessionals. This could mean that despite their own self-confidence, a lack of confidence persists in defining what is professional and what is paraprofessional. On the other hand, it could mean that when confronted with a mixed set of tasks, professionals will opt for sharing or interchanging functions with the paraprofessionals.

The paraprofessionals were also asked to rate the degree of self-confidence displayed by their professional supervisors. The majority of paraprofessionals—73 percent—who see their supervisors as having a high degree of self-confidence, consider this quality relevant to their perceptions that either group could carry out a common set of tasks. This can be seen as a confident sharing of tasks.

The paraprofessional perception of low supervisor self-confidence is more difficult to interpret, although the data indicates a greater tendency to associate low self-confidence on the part of the supervisors with assigning paraprofessionals the more routine tasks. This could reflect the practice of when in doubt, give it to the paraprofessional. Such a tendency may explain the following comments made repeatedly by paraprofessionals:

> Stop treating us like children and let us have a chance to make decisions, since we are the main ones to face the people.
>
> We need more respect from social workers.
>
> Give us credit for a job the social workers will not do.

It is important, however, not to overemphasize the deviant cases when the majority of responses by professionals and paraprofessionals revealed an unusual degree of agreement on task differentiation. The high degree of agreement in the area where tasks overlap—that is, professionals able to do predominantly paraprofessional tasks and vice versa—may indicate more than simply a blurring of roles. A new division of labor is evolving with the arrival of the paraprofessional, and there is mutual agreement that more training is needed in order for both professionals and paraprofessionals to successfully assume their new roles in relationship to the changing division of labor.

WORK ROLE RIGIDITY AND ORGANIZATIONAL STATUS

To develop another perspective on job overlap, independent assessments were developed to determine how rigidly or how flexibly the professional and paraprofessional viewed their work roles. It was hypothesized that due to training and experience, the professional would view his work role with less rigidity than the paraprofessional. It was generally found to be true that a larger proportion of paraprofessionals—91 percent—reflected a higher degree of work role rigidity than did the professionals—49 percent. However, professionals have only a relatively lower degree of work role rigidity than paraprofessionals. The fact that the professionals have been socialized through training and experience to adapt their practice to the requirements of the agency fails to explain a generally more rigid or restricted view of their work role than might be expected. The assumption here is that training and experience should increase flexibility and adaptability, but this is not necessarily so. And yet the almost equal division of the professionals into categories of high—49 percent—and low—51 percent—rigidity may merely represent a modal distribution of responses found in any group of professionals.

On the other hand paraprofessionals, who have had less opportunity to be socialized either through training or experience into the pattern of expectations and pressures of organizational life, tend to express their rigidity by a fear of the unknown and a realistic insecurity over their employment status.

An effort was made to assess job overlap in the light of work role rigidity. It was found that in the group of professionals, evenly divided between high and low levels of work role rigidity, there was a tendency for the less rigid, more flexible professionals to differentiate tasks more often by recognizing the domain of paraprofessional tasks. This tendency represents a flexible approach which can allow paraprofessionals more of a role in managing tasks recognized to be within their domain. It may also represent a sense of territoriality in which the domains of the professional and paraprofessional are clearly delineated and protected.

The concept of role blurring again brings to the surface questions resulting from this study of whether the professional role is being truly shared or is being diluted. For those professionals with low work-role rigidity the role appears to be strengthened and not diluted.

In assessing an organizational relationship between superiors and subordinates, the different perceptions of each group regarding their position in the organizational hierarchy, their worth in terms of salaries, and their informal relations, are important indicators of how labor is divided and rewarded as well as how relationships are maintained. People tend to behave according to their perceptions of how they fit into the organizational hierarchy. Both groups were asked to place the paraprofessional graphically on a simple organization chart. It was assumed that the professionals would place the paraprofessionals below themselves while the paraprofessional would select a position more equal to that of the professional. The pattern of responses is found in Table 16. Proportionately, there is a strong degree of similarity between the two groups' perceptions of paraprofessional organizational status.

Table 16.   Perceptions of Organizational Status of Paraprofessional (Percentages)

	Professionals' View (N = 100)	Paraprofessionals' View (N = 323)
Under Professional and above Secretary	39	36
Under Professional and equal to Secretary	42	35
Equal to Professional and above Secretary	19	22
Missing	0	7
Total	100%	100%

It made little difference to either group of respondents whether or not paraprofessionals were above or equal to secretarial staff. It is significant to note that approximately one-fifth of each group perceived the paraprofessionals as having equal organizational status with the professional. This mutual perception reflected a recognition that each person had his own unique contribution to make to the agency and the clientele. This finding was somewhat surprising in the light of significant differences in salaries.

The topic of equal pay for equal work arose frequently among the paraprofessionals and somewhat less frequently in the professional group. Both the professionals and paraprofessionals were asked to project their own and each other's salaries two years into the future by selecting a starting salary based on a few years of experience. In having each group assess the other's worth, it was assumed that significantly differential perceptions might provide another dimension in gaining an understanding of the professional-paraprofessional relationship.

There was substantial agreement between the professionals —75 percent—and the paraprofessionals—70 percent—that for the year 1971 paraprofessionals ought to receive $6,000 to $8,000 per year. However, there was little consensus on the professional's salary. A large proportion of paraprofessionals —45 percent—felt that $9,000 per year was sufficient for professionals. With little hope for increasing their own salaries, paraprofessionals thought that professionals should receive no more than twice the $4,500 per year paid to paraprofessionals in 1969. The logic was that if they were being poorly paid and doing the same work as professionals, professionals should not be paid significantly more than paraprofessionals. This view can also be explained by the limited information available to paraprofessionals about the rising trend in professional social work salaries. In contrast, the majority of professionals viewed the range of $10,000 to $12,000 as reasonable for the kind of work they were doing.

In drawing conclusions for this dimension, it is significant that both groups projected an increase for paraprofessionals over current salaries. This can be viewed as one indicator of consensus on the contribution being made by paraprofessionals as well as on the inadequacy of the existing poverty-level wages for paraprofessionals.

The informal aspects of the professional-paraprofessional relationship also produced a wide range of attitudes and perceptions. Both groups were asked to estimate the frequency with which they went to lunch with each other on a continuing basis. The responses suggest significantly divergent perceptions of the same phenomenon. The professionals—60 percent—stated that they joined paraprofessionals for informal lunch dates on a weekly basis. In contrast, paraprofessionals—60 percent—stated that they rarely if ever met their professional supervisor for informal lunch dates.

This lack of agreement can be linked to the emotionally charged nature of informal relations with paraprofessionals who generally had expected more informal contact with professionals than they had. The professionals felt that sufficient activity was already taking place. From several of the discussions and interviews it became apparent that the area of informal relations was still very much in flux and subject to the mutual adjustment of expectations around the differences between a colleague relationship and a peer relationship. In some cases, the simple difference in age may have been a factor. In other cases, the issue of racial difference seemed to be significant.

In addition to describing the similarities and differences in perceptions of the professional-paraprofessional relationship, it is important to highlight some day-to-day practices as they reflect a pattern throughout the agencies under study, practices described quite accurately by Gould:

> The typical (paraprofessional) works in the same office or department as his supervisor and sees him daily. However, he does not receive daily work assignments nor does he need to report to his supervisor daily. It is more likely that work assignments are given on a weekly, bi-weekly, or as-needed basis, with the paraprofessional himself substantially planning his own schedule. The supervisor is available for assistance in any area on an as-needed basis. The typical (paraprofessional) found that this was a sufficient amount of supervision to enable him to do the job. In fact, he reports that he (often) feels able to function on the job without supervision.[4]

In many cases, professionals noted that in their daily routines the intensity of their supervision decreased as the paraprofessional gained more experience and confidence in his work. In many cases, professionals as supervisors provided considerable assistance in helping paraprofessionals understand and cope with agency procedure, authority, work habits, and client relations.

While several differences between professionals and paraprofessionals have been discussed in this chapter, the dominant theme is agreement. The differential perceptions around mixed tasks, the relative differences in work role rigidity and paraprofessional effectiveness, and the disagreement over informal relations fail to outweigh the significant agreement found in the mutual perceptions of the division of labor. How will these perceptions be affected by the external factors related to organizational environment? The next chapter addresses the factors which affect the professional-paraprofessional relationship.

Chapter 12

ORGANIZATIONS
MAKE A DIFFERENCE

Relationships within an agency have a personal as well as an organizational dimension. How is Mrs. Smith, a mother of five children, a black, a woman who never graduated from high school, accepted by her supervisor who comes from a white middle-class family and holds a master's degree? Personal factors make a difference; common experiences may help to bridge the gap. However, organizational factors are critical. If an organization reflects strong ideological support for the involvement of paraprofessionals, both the professional and paraprofessional feel important and their relationship is positively influenced by the sanction it receives from the top. Certainly there can be no understanding the relationship between professionals and paraprofessionals without the recognition that it takes place within an organizational climate that is likely to affect the way people see each other and relate to each other.

The matter of organizational influences is very important. The organizational climate of an agency can be changed and planned for by passing rules, revising laws, creating financial inducements, and many other factors. Yet it is difficult to plan in the same systematic fashion to change for better or worse the many different kinds of interpersonal relationships that arise. The acceptance or rejection of this paraprofessional social movement will be very much determined by the way organizational factors are manipulated and the extent to which such factors reflect the adjustments necessary to facilitate the interpersonal elements of the professional-paraprofessional relationship.

The significance of the interdependence between organizations and the people who carry out service objectives has been confirmed throughout the literature of administrative theory and organizational analysis. In recent years the human service sector has received increased attention, especially the relationship of functionaries to the health and welfare establishment.

Most of the research on the differential use of manpower in the human service sector has concentrated on such formal organizations as state mental hospitals, Veterans' Administration hospitals, correctional facilities, and military facilities. In contrast, this study is based on less formal, relatively small, community-based organizations. Such organizations are characterized by small administrative staffs and a high proportion of professionally trained personnel. They are highly subject to community influence and, as a result, citizen interest and pressure from board members, local politicians, and consumers affects the daily operation and responsiveness of the organization.

These data about professionals and paraprofessionals were gathered in six eastern cities[1] from organizations funded or otherwise directly influenced by local antipoverty community action agencies. Essentially, they provide one of three types of service to the community: family services, neighborhood services, or community health services.

The family service category includes both public and private services to families and children. The neighborhood service category includes services to youth and to the aged, and a wide range of neighborhood organization services. The group of community health programs includes services to children and youth, mothers and infants, the emotionally disturbed, and cares for the health needs of the community as found in health department programs. (See Table 17 for the distribution of professionals and paraprofessionals among these organizations.)

Table 17.   Distribution of Agencies and Respondents
(Percentages)

Agency Types and Numbers	Professionals (N = 100)	Paraprofessionals (N = 323)
Family Service (15)	26	17
Neighborhood Service (37)	32	50
Community Health (25)	42	33
Total	100%	100%

While many organizations benefited from federal antipoverty funding, evidence about the impact of such finding on the organizations is still inconclusive. Lambert and Lambert suggest that traditional agencies have been slow to transform their experiences with professionals and paraprofessionals into their regular budgeting and programming practices.[2] In most agencies, for example, paraprofessional salaries were primarily paid with antipoverty funds, and paraprofessionals were noticeably less common on the staffs of the traditional, ongoing services of those agencies funded from other sources such as, public welfare. [3]

It is also important to note that this study was done in relatively small organizations. This smallness is an important factor to remember in assessing the influence of organizational factors or role demands upon the professional-paraprofessional relationship. Hall has noted that the smaller the organization, the greater the tendency for more professional attitudes and practices among the personnel.[4] As a corollary he found that small, relatively nonbureaucratic organizations with strong professional attitudes appear difficult to bureaucratize. As a result, the more professionalized occupations are found in the least bureaucratized settings.[5] Social service agencies were included in his study.

The degree of bureaucratization has also been found to relate to the degree of autonomy of the personnel.[6] When the professionals and paraprofessionals in this study were asked to rate their own and each other's freedom and autonomy, the professionals perceived their own autonomy as medium to low. In contrast, the paraprofessionals perceived the autonomy of professionals as medium to high. This finding, noted in Table 18, will be discussed more fully in the next chapter in the context of the differential perceptions of the professional-paraprofessional relationship.

Table 18.   Differential Perceptions of Professionals' Autonomy (Percentages)

Autonomy for Professionals	High	Medium	Low	Don't Know	Total
Professionals' View (N = 100)	20	50	30	0	100%
Paraprofessionals' View (N = 323)	54	35	11	0	100%

OPEN AND CLOSED ORGANIZATIONS

When applied to organizations, the concepts of "open" and "closed" refer to the attributes of flexibility and initiative. Both concepts represent abstractions that need to be measured operationally. In this study, the openness or closedness of an organization and the resulting impact on the professional-paraprofessional relationship was defined through a combination of the following factors: administrative leadership, communication patterns, paraprofessional staff involvement, community relatedness, and interagency liaison. Again the literature on organizations highlights these important dimensions of organizational life.[7]

In an effort to refine the concepts of openness and closedness, Ricci took the approach that such a categorization of organizations had environmental preconditions.[8] Open organizations were open in large part due to the instability of their environment. Likewise, closed organizations resulted mainly from stable environments. Needless to say, the future of agencies funded by the antipoverty program and of the programs utilized in this study was very uncertain. There was little that could be more unstable in the human service environment.

When the nature of community-based programs was combined with the instability of federal funding, it became apparent that the agencies under study were clearly open. It seemed logical then to determine the degree of openness as reflected in agency procedures and practices.

Without assessing interorganization conflict or the degree of hierarchy in each organization, the study sought the two key perceptions of the professional and of the paraprofessional. The way in which each group assessed its organization's leadership, communication, and community involvement provided important evidence which was useful in assessing the influence of the organization on the professional-paraprofessional relationship.

AGENCY LEADERSHIP AND COMMUNICATION

Professionals and paraprofessionals had different perceptions of the agency administrator. In response to a question about the characterization of the leadership of the top administrator in the agency, 65 percent of professionals in contrast to 46 percent of paraprofessionals perceived the administrator as concerned with broad agency functions and liaison with other agencies—as noted in Table 19. The remaining professionals and paraprofessionals perceived their respective administrator as functioning more narrowly with specific policies and as being more concerned with his own convenience and security. This dichotomy has been described by Selznick as institutional (broad) in contrast to administrative (narrow and managerial) organizational leadership.[9] The prevailing view of broad institutional leadership held by professionals who generally have more contact with the administrator contributed to the adaptability of both the professional and paraprofessional to organizational constraints. The perception of a more narrow managerial leadership held by paraprofessionals requires further research to determine if such perceptions are based on a clearer view of management or insufficient contact with administrators.

Table 19.   Views of Agency Leadership
(Percentages)

	Broad	Narrow	Total
Professionals' View	65	35	100%
Paraprofessionals' View	46	54	100%

There was agreement between the professionals—57 percent—and the paraprofessionals—52 percent—that communication in the agencies flowed in a two-way pattern. These
responses were compiled respectively for the professionals
and paraprofessionals as groups and not by agencies. Many
respondents in both groups felt that good communication
was determined by the issue or information to be com-
municated. Some agency information flowed less easily in
both directions; communication was said to be nonexistent
at some times and sporadic in direction at others—some
communications only up, some only down.

Regarding organizational structure there was general agreement between the professionals—63 percent—and paraprofessionals—60 percent—that paraprofessionals as a group had
been integrated into the agency. But when it came to their involvement in specific staff activities, both the professionals
—62 percent—and the paraprofessionals—52 percent—felt that
the administrator had only involved paraprofessionals in a
marginal way. It is worth noting that more paraprofessionals
—48 percent—felt that they had been involved a great deal by
the administrator than did their professional colleagues—36
percent. When attendance at staff meetings was used as another indicator of involvement, there was strong agreement
between the professionals—79 percent—and paraprofessionals
—76 percent—that they frequently attended such meetings
together. These perceptions of paraprofessional involvement
obviously fail to indicate the amount of actual paraprofessional involvement, which cannot be determined without
some form of measurement external to the professionals and
paraprofessionals.

More important, however, is the old question of whether
or not familiarity breeds contempt. Is it possible that the
more involvement and interaction paraprofessionals experience with professionals and the agency staff the more tension
will result? It is well at least to call into question the frequent
assumption that extensive involvement and interaction is by

definition good. Similarly, the notion that tension resulting from interaction is necessarily bad also needs to be questioned. It has been argued that tension resulting from paraprofessional interaction is positive if the original rationale for paraprofessional involvement in social agencies is fully understood, namely representing the community and its desires to see agency practices changed and improved to serve the clientele better.

In an effort to assess the creative initiative of the agency in relation to unsolved community problems, data was gathered on the extent of the agency's relationship to the community in need of services. The extent to which agencies consulted with neighborhood groups regarding recurring social problems was perceived differently by the two study groups. The majority of professionals—58 percent—thought there was relatively little consultation with neighborhood groups, but only 43 percent of the paraprofessionals agreed. Such differing perceptions may result from the fact that paraprofessionals maintained informal consultation relationships with a wide variety of people in the community. It is difficult to clearly assess who among the professionals and paraprofessionals had the clearest picture of the agency's community relatedness.

In assessing the impact of paraprofessionals on the agency's acceptance in the community, professionals—71 percent—and paraprofessionals—84 percent—strongly agreed that paraprofessionals had significantly increased agency acceptance. Agency-community relatedness, defined in terms of attitudes about agency creativeness, receptiveness to the community, and community acceptance, serves as an important ingredient in providing for a responsive professional-paraprofessional relationship. The more the agency is in tune with the community's needs, the greater is the potential for professionals and paraprofessionals to seek solutions to client problems jointly.[10]

In summary, there was agreement that agencies were more open than closed, although there were several cases of differential perception regarding the functioning of the agencies. Some of these differences between professionals and paraprofessionals might be explained by the greater demands generally placed on professionals to handle organizational matters. Different perceptions of agency operations could easily result from the difference between professional and paraprofessional functions. Pruger and Specht have noted with regard to the agency, the community and staff, that

> obviously, one's location in the service system will determine which set of problems one will know more intimately and, what is more often overlooked, what one will know only superficially or even not at all.[11]

Information gained from informal discussions revealed that opportunities for paraprofessionals to present their clients' problems and needs to the agency in terms of their effect on agency policies were few and far between. Gould has observed that although paraprofessionals are often considered as the agency's links to the community, they are seldom able to affect agency policy, service delivery patterns, or priorities.[12]

On the other hand, agencies reflect a growing awareness that to employ only professionals proves limiting to their service delivery capability. Agencies see themselves as giving more service with the involvement of paraprofessionals. There is also the assumption that the additional paraprofessional manpower has helped to make their services more relevant. Indeed, there is an implicit recognition that the human services require both technical and political aspects of paraprofessional-client relations. This ideology permeates the organization to the extent that administrators wonder how they ever functioned without paraprofessionals.

Nevertheless the mutual perception of a relatively open organization provides one explanation for the atmosphere conducive to the development of a compatable professional-paraprofessional relationship. The impact of the paraprofessional on the professional is the next step in our analysis of the professional-paraprofessional relationship.

Chapter 13

PROFESSIONALISM REVISITED

The impact of paraprofessionals on professional social workers can be evaluated in many different ways. On the most basic level, paraprofessionals have integrated—racially and in terms of social class—the staff of many social service agencies. On a more complex level, they have influenced the practice of social work by providing a new source of knowledge about the realities of the clients' world. This chapter focuses on the dilemmas faced by professionals. The professionals in this study represent a new force in social work practice today. They have generally risked the comforts of secure and safe practice to explore new ways of serving their clients with the help of paraprofessionals. While some viewed the paraprofessionals as another set of hands to do both the old jobs and the jobs for which there had never been enough time, others seized the opportunity to experiment with new approaches to serving the client population.

Recently, professionals have had to reexamine the basis of their sense of security, grounded in their credentials, as people without professional training have, under certain circumstances, begun to perform traditionally professional functions. The medical profession experienced the need for reassessment during World War II when there was an influx of medical orderlies, as well as when nurses assumed some of the traditional duties of doctors. In the case of social work, not only are paraprofessionals assuming traditional social work functions, but other professionals, as well, have begun to perform in domains traditionally identified as social work areas—for example, public health nurses, school guidance counselors, and correctional officers. The introduction of paraprofessionals has dramatically brought to the surface an issue which has always existed in the social work profession, namely, to what extent is a particular route of professional training essential or at least preferable for the performance of social service functions?

The professionals have been required to overcome both real and imaginary obstacles in forming a workable relationship with paraprofessionals. The first obstacle has its parallel in industry, where a foreman earns his position through on-the-job experience. Professionals have had to demonstrate that in spite of their own lack of specific experience as indigenous paraprofessionals, they could demonstrate the basic ingredients of the paraprofessional role. In doing so, they had to adjust many of their preconceived notions about good social work practice skills being those acquired only through graduate education. They had to unlearn what they had been socialized to believe in graduate school. For some professionals, both old and young, this process of unlearning had already begun prior to the arrival of paraprofessionals. Since a great deal of time and energy had been invested in acquiring professional training, the uncertainty about how much difference in competence really existed between professionals and paraprofessionals was a new source of difficulty which needed to be confronted.

Serving as a role model for the paraprofessional proved to be quite demanding for the professional. The problem of motivating paraprofessionals to aspire to higher levels of performance and position when both salary incentives and new positions were in short supply proved to be overwhelming for the client-oriented social work practitioner, as well as for the paraprofessional. Compounding this dilemma was the age factor, as the majority of paraprofessionals were older than the majority of professionals. Difficulty in establishing rapport and compassion was complicated by great differences in personal and educational backgrounds as well as in racial and ethnic origins. It should also be noted that the paraprofessionals served as role models for professionals. Whether it is freely admitted or not, professionals perceive paraprofessionals as having close contact with their own communities with access to community power, prestige, and resources inaccessible to professionals.

The impact of the paraprofessional upon the professional varies also in terms of such intangible factors as professional values, career objectives, and reference group identification. These issues arise when the professional's job investment appears to be total and the paraprofessional's investment, when cultural styles and family commitments affect his/her job, is interpreted as something less than total. The reverse pattern was also observed where paraprofessional job investment exceeded that of the professionals. Similarly, the expectations of the two groups concerning their informal relations vary considerably as noted earlier. The paraprofessional seeks admittance to the professional's reference group and, when rebuffed, tends to restrict the admittance of the professional into his own reference group. When the hiring of a paraprofessional in the agency is interpreted as of value strictly on the basis of his reference group connections, the impact on the professional can be profound and, at times, quite negative. For example, resentment surfaces most clearly when the professional observes that, "I made it professionally on the basis of hard work and study, while he made it paraprofessionally on the basis of reference group."

In essence, paraprofessionalism confronted the professional social worker with a new set of influences and expectations. At the same time that paraprofessionals were influencing the agency and the clientele, new expectations began to form for professional practice. The paraprofessionals were not a new type of client population, yet some were treated as such. Professionals were expected to lead a team of paraprofessional client helpers, not just serve as client-centered helpers themselves. Professionals began to assume new supervisory roles, different from the kind of supervision provided to other, less experienced professionals. They were forced to assume more administrative responsibility for staff development by newly adopted consultation and training functions. In general terms, the old and new influences might be diagrammed as in Figure 5, in which the paraprofessional represented the new element impacting on the role of the professional.

Figure 5.

Factors Affecting the Professional Social Worker

When assessing the wide range of factors affecting the professional social worker, the issue is not that the past training methods for professional practice are irrelevant but that we have not yet developed techniques with which to evaluate a particular training approach as it relates to a particular level of professional performance. This does not mean that we should abolish standards; rather it addresses the question of how the public can best be served, that is, the issue of efficient and effective utilization of sufficiently trained man-power. In the area of social service delivery, where many professionals have felt secure in developing and enforcing standards of practice and service, the introduction of para-professionals has resulted in reopening issues of professional performance in delivering service in sufficient quantity and with the highest quality.

THE RESPONSES OF PROFESSIONALS

Several patterns of response have been noted by other re-searchers. Like all abstractions, they suffer from imprecision because of the inherent difficulty of generalizing individual response patterns into group patterns. Gould suggests that there are primarily two types of responses in which a new supervisory model emerges on the basis of an open and en-thusiastic personality, more freedom on the job for sub-ordinates, and a team approach to task management.[1] This model is contrasted with the old supervisory model that represents the traditional ways of doing things, close control over subordinates, the procedural orientation, and generally more closed, inflexible personality. Gould found that the majority of supervisors interviewed represented the new supervisory model.

Denham and Shatz also identified patterns of professional response.[2] Three patterns were derived by first making ex-plicit the commonly held expectations of the parapro-fessional for the role of the professional.

> As a subordinate in the relationship, he [the parapro-
> fessional] tended to look for five kinds of helping inputs
> from the professional: (1) help in surviving in a highly
> tenuous role, (2) help in developing practical skills and
> acquiring knowledge to meet the task requirements, (3)
> help in learning to negotiate his way in the agency, (4) help
> in realizing his aspirations for advancement in the event he
> was motivated in this direction, and (5) respect, support
> and recognition as a worker with the rights and privileges
> attendant thereto.[3]

While it is apparent that these expectations could be
considered universals for all levels of staff, three professional response patterns were developed and referred to as the
"doubters," the "idealists," and the "pragmatic experimentalists." The doubters had low expectations of the
paraprofessionals and cast them in the role of dependent
handymen. The idealists had overly high expectations of
the paraprofessionals and ascribed to paraprofessionals the
ability to outperform the professional as the "all-American
indigenous worker." The pragmatic experimentalists, like
Gould's new supervisor model, represented the majority of
professionals studied. They were characterized as more
cautious about fixing the expectations of paraprofessional
potential at any given level, and oriented toward matching
the learning needs of paraprofessionals with the tasks and
evaluating performance accordingly.

Both the two-part and three-part models were kept in
mind as the data in this study were analyzed. The data was
collected to yield information on the nature of the professionals' orientation to supervision, their academic orientation, their preferences in organizational role-taking, and
their perceptions of their supervisory experience. All these
dimensions relate to the third hypothesis in this study:
namely, that when it comes to supervising paraprofessionals
a high proportion of professionals will be predisposed to
strong supervisory control and thereby more bureaucratically
oriented than professionally oriented. The reverse of this

hypothesis, in which the professional orientation prevailed, was found to be true. The findings described below illustrate the response of professionals to the experience of supervising paraprofessionals.

PROFESSIONAL VERSUS BUREAUCRATIC ORIENTATION

In an effort to determine the professionals' orientation to work and their role in the agency, a scale was developed for this case study from Scott's research on reactions to supervision.[4] Questions were designed to elicit the varying degrees to which professionals perceive their supervisory roles in either professional or bureaucratic terms. The professionally oriented supervisor is more concerned with issues of staff development, whereas the bureaucratically oriented supervisor places more emphasis on issues of agency policy and accountability. Specific information was sought in the following areas: (1) reliance on psychosocial theory as a framework for professional practice; (2) the degree of autonomy for subordinates to make decisions; (3) the extent of supervisory review of subordinate's work; and (4) the reliance on skills in teaching casework. As might be expected, determining distinctly bureaucratic or professional orientations was exceedingly difficult since different times and circumstances produced different orientations. Nevertheless, 60 percent of the professionals displayed a strong professional orientation, while 40 percent perceived their roles more in bureaucratic terms.

The paraprofessionals were asked for their views of their supervisors, and the following profile emerged, reflecting in percentages the degree of paraprofessional consensus. Professional supervisors were generally seen as quite self-confident—73 percent—with good control over the work situation —50 percent—and with demonstrated commitment to backing up paraprofessionals in conflicts with clients—50 percent.

Supervisors were rarely perceived by paraprofessionals as impatient with loss of temper and were seen as generally secure in making decisions with minimal reluctance. The remaining percentages for each perception simply reflected the occasional absence of these supervisory characteristics. In total, the paraprofessionals viewed their supervisors quite positively.

To account for some of the variation found in the professionals' perceptions of their own orientations, the findings on work role rigidity were used. In this case, there is a strong correlation between the professional orientation and low work role rigidity, and a somewhat weaker correlation between the bureaucratic orientation and high work role rigidity.

While several interpretations are possible, the explanation of the greatest variation seems most apparent, namely that work role flexibility—or low rigidity—is a necessary ingredient of a professional orientation to supervision. Meeting the needs of other staff members appears to require a more flexible sense of one's own work role than does meeting the bureaucratic needs of an agency. Some of the earlier findings on task agreement can be further explained by the fact that a majority of the social workers working with paraprofessionals have a professional orientation to supervision that is supported by similar perceptions on the part of paraprofessionals.

ACQUIRING NEW ROLES

As another way of assessing the professional's response to paraprofessionals, a list of items was developed that included knowledge areas related to beginning social work practice. While this list (Table 20) yielded important information about where such subjects should be taught, it was even more interesting to use the items as an index of the professionals' receptivity to assuming a greater teaching function. The scores for the professionals showed that 64 percent defined nearly all of the items as curriculum content for college or in-service training sessions. Only 34 percent saw the bulk of these subjects as topics to be handled in supervisory meetings. In essence, training responsibilities were generally perceived as falling outside the domain of the professionals' responsibilities.

Table 20.   Curriculum Questions

Where should the following subjects be taught to paraprofessionals?

		College	In-service Training	Supervisory Meetings
A.	Community problems	1	2	3
B.	Human growth and development	1	2	3
C.	Interviewing skills	1	2	3
D.	Strategies in community work	1	2	3
E.	Elementary casework skills	1	2	3
F.	Agency resources and referrals	1	2	3
G.	Introduction to psychotherapy	1	2	3
H.	Sensitivity training	1	2	3
I.	Writing program reports	1	2	3

Again several interpretations are possible. Since the topics were designed to represent beginning-level content in social work education, it is possible that the professionals were caught in their own frame of reference, namely, "I learned it in college; therefore you should have learned it too." On the other hand, professionals may have perceived paraprofessional training as so specialized and extensive   that there would be insufficient time in supervisory meetings to handle the range of material needed by paraprofessionals. It was found also that some professionals saw themselves as ill-equipped to assume an active teaching function as a part of their supervisory responsibilities.

To complement the academic orientation, data were also collected from both professionals and paraprofessionals regarding their views on certifying paraprofessionals. For paraprofessionals to advance in a highly credentialed society, some form of certification would be necessary even if only to allow the paraprofessional to move from one city to another. Both the professionals—55 percent—and the paraprofessionals —55 percent—felt that paraprofessionals should be certified through a college or through a governmental agency. Both the remaining professionals and paraprofessionals felt that the local agency and/or local paraprofessional association should do the certifying. With opinion obviously divided, there appears to be no clear consensus; however, it is important to note that there is substantial support in both groups for a local, nonacademic form of certification.

The concept of organizational role-taking represents a combination of the demands of the organization on the professional blended with his own personality and the nature of communication with supervisors, peers, and subordinates. The concept of organizational role-taking provided the framework for gathering data on the perceptions of professionals and paraprofessionals regarding the roles assumed by professionals. Were professionals mainly consultants, or teachers, or managers?

As Table 21 indicates, there was strong agreement between professionals—64 percent—and paraprofessionals—62 percent —that the dominant role of the professional was that of consultant. There was less agreement on the teaching role, as professionals—40 percent—viewed themselves more consistently as teachers than did the paraprofessionals—27 percent. There was no consensus in either group about the role of manager, with some indication that this role was either rarely assumed by professionals or simply not recognized.[5]

Table 21. Perceptions of Organizational Roles Assumed
by Professionals
(Percentages)

	Usually	Sometimes	Seldom	Don't Know	Total
Consultant Role					
Professionals' View (N=100)	64	28	4	4	100%
Paraprofessionals' View (N=323)	62	17	4	17	100%
Teacher Role					
Professionals' View	40	51	3	6	100%
Paraprofessionals' View	27	28	15	30	100%
Manager Role					
Professionals' View	22	28	39	11	100%
Paraprofessionals' View	22	17	26	35	100%

Despite the paraprofessionals' high percentage of "don't know" responses, they seemed more secure when viewing professionals as consultants and colleagues than when viewing them as teachers or managers, roles which imply a superior-subordinate relationship. Similarly, professionals wanted to appear less threatening and perceived the consultant role as allowing more latitude in organizational role-taking. Professionals saw themselves more often as teachers than did the paraprofessionals. This might reflect the paraprofessional's resistance to assuming the student role or the professional's failure to convey his teaching role successfully.

The attractiveness of the consultant's role to both the professional and paraprofessional seems to reflect a new dimension in the traditional superior-subordinate relationship. Rather than favoring the managerial role of organizing the work load, both seem to favor the consulting and, in part, the teaching roles, which focus more heavily on organizing for peak performance. This distinction gains importance as the findings on the professionals' assessments of the supervisory role are analyzed. One of the respondents in the professional group voiced these concerns in her attempt to support the role of the paraprofessional and to show compassion for a coworker:

> The ratio of paraprofessional to professional should be about one-to-one. Otherwise a sensitive and dedicated health aide will uncover so many overwhelming situations that she will experience much frustration (and so will the client) unless her situations can be met promptly and coped with effectively.

This is the spirit with which the majority of professionals have approached their supervisory responsibilities of paraprofessionals.[6]

In the light of these generally positive appraisals, it is important to note the manner in which professionals first assumed responsibility for supervising paraprofessionals. Interestingly enough, 61 percent of the professionals were originally assigned by their agencies to this responsibility; 12 percent volunteered for the assignment. The remaining proportion of professionals—27 percent—reported that a combination of circumstances led to their assuming these responsibilities, but the majority of these cases reflected a highly voluntary dimension to supervisory responsibilities. The current high degree of job satisfaction, despite the limited initiative displayed by the professionals to volunteer for such supervisory duty, is open to multiple interpretations. At the beginning there might have been apprehension possibly resulting from fear of and doubt about the abilities of paraprofessionals. Similarly, the generally widespread satisfaction today may be more a function of professional control over the paraprofessionals than anything else.

The early hesitancy to get involved with paraprofessionals and the resulting high rate of assignment by agency administration could be interpreted still another way. Many professionals—76 percent—felt that their social work training had only minimal relevance to their supervisory responsibilities. Many others commented that their lack of course work and field experience in the area of supervision was a major shortcoming in their training and keenly felt a void in their range of practice skills. This perception of deficiency in their own skills might have affected the early willingness of professionals to get involved with paraprofessionals. It can be assumed from such comments as, "I don't know how we ever functioned without paraprofessionals," and "They are my primary souce of support . . . [rather than] the agency or the funding source" that the positive job satisfaction is based on some rather rewarding experiences. Many professionals commented that their satisfactions derived from their first real opportunity to see teamwork actually taking place.

In general, the professional social workers accepted both the presence of paraprofessionals and their performance of many duties that professionals in the past had thought of as part of their monopoly. This nonunion, nonmonopoly approach on the part of the professionals is related in part to an ideological assumption that the involvement of paraprofessionals is good and justifiable in terms of client needs. Social services performed by individuals who lack professional training is seen as a positive development provided there is some degree of professional supervision. In reality, the professionals are willing to go rather easy on this supervisory process as long as their symbolic dominance is accepted. In this regard, there is a great deal of similarity in behavior between social workers and doctors. Nurses are often given great responsibility for the management of patients on hospital wards. The status difference is denoted by both salary differences and educational experience.

It is now possible to reassess the patterns of response in the light of the models developed by Gould and by Denham and Shatz from the findings and interpretations on supervisory orientations, academic orientations, organizational role-taking, and the overall views of the professionals. The implications of the data presented lead to the conclusion that professional social workers in this study responded to the use of paraprofessionals with a varying degree of experimentation. Gould's new and old supervisor model does not really capture the essence of the professional response except for its component of work role flexibility. The Denham and Shatz approach develops a trichotomy which also falls short of describing this sample of professionals except for its notion of experimentation. The concepts of "doubters" and "idealists" were set up as extremes, and it is therefore possible that applicability of the concepts was limited.

From the findings in this study, the responses of professionals to supervising paraprofessionals can be placed on a continuum of professional practice that includes a low degree of experimentation at one end and a high degree at the other. In this case, experimentation refers to that quality of professional practice that allows professionals the freedom to work out compatible relationships with coworkers who in some way represent the client population, for the purpose of improving the effectiveness of service delivery. It is that quality of flexibility in a professional that permits an untrained coworker to provide both personal and client feedback sufficient to change and improve his practice as well as the routines of his agency.

It is possible to identify all types of professionals by placing them on a continuum of degree of experimentation.

They range from those who experiment very little, are primarily bureaucratic in orientation with limited teaching skills, and use predominantly management skills to those with a highly professional staff development orientation, definite teaching skills, and the ability to turn the supervisory role into a consultative role.

It should be remembered that a large majority of the professionals in this study represent one of the groups of social workers most experienced in the use of paraprofessionals. The keynote of this experience has been the mutual adjustment of expectations. These professionals are surviving amidst severe criticism of the profession coming especially from paraprofessionals who are adjusting their own perceptions of social work skills. At the same time, paraprofessionals are becoming more realistic about the capabilities and limitations of paraprofessional practice. As some professionals have noted, many paraprofessionals are performing quite adequately and should not be encouraged to go back to college where academic failure could undermine their intuitive practice skills.

CENTRAL QUESTIONS REVISITED

On reviewing the central questions, it is possible to suggest both refinements and additional avenues of inquiry. There is lack of evidence to support the hypothesis that professionals perceive a rather narrow scope of paraprofessional capability, resulting in their reserving a greater number of tasks for themselves. This absence indicates that there is more agreement on task sharing than was suspected. Several questions still remain. Why did the professionals fail to identify more tasks as specifically paraprofessional when the list of tasks was slanted in the paraprofessional direction? Is it possible that to identify clearly paraprofessional tasks might undermine professional practice? Could professionals, in part, be protecting their own practice from scrutiny while limiting the development of paraprofessional tasks and skills? Or do professionals simply perceive more nuances in certain agency activities which lead them to draw conclusions about the complexity of human service work?

The findings on task differentiation and overlap suggest the development of interchangeable functions necessary for teamwork, but also raise a question about the development of a paraprofessional identity. It is possible that the more paraprofessionals overlap their tasks and functions with the social work profession, the greater will be their difficulty in gaining both organizational and community acceptance for establishing their own career ladders and independent practice. While task differentiation is an important variable, it was discovered that other variables also need to be taken into account.[7]

The second part of the central question was concerned with work role rigidity. It was found that paraprofessionals displayed more work role rigidity than did the professionals. While the hypothesis was generally supported, additional questions should be raised. To what extent have paraprofessionals been frightened into a rigid definition of their work roles? To what extent are they actually intimidated by the rituals of organizational life? Have professionals contributed to any feelings of second-class citizenship among paraprofessionals? Such questions could not be answered with the evidence from the work role rigidity scale, but might provide still another fruitful area for further research.

It seems evident that the quality of professional practice must also be raised as an issue in any discussion of work role. This might mean developing measurements which assess both the direct service skills of the professional and his supervisory skills. What became most apparent in this study was that these are two separate sets of skills. Supervisory skills in relationship to paraprofessionals are reported to be significantly different from the traditional social work skills in casework, group work, or community work.

On the topic of supervision, another part of the central question concerned the degree to which professionals would be predisposed to strong supervisory control over the relatively untrained paraprofessionals. This predisposition did not surface significantly. A majority of professionals viewed their orientation to supervision through professional, nonbureaucratic lenses. Additional research in which professional supervisory behavior is actually monitored to check the validity of these perceptions is needed. What seemed to emerge most clearly was not so much bureaucratic orientation on the part of professionals as basic insecurity in knowing how much freedom paraprofessionals need and want. The distinction between needs and wants is crucial.

While paraprofessionals repeatedly complained about lack of support and recognition, the professionals repeatedly mentioned the unanticipated amount of time and energy required to work on both the paraprofessionals' personal problems and their adjustment to organizational life. Further research on the professional-paraprofessional relationship should yield both interpersonal and organizational models relevant to the promotion of an effective working relationship.

This study has been made in the context of an emerging social movement. It still remains to be seen exactly how this movement either establishes itself formally or disappears. The crucial questions about decay and reorganization are as yet unanswered. Does this movement reflect a major innovative thrust in human service delivery? Are both the quality and quantity of service affected significantly by the combined efforts of professionals and paraprofessionals? These questions require further assessment of the movement's ideology. If the professionals and paraprofessionals are as effective as they think they are, why is it taking agencies so long to adapt their administrative practices to this new personnel thrust? Why is it so difficult to develop educational leave and support programs for paraprofessionals when such procedures have long been in effect for professionals? When social agencies are so concerned about the material and psychological supports needed by their clients, why is it so difficult to translate that awareness into personal practices benefiting paraprofessionals, such as sick leave, retirement benefits, merit increases, and so forth?

These are just a few of the unanswered organizational questions whose answers will have impact upon the ideology as well as the survival of the movement. It will also be important to assess the turnover rate of professionals supervising paraprofessionals. Does this supervisory experience burn out professionals any more than or in a different way from other human service experiences? Related to turnover is the question of the involvement of the social work profession as a whole. Why aren't more social workers working with paraprofessionals? Some of the respondents in this study suggested that other social workers regard themselves as too good to get involved with such new and trying forms of practice. Others suggested that professionals no longer have time for direct casework practice and are retreating from "good" practice. The implication seems to be that the supervision of paraprofessionals takes less skill than that required in the personal delivery of casework services to clients. Is there any evidence for these interpretations?

Related to questions of skill are similar questions about function. One professional stated, "Paraprofessionals carry out semi-casework and semi-group work responsibilities, and I carry out administrative responsibilities." If this is so, who actually does the casework? Is traditional casework relevant for the type of situations in which paraprofessionals find themselves?

Another professional felt, "The personality characteristics, personal interests, and special talents of the good paraprofessionals are the key determinants in making good, effective use of paraprofessionals." Does this also apply to professionals? If so, what are the criteria for a professional's suitability for supervising paraprofessionals?

Agencies and professionals have prided themselves on selecting the most articulate and knowledgeable paraprofessionals for their staffs. Yet there are several unresolved issues related to these qualities. How does an agency prepare for the large-scale introduction of untrained and strongly articulate workers? How is an atmosphere maintained that will preserve the perspectives of the paraprofessional so that he is not co-opted into the ways of the agency or the ways of the professionals? Is such co-optation a positive development, perhaps?

It is necessary to raise certain questions about screening. Some have argued that the employment of paraprofessionals was simply a work relief activity for the previously unemployed. It has been shown in this study that the paraprofessionals represented the working poor and not the unemployed poor. However, other issues come to light regarding the quality of applicants and the extent to which they represented the communities to be served. Some professionals felt that screening was too loose, and that there were many troubled people hired who had few human relations skills. If this is so, what screening criteria should be developed? The early requirements for paraprofessionals included residence in the area served by the agency, a stipulation which proved to be both a blessing and a curse. Whereas paraprofessionals were knowledgeable about conditions in the community, their indigenous status also hampered their effectiveness in their relationships with clients. Since professionals are not subject to such requirements, why are paraprofessionals? Is the residential location of the paraprofessional more important than his human service abilities?

These questions lead to a final set of problems for further research. To raise an old but nagging question, what is the best relationship between credential and performance? A professional from Baltimore noted, "There are many paraprofessionals who are much more capable and concerned than many professionals, and it is unfortunate that the lack of a degree places paraprofessionals in a position which inhibits their creativity and thus limits their contribution to the success of the program." Have we rediscovered the therapeutic personality in an age of credentialism? A paraprofessional, reflecting some of the anguish inherent in the credentialism issue, emphatically stated, "When given a job, let paraprofessionals use their own ideas as far as possible and don't make them feel like they are children needing to be told everything as if they don't know anything." The related issues of training for both professionals and paraprofessionals also require further attention.

TRAINING FOR PROFESSIONAL–PARAPROFESSIONAL SERVICES

The process of role-blurring, in which functions become interchangeable, poses difficulties for the training of professionals and paraprofessionals. The problems of training people for changing tasks and interchangeable functions seems no different from the problem of preparing people today for practice in future decades. Yet all training programs will be changing in order to meet the job requirements resulting from the redefinition of social services.

Role differentiation also accompanies role-blurring. While there are benefits to interchangeable functions, each person usually requires his own area of competence. This distinction can become very unclear, as demonstrated by the following comments of two professionals:

> I handle primarily emergency and treatment cases while paraprofessionals do the ongoing follow-up and monitoring of cases.

> Paraprofessionals do crisis, on-the-spot tasks while professional caseworkers do more continuous follow-up.

These two perceptions, which appear to contradict each other, in fact may not. The key determinant is the degree of communication and expectation found in the individual relationships. The paraprofessional's activities might include both follow-up and crisis work; so might the professional's. It becomes clear, then, that training for role-blurring should emphasize skills in communication and in assessing the expectations of colleagues. Training for role differentiation also requires special attention to skill development for both the professional and the paraprofessional.

The effective use of casework and group work skills with clients and their problems have been the central function of social work as a profession. These skills are not obsolete; they merely require redirection when used with paraprofessionals. Individualizing the progress of a paraprofessional co-worker requires many of the same skills required for professional practice. It can happen both in continuing education programs and in existing programs of professional education.

As a result of this study, it has become increasingly apparent that the professional social worker serves as one of the major gatekeepers for paraprofessional advancement. That this function is not yet clear in the minds of the professionals is in part due to the lack of experience with such a new manpower pool. What is more clear to the professionals is their lack of training and, in some cases, of skills in the areas of supervision, consultation, administration, and teaching. The administrative skills necessary to assist both paraprofessionals and agencies in the development of career ladders, for example, were found to be in short supply. The same might be said for teaching and program consultation skills.

What content should be handled at in-service training meetings and what teaching materials are needed? What should paraprofessionals be gaining from their community college experience? What is the difference between an associate of arts degree and a bachelor of arts degree in the human services? These questions and others need the attention of trained social workers. Such an assessment requires training beyond the traditional methods of casework and group work. If the professional social worker is to continue to serve the needs of both the client population and the paraprofessional staff, university training programs must redirect their instructional goals toward the present and future needs of social workers who must handle the demands of supervision, consultation, administration, and teaching. The identity crisis in the social work profession, mentioned earlier, will continue to grow if these training needs are not met.

Many paraprofessionals in the study admitted that they "could rap but couldn't scribe." It is evidence of a communication problem if the meaning of this statement is not clear to the professional social worker. It means that paraprofessionals feel much more skillful with their interpersonal relation skills than with their ability to write. It is part of the psychic stretch mentioned earlier when the lack of good education results in built-in frustrations in organizational life.

The old antidote of college education has been used as the remedy for this situation. However, this too is proving to increase the frustrations in many cases. The combination of weak educational backgrounds, of older paraprofessionals competing with younger and better educated community college students, of child-rearing demands at home, and of insufficient agency support produces new increments of frustration. The problem of the pressures of college is compounded by the difficulties of integrating course content into daily practice. The paraprofessionals are learning the language of the classroom but are having difficulty in translating their new knowledge into practice.

This difficulty highlights the potential translator role of the professional, provided that he has sufficient awareness of learning approaches and differential levels of understanding. To handle the frustrations of the paraprofessionals, professionals have retreated to the comfort of the domain of their own skills by handling primarily the emotional problems and fears of the paraprofessional but tending to give much less attention to the problems and the processes of learning.

Recent developments in the field of education seem to reflect a growing interest in unionization. Is this the direction in which this emerging social movement will go? Future training programs may need to devote attention to labor-management relations in the human service sector.

More research and improved training will still provide only some of the answers to the questions about the organization and ideology of the professional-paraprofessional relationship as part of an emerging social movement. Both sets of participants recognize their roles in serving their fellow man. Both identify with the art and science of the helping process. While the future directions of this emerging social movement are unclear, the process of change is inevitable. Those professionals who have displayed a highly experimental orientation will provide one of the key ingredients necessary to making the professional-paraprofessional relationship a unique blend of talent in service to all segments of our society.

[Notes Part 1]

1 Robert Reiff, "Dilemmas of Professionalism," in *Nonprofessionals in the Human Services*, eds. Charles Grosser et al, (San Francisco: Jossey-Bass, 1969), pp. 57-65.

[Chapter 1]

1 The human services provided to people in need include everything from the provision of foster care for neglected children to the rehabilitation of the adult offender. In many states human service agencies include programs for the welfare recipient, the mentally ill, the physically disabled, the mentally retarded, the juvenile offender, malnourished elderly, and the attached.

2 While paraprofessionals work in the fields of public education, law, employment, and health, primary emphasis in this book is placed on paraprofessionals in social welfare settings. Therefore, a para-professional is defined as a person who works along side of a professional, in this case a trained social worker with a master's degree, associated in an auxiliary, relatively independent role, performing some functions also performed by professionals and who is without the formal training and sanctions of traditional certifying bodies.

[3] As will be noted later, the paraprofessionals are now suffering the consequences of this development in an era when college education is the primary ticket for advancement.

[4] M.A. Thompson, "The Professionalization of New Careerists," (master's thesis, University of Minnesota, 1969).

[5] The research noted in Part III is based primarily on social workers who had left traditional middle-class agencies due to the appeal of the War on Poverty. They are defined as social workers with master's degrees engaged in a field of practice requiring specialized knowledge based on academic preparation, operating under community sanctions and authority, abiding by a code of ethics, and belonging to a particular subculture of the helping professions.

[6] A. Flexner, "Is Social Work a Profession?" *Proceedings of National Conference on Charities and Corrections* (Chicago: University of Chicago Press, 1915).

[7] E. Greenwood, "Attributes of a Profession," *Social Work* (July,.1957).

[8] Thomas Marshall, "Professionalism and Social Policy," in *Man, Work and Society*, eds. S. Nosow and W. Form (New York: Basic Books, 1962).

[9] Everett Hughes, *Men and Their Work* (Glencoe, Ill.: Free Press, 1958).

[10] Theodore Caplow, *The Sociology of Work* (Minneapolis: University of Minnesota Press, 1954).

[11] William Goode, "Community Within a Community: The Professions," *American Sociological Review* (April 1957); W. Goode, "Encroachment, Charlatanism, and the Emerging Professions," *American Sociological Review* (December 1960).

[12] Rue Bucher and Anselm Strauss, "Professions in Process," *American Journal of Sociology* (January 1961).

[13] William Goode, "The Protection of the Inept," *American Sociological Review* (February 1967).

[14] Roy Lubove, *The Professional Altruist* (Cambridge: Harvard University Press, 1965).

[15] Mary Richmond, *Social Diagnosis* (New York: Harper & Row, 1917).

[16] Roy Lubove, *Professional Altruist*, p. 118.

[17] Harry Lurie, "The Responsibility of a Socially Oriented Profession," in *New Directions in Social Work*, ed. C. Kasius (New York: Harper & Bros., 1954).

[18] *Ibid.*, p. 31.

[19] *Ibid.*, p. 36.

[20] Werner Boehm, "Relationship of Social Work to Other Professions," in *Encyclopedia of Social Work*, H. Lurie (New York: National Association of Social Work, 1965).

[21] Harry Lurie, "Responsibility of a Socially Oriented Profession," p. 40.

[22] Harold Wilensky and Charles Lebeaux, *Industrial Society and Social Welfare* (New York: Free Press, 1958).

[23] Joseph W. Eaton, "Whence and Whither Social Work? A Sociological Analysis," *Social Work* (January 1956).

[24] Alfred Kadushin, "The Knowledge Base of Social Work," in *Issues in American Social Work,* ed. A. Kahn (New York: Columbia University Press, 1959).

[25] Harold Wilensky and Charles Lebeaux, *Industrial Society and Social Welfare*, p. 306.

[26] Peter Blau and W. Richard Scott, *Formal Organizatons: A Comparative Approach* (San Francisco: Chandler Publishing, 1962).

[27] Harold Wilensky and Charles Lebeaux, *Industrial Society and Social Welfare*, p. 302.

[28] *Ibid*., pp.303-308.

[29] Henry Meyer, "Professionalization and Social Work," in *Issues in American Social Work,* ed. A Kahn (New York: Columbia University Press, 1959).

[30] Eleanor Cockerill, "The Interdependence of the Professions in Helping People," *Social Casework* (November 1953).

[31] Alexander Carr-Saunders and P. Wilson, *The Professions* (Oxford: Clarendon Press, 1933).

[32] Henry Meyer, "Professionalization and Social Work," p. 330.

[33] Harold Wilensky and Charles Lebeaux, *Industrial Society and Social Welfare*, pp. 318-323.

[34] Lydia Rapaport, "In Defense of Social Work: An Examination of Stress in the Profession," *Social Service Review* (March 1960).

[35] Charles Frankel, "Social Philosophy and the Professional Education of Social Workers," *Social Service Review* (December 1959).

[36] Harold Wilensky and Charles Lebeaux, *Industrial Society and Social Welfare*, p. 333.

[37] Alva Myrdal and V. Klein, *Women's Two Roles* (London: Routledge & Kegan, 1956).

[38] *Ibid.*, p. 2.

[39] M. Cogan, "The Problem of Defining a Profession," *Annals of the American Academy of Political and Social Sciences* (January 1955).

[40] Harold Wilensky, "The Professionalization of Everyone," *American Journal of Sociology* (September 1964).

[41] Carr-Saunders and Wilson, *The Professions*, p. 10.

[Chapter 2]

[1] Dorothy Daly, *Closing the Gap . . . in Social Work Manpower* (Washington: Department of Health, Education, and Welfare, 1965).

[2] Jean Szoloci, "Some Conceptual Issues in Social Welfare Manpower Statistics," *Welfare Review* (March 1967); August Bolino, *Manpower and the City* (Cambridge: Schenkman, 1969).

[3] Richard Lester, *Manpower Planning in a Free Society* (Princeton: Princeton University Press, 1966).

[4] Eli Ginzberg, "Manpower in a Service Economy," in *Training Health Service Workers: The Critical Challenge*, ed. Lucy Kramer (Washington: Department of Labor and Department of Health, Education, and Welfare, 1966).

[5] Anthony Downs, *Inside Bureaucracy* (Boston: Little, Brown, 1967).

[6] David Novick, ed., *Program Budgeting* (Washington: Bureau of the Budget, 1965).

[7] F. William Howton, *Functionaries* (Chicago: Quadrangle Books, 1969).

[8] William Whyte, *The Organization Man* (New York: Doubleday, 1956).

[9] Howton, *Functionaries.*

[10] Ginzberg, "Manpower in a Service Economy," pp. 17-18.

[11] Daly, *Closing the Gap;* Edward Schwartz, ed., *Manpower in Social Welfare: Research Perspectives* (New York: National Association of Social Workers, 1966).

[12] Joseph Bensman and Bernard Rosenberg, *Mass, Class, and Bureaucracy* (Englewood Cliffs, N.J.: Prentice-Hall, 1963).

[13] Louis Orzack, "Social Change: Implications for Welfare Manpower," in *Manpower and Social Welfare*, ed. E. Schwartz (New York: National Association of Social Workers, 1966).

[14] Bensman and Rosenberg, *Mass, Class, and Bureaucracy*, p. 513.

[15] Oswald Hall, "Organization of Manpower in Some Helping Professions," in *Manpower in Social Welfare*, ed. E. Schwartz (New York: National Association of Social Workers, 1966).

[16] Samuel Mencher, "Social Policy and Welfare Manpower," in *Manpower in Social Welfare*, ed. E. Schwartz (New York: National Association of Social Workers, 1966).

[17] Henry Meyer, "The Effect of Social Work Professionalization on Manpower," in *Manpower in Social Welfare*, ed. E. Schwartz (New York: National Association of Social Workers, 1966).

[18] Mencher, "Social Policy and Welfare Manpower," p. 40.

[19] Peter Clark and James Wilson, "Incentive Systems: A Theory of Organizations," *Administrative Science Quarterly* (September 1961).

[20] Arnold Gurin, *Outline of Recommendations on Curriculum Content for Community Organization,* (New York: Council on Social Work Education, 1968).

[21] Howard Vollmer and Donald Mills, eds., *Professionalization* (Englewood Cliffs, N.J.: Prentice-Hall, 1966); Amitai Etzioni, *The Semi-Professions and Their Organization* (New York: Free Press, 1969).

[22] Samuel Mencher, "Social Policy and Welfare Manpower," p. 40.

[23] Joseph W. Eaton, *Stone Walls Not a Prison Make* (Springfield, Ill.: Charles C. Thomas, 1962).

[24] Arthur Pearl and Frank Riessman, *New Careers for the Poor* (New York: Free Press, 1965); Frank Riessman and Hermine Popper, *Up From Poverty: New Career Ladders for Nonprofessionals* (New York: Harper & Row, 1968); C. Grosser, W. Henry, and J. Kelly, eds., *Nonprofessionals in the Human Services* (San Francisco: Jossey-Bass, 1969).

[25] Harry Specht, et al., "The Neighborhood Subprofessional Worker," *Children* (January-February 1968).

[26] Neil Gilbert, *Clients or Constituents: A Case of Pittsburgh's War on Poverty* (San Francisco: Jossey-Bass, 1970); David Moynihan, *Maximum Feasible Misunderstanding* (New York: Free Press, 1968); Council on Social Work Education, *Personnel in Anti-Poverty Programs: Implications for Social Work Education* (New York 1967); Kenneth Clark, *A Relevant War on Poverty* (New York: Metropolitan Research Council, 1969).

[27] Daly, *Closing the Gap*, p. 57.

[28] Schwartz, *Manpower in Social Welfare*, pp. 149-150.

[29] Henry David, "Manpower Theory and Conceptualization," in *Manpower for Mental Health*, ed. Franklin Arnoff et al. (Chicago: Aldine, 1969).

[30] Kenneth E. Boulding, "The Concept of Need for Health Services," *Milbank Memorial Fund Quarterly* (October 1966).

[31] Alfred Kahn, *Theory and Practice of Social Planning* (New York: Russel Sage, 1969).

[32] *Ibid.*, p. 231.

[33] Schwartz, *Manpower in Social Welfare*, p. 146.

[34] *American Journal of Public Health* (September 1969), p. 1660.

[35] Arthur Pearl and Frank Riessman, *New Careers for the Poor*.

[36] Lester, *Manpower Planning*, p. 207.

[37] D. Braybrooke and C. Lindblom, *A Strategy of Decision* (New York: Free Press, 1963).

[Chapter 3]

[1] Salvador Minuchin, "The Paraprofessional and the Use of Confrontation in the Mental Health Field," *American Journal of Orthopsychiatry* (October 1969).

[2] Another interpretation of the "psychic stretch" is that paraprofessionals were hired to both help their brothers and keep the lid on dissatisfaction and revolt, truly a "psychic," if not moral stretch.

[3] Rue Bucher and J. Stelling, "Characteristics of Professional Organizations," *Journal of Health and Social Behavior* (March 1969).

[4] With the following exceptions: William Denham and Eunice Shatz, "Impact of the Indigenous Nonprofessional on the Professional's Role," in *Human Services and Social Work Responsibility*, ed. Willard Richan (New York: National Association of Social Work, 1969); M.L. Birnbaum and C.H. Jones, "Activities of the Social Work Aides," *Social Casework* (June 1967); Charles F. Grosser, "Local Residents as Mediators Between Middle-Class Professionals and Lower-Class Clients," *Social Service Review* (January 1966).

5 Charles F. Grosser, et al., eds., *Nonprofessionals in the Human Services* (San Francisco: Jossey-Bass, 1969), p. 6.

6 William B. Cameron, *Modern Social Movements: A Sociological Outline* (New York: Random House, 1966); Rudolf Heberle, *Social Movements: An Introduction to Political Sociology* (New York: Appleton-Crofts, 1951); C. Wendell King, *Social Movements in the United States* (New York: Random House, 1956); Kurt and Gladys Lang, *Collective Dynamics* (New York: T. Y. Crowell, 1961); Neil Smelser, *Theory of Collective Behavior* (New York: Free Press, 1963); Hans Toch, *The Social-Psychology of Social Movements* (Indianapolis: Bobbs-Merrill, 1966).

7 Joseph W. Eaton, *Stone Walls Not a Prison Make* (Springfield, Ill.: Charles C. Thomas, 1962).

8 Daniel P. Moyniham, *Maximum Feasible Misunderstanding* (New York: Free Press, 1969).

9 *Ibid.*, p. 25. However, it has been noted that social workers were distinctively absent from the early formulation of the poverty program.

10 Joseph W. Eaton, *Stone Walls*, p. 15.

11 *Ibid.*, pp. 39-41.

12 Michael Harrington, *The Other American: Poverty in the United States* (New York: Macmillan, 1962).

13 Joseph W. Eaton, *Stone Walls*, p. 41.

14 *Ibid.*, p. 40.

15 Arthur Pearl and Frank Riessman, *New Careers for the Poor* (New York: Free Press, 1965).

16 Joseph W. Eaton, *Stone Walls*, p. 40.

17 In some instances paraprofessional jobs have been formally established. However, in these cases there is a significant reduction in the sense of mission which flavored the first entry of paraprofessionals into social agencies. The formalism has taken on the colors of the bureaucratic civil service system. The result has been a formalizing of entry-level jobs with little or no structure for upward mobility within the personnel system. These obstacles have forced paraprofessionals to return to college to seek alternative forms of advancement in attempting to move out of their professional status.

18 Joseph W. Eaton, *Stone Walls*, p. 41.

[Chapter 4]

[1] Ivan Berg, *Education and Jobs: The Great Training Robbery* (New York: Praeger, 1970); Ivan Illich, *Deschooling Society* (New York: Harper and Row, 1971); S.M. Miller, "Breaking the Credentials Barrier," in *Managing People at Work*, ed. S.M. Miller (New York: Macmillan, 1971).

[2] Charles F. Grosser, "Manpower Development Programs," in *Nonprofessionals in the Human Services*, Charles Grosser, William E. Henry, and James G. Kelly, eds., (San Francisco: Jossey-Bass, 1969).

[3] Yosef K. Katan, "The Utilization of Indigenous Nonprofessionals in Human Service Organizations and the Factors Affecting It—An Exploratory Study," (Ph.D. dissertation, University of Michigan, 1972).

[4] J.A. Chester, *New Careers and HEW*, mimeographed (Washington: Office of New Careers, Department of Health, Education and Welfare, 1970).

[5] Raymond A. Katzell, A. Korman, and E. Levine, *Research Report No. 1: Overview Study of the Dynamics of Worker Job Mobility*, (Washington: U.S. Government Printing Office, 1971).

[6] Louis A. Ferman, *Job Development for the Hard-to-Employ* (Ann Arbor: Institute of Labor and Industrial Relations, University of Michigan—Wayne State University, 1968).

[7] Edward E. Schwartz, "A Strategy of Research on Manpower Problems," in *Manpower in Social Welfare*, ed. Edward E. Schwartz (New York: National Association of Social Work, 1966).

[8] Robert L. Barker and Thomas L. Briggs, *Trends in the Utilization of Social Work Personnel: An Evaluative Research of the Literature*, Research Report No. 2 (New York: National Association of Social Work, 1966).

[9] Bertram M. Beck, "Nonprofessional Social Work Personnel," in *Nonprofessionals in the Human Services*, eds. Charles Grosser, William Henry, and James Kelly (San Francisco: Jossey-Bass, 1969).

[10] Richard A. Cloward and C. Epstein, "Private Social Welfare's Disengagement from the Poor," in *Community Action Against Poverty*, eds. G. Brager and F. Purcell (New Haven: College and University Press, 1967).

[11] Ivan Illich, *Deschooling Society*.

[12] Robert Reiff and Frank Riessman, *The Indigenous Nonprofessional: A Strategy of Change in Community Action and Community Mental Health Programs* (New York: National Institute of Labor Education, 1964); Arthur Pearl and Frank Riessman, *New Careers for the Poor* (New York: Free Press, 1965).

[13] Marie Haug and Marvin B. Sussman, "Professional Autonomy and the Revolt of the Client," *Social Problems*, 17:153-161; R. Reiff, "Dilemmas of Professionalism," in *Nonprofessionals in the Human Services*, eds. Charles Grosser, William Henry, and James Kelly (San Francisco: Jossey-Bass, 1969).

[14] Y. Brozen, "Toward an Ultimate Solution," *Saturday Review* (May 23, 1970), 30-61.

[15] Reference is made here to legislation such as the Nelson Amendment to EOA (1965), the Scheuer Amendment to EOA (1966), the 1967 Amendments to the Higher Education Act and the Elementary and Secondary Education Act, the Harris Amendment to the Social Security Act (1967), and 1968 Amendments to the Vocational Education Act, and many others.

[16] Frank Riessman, "The 'Helper' Therapy Principle," *Social Work*, 10:27-32.

[17] Perhaps the best recent definition of indigenous workers is "those who reside in the target area, engage in social, economic, and political processes similar to those of program participants and are matched with them on such characteristics as social class, race, ethnicity, religion, language, culture, and mores." Charles Grosser, *op. cit.*, p. 123.

[18] Yosef Katan, "Utilization of . . . Paraprofessionals."

[19] In Katan's original work, he identified seven major motives. Since several of these were considered to be highly interrelated, we have synthesized them into the five we are presently using.

[20] E.F. Lynton, *The Subprofessionals: From Concepts to Careers*. A report of a Conference to Expand and Develop Subprofessional Roles in Health, Education, and Welfare, National Conference on Employment of Youth (New York: 1967).

[21] The baccalaureate degree is the minimum educational requirement for membership in the National Association of Social Workers (NASW).

[22] This refers to the broad field of human services and not just to the social work and social welfare services.

[23] These data were tabulated at the request of Senator Harris and were available, in limited quantities, in mimeographed format.

[24] Alan Gartner, *Do Paraprofessionals Improve Human Services: A First Critical Appraisal of the Data* (New York: New Careers Development Center, New York University, 1969).

[25] University Research Corporation, *Human Resources and Manpower Development: A Curriculum Approach* (Washington: University Research Corporation, 1970).

[26] To be sure, studies in the literature vary in terms of the types of variables they include and in the ways in which they define them.

[27] J.D. Wilson, J.R. Fishman, and L.E. Mitchell, *An Assessment of Technical Assistance and Training Needs in New Careers Projects Being Sponsored by the United States Training and Employment Service, Manpower Administration, Department of Labor* (Washington: University Research Corporation, 1969). This sample includes the SRS Harris Amendment survey mentioned earlier and a national survey of New Careers Programs.

[28] P. Larson, M. Bible, and R.F. Falk, *Down the Up Staircase: A Study of New Careers Dropouts.* Recommendations and summary reprinted in *New Career Perspectives*, reprint Series No. 10 (Washington: University Research Corporation, 1969).

[Chapter 5]

[1] Sidney A. Fine, "Guidelines for the Design of New Careers," in *Up From Poverty: New Career Ladders for Nonprofessionals*, Frank Reissman and Hermine Popper, eds. (New York: Harper and Row, 1968).

[2] Robert J. Teare and Harold I. McPheeters, *Manpower Utilization in Social Welfare* (Atlanta: Southern Regional Education Board, 1970).

[3] "Homogeneous" tasks are those which are similar in task content or in level of difficulty.

[4] William H. Denham and Eunice O. Shatz, "Impact of the Indigenous Nonprofessional on the Professional's Role," in *Human Services and Social Work Responsibility*, Willard Richan, ed. (New York: National Association of Social Workers, 1969).

[5] Alan Gartner, *Paraprofessionals and Their Performance* (New York: Praeger, 1971).

[6] Sidney A. Fine, "Guidelines."

[7] William Denham and Eunice Shatz, "Impact of the Indigenous Non-professional."

[8] Robert L. Barker and Thomas L. Briggs, "Trends in the Utilization of Social Work Personnel: An Evaluative Research of the Literature," *Research Report No. 2*, mimeographed (New York: National Association of Social Work, 1966).

[9] Robert L. Barker and Thomas L. Briggs, *Differential Use of Social Work Manpower: An Analysis and Demonstration Study* (New York: National Association of Social Work, 1968).

[10] Samuel Finestone, "Major Dimensions and Alternatives in Differential Use of Casework Staff," in *Experimentation in Differential Use of Personnel in Social Welfare* (New York: National Association of Social Work, 1964).

[11] *Ibid.*

[12] Aside from the formidable technical difficulties of defining task boundaries in the social service field, there is a good deal of uncertainty concerning the dimensions on which task difficulty or complexity would be based. Some research has been started in this area. See Thomas L. Briggs, D.E. Johnson, and E. Lebowitz, *Research on the Complexity-Responsibility Scale* (Syracuse: School of Social Work, Syracuse University, 1970).

[13] Willard C. Richan, "Utilization of Personnel in Social Work: Those with Full Professional Education and Those Without," *Final Report of the Subcommittee on Utilization of Personnel* (New York: National Association of Social Work, 1962).

[14] Robert Barker and Thomas Briggs, "Differential Use of Social Work Manpower."

[15] D. Anderson and J. Dockhorn, "Differential Use of Staff: An Exploration with Job Trained Personnel," *Personnel Information* 8 (1965).

[16] Robert J. Teare and Harold McPheeters, *Manpower Utilization in Social Welfare.*

[17] These roles are described and defined in the next section of this chapter.

[18] Willard Richan, "Utilization of Personnel in Social Work."

[19] Robert Reiff and Frank Riessman, *The Indigenous Nonprofessional: A Strategy of Change in Community Action and Community Mental Health Programs* (New York: National Institute of Labor Education, Mental Health Program, 1964).

[20] See the following for a detailed analysis of the concept "indigenousness": Charles F. Grosser, "Local Residents as Mediators Between Middle-Class Professionals and Lower-Class Clients," *Social Service Review*, January 1966.

[21] Robert Reiff and Frank Riessman, *The Indigenous Nonprofessional*, p. 2.

[22] Jack Otis, "Problems and Promise in the Use of Indigenous Personnel," *Welfare in Review*, Vol. 3, No. 6, June 1965, 12-19.

[23] P. Elston, *New Careers in Welfare for Professionals and Nonprofessionals: A Proposal for Staffing Reorganization Linked to Programs for the Improvement and Expansion of Welfare Services* (New York: New Careers Development Center, New York University, 1967).

[24] These processes, when implemented fully, can give rise to problems for the indigenous worker. A related article (see David Hardcastle, "The Indigenous Nonprofessional in the Social Service Bureaucracy: A Critical Examination," *Social Work*, April 1971, 16, 2:56-63.) indicated that these methods of integrating indigenous workers into agency structures can hasten the loss of their uniqueness, the capability to serve as a link with clients and the community. Hardcastle recommends some staffing patterns that may serve as short-range solutions to the problems.

[25] P. Larson, N. Belding, and R. Falk, *A Functional Model for the Use of Paraprofessional Personnel*, mimeographed (Minneapolis: New Careers Research, University of Minnesota Center for Sociological Research, 1968).

[26] Robert J. Teare and Harold McPheeters, *Manpower Utilization in Social Welfare*.

[Chapter 6]

[1] See William H. Denham and Eunice O. Shatz, "Impact of the Indigenous Paraprofessional on the Professional's Role," in *Human Services and Social Work Responsibility*, Willard Richan, ed. (New York: National Association of Social Workers, 1969); T.M. Gannon, "The Role of the Nonprofessional in the Harlem Domestic Peace Corps," *Sociology and Social Research*, 52 (1968); Emanuel Hallowitz and Frank Riessman, "The Role of the Indigenous Nonprofessional in a Community Mental Neighborhood Service Center Program," *American Journal of Orthopsychiatry* (July 1967);

Perry Levinson and John Schiller, "The Indigenous Non-Professional—Research Issues," (Washington: U.S. Department of Health, Education and Welfare, 1965).

[2] Frank Riessman, "Strategies and Suggestions for Training Nonprofessionals," *Community Mental Health Journal*, 3, no. 2 (Summer 1967).

[3] Adele C. Brody, Nadine Felton, and Frank Riessman, "A New Careers Approach to Training," in *Up From Poverty*, eds. Riessman and Popper, (New York: Harper and Row, 1968), pp. 288-289.

[4] Eunice Shatz et. al., *New Careers: Generic Issues in the Human Services: A Sourcebook for Trainers* (Washington: University Research Corporation, 1968); Leon Ginsberg, Margaret Emery, and John Isaacson, *Syllabus on Orientation and Training of Beginning Workers to Provide Social and Rehabilitation Services*, prepared for the use of the Office of Manpower Development and Training, DHEW, Social and Rehabilitation Service (West Virginia: West Virginia University School of Social Work, 1971); California Community Colleges, *Social Services: A Suggested Associate Degree Curriculum* (Sacramento: California Community Colleges, Chancellor's Office, 1971); Rose C. Thomas, *Public Service Careers Program Training Manual for Case Aide Trainees* (New York: City of New York Department of Social Services, 1968).

[5] Malcolm S. Knowles, *The Modern Practice of Adult Education* (New York: Association Press, 1970), pp. 37-55.

[6] Rolf P. Lynton and Udai Pareek, *Training for Development* (Homewood, Illinois: The Dorsey Press, 1967)., p. 19.

[7] Leslie J. Briggs, *Handbook of Procedures for the Design of Instruction* (Pittsburgh: American Institute of Research, 1970).

[8] Leslie Button, *Discovery and Experience: A New Approach to Training, Group Work, and Teaching* (New York: Oxford University Press, 1971), pp. 12-13

[9] John D. Ingalls, *A Trainer's Guide to Andragogy* (Washington: USDHEW, Social and Rehabilitation Service, 1973), p. 11.

[10] See, for example, California Community Colleges, *Social Services: A Suggested Associate Degree Curriculum* (Sacramento: California Community Colleges, Chancellor's Office, 1971); Steven J. Danish and Allen L. Hauer, *Helping Skills: A Basic Training Program* (New York: Behavioral Publications, 1973); Leon Ginsberg, Margaret Emery, and John Issacson, *Syllabus on Orientation and Training of Beginning Workers to Provide Social and Rehabilitation Services*,

258 PROFESSIONALS AND PARAPROFESSIONALS

prepared for the use of the Office of Manpower Development and
Training, DHEW, Social and Rehabilitation Service (West Virginia:
West Virginia University School of Social Work, 1971); Gertrude S.
Goldberg et al., *New Careers: The Social Service Aide: A Manual
Michael D. Lewis and G. Edward Stormer, *Human Services: A
Common Core Curriculum for Human Service Workers* (Illinois:
Governors State University, 1972); Louis Lowy, *Training Man-
(Boston: United Community Services of Metropolitan Boston and
Boston University School of Social Work, 1968); Janet Rosenberg,
*Breakfast: Two Jars of Paste: A Training Manual for Workers in
1972); Seymour J. Rosenthal et al., *Curricula and Training of
Paraprofessional Employees of Public Housing Authorities* (Wash-
1972); Eunice Shatz et al., *New Careers: Generic Issues in the
Human Services: A Sourcebook for Trainers* (Washington: Uni-
Service Careers Program Training Manual for Case Aide Trainees*
(New York: City of New York Department of Social Services,
1968).

[11] See Yosef K. Katan, *The Utilization of Indigenous Nonprofessionals
Exploratory Study* (Ph.D. dissertation, University of Michigan,
1972).

[12] Robert J. Teare and Harold L. McPheeters, *Manpower Utilization in
Social Welfare* (Atlanta: Southern Regional Education Board,
1970).

[13] Michael J. Austin, Alexis H. Skelding, and Philip L. Smith, *Deliver-
York: Harper and Row, 1977).

[Chapter 7]

[1] Alfred Kadushin, "Games People Play in Supervision," *Social Work*,
13 (March 1968).

[2] *Ibid.*, p. 24.

[3] Irving Miller, "Supervision in Social Work," *Encyclopedia of Social
Work* (New York: National Association of Social Work, 1971),

[4] Herbert H. Aptekar, "Supervision and the Development of Professional Responsibility: An Application of Systems Thought," (Paper presented at the Institute for Field Instructors, Yeshiva University, New York, April 29, 1965), p. 8.

[5] *Ibid.*, p. 12.

[6] Harry Wasserman, "The Professional Social Worker in a Bureaucracy," *Social Work* 16 (January 1971) pp. 90-91.

[7] Donald A. Davis, "Teaching and Administrative Functions in Supervision," *Social Work* (April 1965) p. 83.

[8] Lucille N. Austin, "Basic Principles of Supervision," *Social Casework* 34 (October 1958) p. 445.

[9] Ruth Fizdale, "Peer-Group Supervision," *Social Casework* 34 (December 1952) p. 415.

[10] Frances Scherz, "A Concept of Supervision Based on Definition of Job Responsibility," *Social Casework* 39 (October 1958) p. 440.

[11] Social and Rehabilitation Services, *Operational Planning Manual: FY '73* (Washington, HEW, 1972).

[12] *Ibid.*, p. 37.

[13] Edwina T. Leon, "The MSW as a Supervisor of Paraprofessionals," in *Educating MSW Students to Work with Other Social Welfare Personnel*, Margaret Purvine, ed. (New York: Council on Social Work Education, 1973).

[14] *Ibid.*, p. 41.

[15] *Ibid.*, p. 43.

[16] Malcolm Knowles, *The Modern Practice of Adult Education* (New York: Association Press, 1970).

[17] John D. Ingalls, *A Trainer's Guide to Andragogy* (Washington: U.S. Government Printing Office, 1973).

[18] *Ibid.*, p. 11.

[19] For a discussion of these models see: Sidney A. Fine and Wretha W. Wiley, *An Introduction to Functional Job Analysis* (Washington: The W.E. Upjohn Institute for Employment Research, 1971); Robert J. Teare and Harold L. McPheeters, *Manpower Utilization in Social Welfare* (Atlanta: Southern Regional Education Board, 1970); Robert L. Barker and Thomas R. Briggs, *Using Teams to Deliver Social Services* (Syracuse: School of Social Work, Syracuse University, 1969).

[20] Jean Szalcozi Fine, "Issues in Manpower Development Program Planning," *Working Papers No. 1* (Washington: Department of Health, Education, and Welfare, 1971).

[21] Teare and McPheeters, *Manpower Utilization in Social Welfare.*

[22] Michael J. Austin, Edward Kelleher, and Philip L. Smith, eds., *The Field Consortium: Manpower Development and Training in Social Welfare and Corrections* (Tallahassee, Florida: Board of Regents, 1972).

[23] T. David Ainsworth and Katherine L. Goldsmith, *Occupational Analysis of Social Service in Medical Care Facilities* (Los Angeles: U.C.L.A. Allied Health Profession Project, 1971).

[24] Michael J. Austin and Philip L. Smith, "Manpower Utilization and Educational Articulation: The Florida Experiment in Collaborative Planning," in *Approaches to Innovation in Social Work Education* (New York: Council on Social Work Education, 1974).

[25] See the following references for more complete discussions of functional job analysis: Sidney A. Fine, *A Systems Approach to Task Analysis and Job Design—Seminar Workshop Workbook* (Kalamazoo, Michigan: The W.F. Upjohn Institute for Employment Research, 1967); Sidney A. Fine and Wretha W. Wiley, *An Introduction to Functional Job Analysis: A Scaling of Selected Tasks from the Social Welfare Field* (Kalamazoo, Michigan: The W.F. Upjohn Institute for Employment Research, 1971); Wretha W. Wiley and Sidney A. Fine, *A Systems Approach to New Careers: Two Papers* (Kalamazoo, Michigan: The W.F. Upjohn Institute for Employment Research, 1969).

[26] Philip Smith, "Using Functional Job Analysis to Redesign Jobs," in *Statewide Career Planning in a Human Service Industry*, M. Austin and P. Smith, eds. (Tallahassee, Florida: Board of Regents, 1973).

[27] Fine and Wiley, *An Introduction to Functional Job Analysis.*

[Chapter 8]

[1] Karolyn R. Gould, *Career Mobility for Paraprofessionals in Human Service Agencies* (Washington: U.S. Department of Labor, 1969), p. 113.

[2] National Association of Social Workers, *Standards for Social Service Manpower* (Washington: National Association of Social Workers, 1973).

3Myrna Bordelon Kassel, *Career Systems in State Human Service Agencies* (Chicago: Human Services Manpower Career Center, 1971).

4*Ibid.*, p. 2.

5 Raymond Katzell, Abraham Korman, and Edward Levine, *Research Report No. 1, Overview Study of the Dynamics of Worker Job Mobility* (Washington: Department of Health, Education, and Welfare, 1971), p. 4.

6American Hospital Association, *Career Mobility: A Guide for Program Planning in Health Occupations* (Chicago: American Hospital Association, 1971), p. 1.

7Eli Ginzberg, "Forward," in Charles Brecher, *Upgrading Blue Collar and Service Workers* (Baltimore: John Hopkins University Press, 1972).

8*Ibid.*, p. xi.

9*Ibid,.* Brecher, p. 62.

10U.S. Department of Health, Education, and Welfare, "Social Services '75: A Citizen's Handbook to Program Options and Public Participation under Title 20 of the Social Security Act (PL93-647)" (Washington: U.S. Government Printing Office, 1975).

11Charles Brecher, *Upgrading Blue Collar and Service Workers* (Baltimore: John Hopkins University Press, 1972), p. 107.

12Edward E. Schwartz and William C. Sample, *The Midway Office: An Experiment in the Organization of Work Groups* (New York: National Association of Social Workers, 1972).

[Chapter 9]

1Alvin Gouldner, "Organizational Analysis," in *Sociology Today*, eds. R. Merton et al. (New York: Basic Books, 1959).

2Chester Barnard, *The Functions of the Executive* (Cambridge: Harvard University Press, 1938).

3George Homans, *The Human Group* (New York: Harcourt, 1950).

4See for example, James Thompson, *Organizations in Action* (New York: McGraw-Hill, 1967) and Robert Presthus, *The Organizational Society* (New York: Random House, 1962).

5W. Richard Scott, "Theory of Organizations," in *Handbook of Modern Sociology*, ed. R. Faris, (Chicago: Rand McNally, 1964).

[6] S. Udy, "Comparative Analysis of Organizations," in *Handbook of Organizations*, ed. J. March (Chicago: Rand McNally, 1965).

[7] Charles Perrow, "Hospitals: Technology, Structure, and Goals," in *Handbook of Organizations*, ed. James March (Chicago: Rand McNally, 1965).

[8] Richard Scott, "Theory of Organizations," p. 489.

[9] Robert Merton, *Social Theory and Social Structure* (Glencoe, Ill.: Free Press, 1959).

[10] Some of the most significant work in developing and understanding the link between the individual and the organization has been done by Gouldner on the organizational roles of "cosmopolitan" and "local." He focuses upon the latent or less apparent qualities of social roles as found in the organizational roles of college teachers. Cosmopolitans are defined as those persons low on loyalty to the employing organization, high on commitment to specialized role skills, and likely to use an outer reference group orientation. Locals are defined as those high on loyalty to the employing organization, low on commitment to specialized role skills, and likely to use an inner reference group orientation. See Alvin Gouldner, "Cosmopolitans and Locals: Toward an Analysis of Latent Social Roles," *Administrative Science Quarterly* (December 1957) and (March 1958). Also Leonard Riessman, "A Study of Role Conceptions in Bureaucracy," *Social Forces* (March 1949).

[11] Robert Merton, *Social Theory*, chapter 6.

[12] William Kornhauser, *Scientists in Industry: Conflict and Accommodation* (Berkeley: University of California Press, 1963).

[13] Amitai Etzioni, *A Comparative Analysis of Complex Organizations* (New York: Free Press, 1961).

[14] Erving Goffman, *Asylums* (New York: Doubleday, 1961).

[15] W. Richard Scott, "Professionals in Bureaucracies—Areas of Conflict," in *Professionalization*, eds. H. Vollmer and D. Mills (Englewood Cliffs, N.J.: Prentice-Hall, 1956).

[16] Ronald Corwin, *A Sociology of Education* (New York: Appleton-Century-Crofts, 1965). See also C. Bidwell, "The School as A Formal Organization," in *Handbook of Organizations*, ed. J. March (Chicago: Rand McNally, 1965).

[17] The issues raised in Corwin's study bring to the surface another wide range of issues in organization theory which will be merely mentioned here, since they constitute a considerable area of discussion. The concepts of discretion, predictability of work, management

control, and communication have been major areas of study in the administrative sciences. The issues around supervision, interpersonal relations, productivity, and organizational leadership have also received extensive attention. See also J. March and H. Simon, *Organizations* (New York: J. Wiley, 1958); G. Bell, "Formality Versus Flexibility in Complex Organizations," in *Organizations and Human Behavior*, ed. G. Bell (Englewood Cliffs, N.J.: Prentice-Hall, 1967); R. Day and R. Hamblin, "Some Effects of Close and Punitive Styles of Supervision," *American Journal of Sociology* (March 1964). Also D. Miller, "Supervision: Evolution of an Organizational Role," in *Organizations and Human Behavior*, ed. G. Bell (Englewood Cliffs, N.J.: Prentice-Hall, 1967); Philip Selznick, *Leadership in Administration* (New York: Row, Peterson and Co., 1957).

[18] Robert Pruger and Harry Specht, "Establishing New Careers Programs: Organizational Barriers and Strategies," *Social Work* (October 1968).

[19] Herbert Simon, *Administrative Behavior* (New York: Free Press, 1957).

[20] George Brager, "The Indigenous Worker: A New Approach to the Social Work Technician," *Social Work* (April 1965).

[21] David Sills, *The Volunteers* (Glencoe, Ill.: Free Press, 1957).

[22] Neal Gross, Ward Mason, and Alexander McEachern, *Explorations in Role Analysis* (New York: J. Wiley, 1958).

[23] *Ibid.*, p. 17.

[24] H.H. Gerth and C.W. Mills, *Character and Social Structure* (New York: Harcourt, Brace & World, 1953).

[25] Gerth and Mills, *Character and Social Structure*, p. 172; also Erving Goffman, *Presentation of Everyday Self* (New York: Doubleday, 1959). In designing the research instrument, questions were developed to gather data about the "three persons" in an effort to determine how each member of the relationship viewed himself, was viewed by others, and how he thought others viewed him.

[26] Roger Brown, *Social Psychology* (New York: Free Press, 1965).

[27] Daniel Levenson, "Role, Personality, and Social Structure in the Organizational Setting," *Journal of Abnormal and Social Psychology* (March 1959).

[28] Sidney Fine, "Guidelines for the Design of New Careers," in *Up From Poverty: New Career Ladders for Nonprofessionals*, eds. F. Riessman and H. Popper (New York: Harper and Row, 1968).

[29] Amitai Etzioni, *Modern Organizations* (Englewood Cliffs, N.J.: Prentice-Hall, 1964).

[30] Arthur Pearl and Frank Riessman, *New Careers for the Poor* (New York: Free Press, 1965), p. 63.

[31] Herbert Simon, *Administrative Behavior*, p. 33.

[32] G. Weber, "Conflicts Between Professional and Non Professional Personnel," in *Professionalization*, eds. H. Vollmer and D. Mills (Englewood Cliffs, N.J.: Prentice-Hall, 1966).

[33] Arthur Pearl and Frank Riessman, *New Careers for the Poor*, p. 124.

[34] Hubert Jones, "Beyond Romanticism: A Critical Look at the Use of Indigenous Workers," mimeographed (San Francisco: N.A.S.W. Second Symposium on Human Services and Professional Responsibility, May 1968).

[Chapter 10]

[1] Daniel Katz and Robert Kahn, *The Social Psychology of Organizations* (New York: J. Wiley, 1966).

[2] *Ibid.*, p. 187.

[3] Robert Pruger and Harry Specht, "Establishing New Careers Programs: Organizational Barriers and Strategies," *Social Work* (October 1968), p. 24.

[4] J.C. Wilson et al., "An Assessment of Technical Assistance and Training Needs in New Careers Projects," (Washington: University Research Corporation, 1969).

[5] Calvin Hall and Gardner Lindzey, *Theories of Personality* (New York: J. Wiley, 1957), pp. 457-499.

[6] M.L. Kohn and C. Schooler, "Class, Occupation, and Orientation," *American Sociological Review* (October 1969), pp. 667-699.

[7] This was in contrast to nursing (5 percent), teaching (8 percent), business (8 percent), law (4 percent), and other fields (5 percent). The choice of social work was equally high for men (68 percent) and for women (70 percent) as well as for blacks (71 percent) and whites (72 percent). However, those thirty-nine years old and under were less enthusiastic (57 percent) than those forty years old and above (74 percent).

[8] Over 60 percent had received their degrees during the 1960s and the total population included those trained in casework (69 percent), group work (16 percent), community organizations (5 percent), or a combination of methods (10 percent).

[Chapter 11]

[1] There is a danger of overemphasizing the tasks at the expense of the objectives of the services. It is important to define the tasks which were used to measure both overlap and differentiation in the professional/paraprofessional relationship. When two differently trained persons approach a similar task, it is necessary to refer to different levels. In this case, the level of complexity of the problem, the level of difficulty of the task regarding skills and knowledge, and the level of risk to the client regarding poorly performed services become crucial to task analysis. See R.J. Teare, "Roles and Functions of Different Levels of Social Welfare Workers," mimeographed (Athens, Georgia: University of Georgia, 1969).

[2] The response category "either" could reflect ambivalence and therefore constitutes a "catch all" category, or it could reflect confidence on the part of both sets of respondents that either professionals or paraprofessionals can perform the task.

[3] As noted in the profiles of participants, blacks represented 43 percent of the professional group and 76 percent of the paraprofessional group.

[4] K. Gould et al., *Where Do We Go From Here?* (New York: National Committee on Employment of Youth, 1969).

[Chapter 12]

[1] The majority of the organizations included in the study were receiving anti-poverty funds to carry out programs involving professionals and paraprofessionals. Other sources of support included the United Fund; Children's Bureau; Health, Community Mental Health Act; Older Americans Act; and the state and local public sources.

[2] Camille Lambert and Leah Lambert, "Impact of Poverty Funds on Voluntary Agencies," *Social Work* (April 1970).

[3] *Ibid.*, p. 58.

[4] Richard Hall, *Occupations and the Social Structure* (Englewood Cliffs, N.J.: Prentice-Hall, 1969).

[5] *Ibid.*, p. 125.

[6] Fred E. Katz, *Autonomy and Organization: The Limits of Social Control* (New York: Random House, 1968).

[7] While the literature reflects both the study of organizational constraints on the individual and the individual's impact on the organization, information for this study focused only on the influence of the organization on the professional-paraprofessional relationship.

[8] Edmund Ricci, *Organizational and Professional Influences upon Work-Role Conception and Work Interaction* (Ph.D. dissertation, University of Pittsburgh, 1967).

[9] Philip Selznick, *Leadership in Administration* (New York: Row, Peterson, and Co., 1957).

[10] With regard to interagency liaison, there was general agreement throughout the population of respondents in the six cities that liaison with other agencies was quite active regarding health, welfare, school, and other voluntary agencies. Much less liaison was reported with the probation and police departments.

[11] Robert Pruger and Harry Specht, "Establishing New Careers Programs: Organizational Barriers and Strategies," *Social Work* (October 1968), p. 25.

[12] Karolyn Gould et al., *Where Do We Go From Here?* (New York: National Committee on Employment of Youth, 1969).

[Chapter 13]

[1] Karolyn Gould et al., *Where Do We Go From Here?* (New York: National Committee on Employment of Youth, 1969).

[2] William H. Denham and Eunice O. Shatz, "Impact of the Indigenous Nonprofessional on the Professional's Role," in *Human Services and Social Work Responsibility*, ed. Willard Richan (New York: National Association of Social Workers, 1969).

[3] *Ibid.*, p. 184.

[4] W. Richard Scott, "Reactions to Supervision in a Heteronomous Professional Organization," *Administrative Science Quarterly* (June 1965).

[5] Some professionals even reported that their paraprofessionals referred to them as their "mascots," based on an obviously close working relationship with little of the managerial or "boss" atmosphere.

[6] Some might also argue that this compassion reveals the typical overprotection frequently observed in social work supervision.

[7]With task analysis receiving increased research attention throughout the country, it is hoped that work role compatability and personality factors relevant to both the supervisor and the supervisee will also receive attention. From this study it appears that one area of analysis without the other would be misleading.

BIBLIOGRAPHY

Books

Ainsworth, T. David, and Goldsmith, Katherine L. *Occupational Analysis of Social Service in Medical Care Facilities.* Los Angeles: U.C.L.A. Allied Health Profession Project, 1971.

American Hospital Association. *Career Mobility; A Guide for Program Planning Health Occupations.* Chicago: American Hospital Association, 1972.

Austin, Michael; Kelleher, Edward; and Smith, Philip, eds. *The Field Consortium: Manpower Development and Training in Social Welfare and Corrections.* Tallahassee, Florida: Board of Regents, 1972.

Barker, Robert, and Briggs, Thomas R. *Differential Use of Social Work Manpower: An Analysis and Demonstration Study.* New York: National Association of Social Workers, 1968.

Barker, Robert L., and Briggs, Thomas R. *Using Teams to Deliver Social Services.* Syracuse: School of Social Work, Syracuse University, 1969.

Barnard, C. *The Functions of the Executive.* Cambridge: Harvard University Press, 1938.

Becker, H. *The Outsider.* New York: Free Press, 1963.

Benjamin, Judith; Freedman, Marcia; and Lynton, Edith. *Pros and Cons: New Roles for Nonprofessionals in Corrections.* Washington: U.S. Department of Health, Education, and Welfare, Welfare Administration, Office of Juvenile Delinquency and Youth Development, 1966.

Bensman, J., and Rosenberg, B. *Mass, Class, and Bureaucracy.* Englewood Cliffs, N.J.: Prentice-Hall, 1963.

Berg, I. *Education and Jobs: The Great Training Robbery.* New York: Praeger, 1970.

Billingsley, Andrew. *The Social Worker in a Child Protective Agency.* New York: National Association of Social Workers, 1964.

Blau, Peter. *The Dynamics of Bureaucracy.* Chicago: University of Chicago Press, 1955.

Blau, Peter, and Scott, W.R. *Formal Organizations: A Comparative Approach.* San Francisco: Chandler Publishing, 1962.

Bolino, August. *Manpower and the City.* Cambridge: Schenkman, 1969.

Braybrooke, David, and Lindblom, Charles. *A Strategy of Decision.* New York: Free Press, 1963.

Briggs, Leslie J. *Handbook of Procedures for the Design of Instruction.* American Institute of Research, 1970.

Briggs, Thomas L.; Johnson, D.E.; and Lebowitz, E. *Research on the Complexity-Responsibility Scale.* Syracuse: School of Social Work, Syracuse University, 1970.

Brown, Roger. *Social Psychology.* New York: Free Press, 1965.

Button, Leslie. *Discovery and Experience: A New Approach to Training, Group Work, and Teaching.* New York: Oxford University Press, 1971.

California Community Colleges. *Social Services: A Suggested Associate Degree Curriculum.* Sacramento: California Community Colleges, Chancellor's Office, 1971.

Cameron, William B. *Modern Social Movements: A Sociological Outline.* New York: Random House, 1966.

Caplow, Theodore. *The Sociology of Work.* Minneapolis: University of Minnesota Press, 1954.

Carr-Saunders, A., and Wilson, P. *The Professions.* Oxford: Claredon Press, 1933.

Chester, J.A. *New Careers and HEW.* Mimeographed. Washington: Office of New Careers, Department of Health, Education, and Welfare, 1970.

Clark, Kenneth. *A Relevant War on Poverty.* New York: Metropolitan Research Council, 1969.

Community Service Administration. *Draft Revisions of Chapter II, Title 45 of the Code of Federal Regulation, Part 220—Service Programs for Families and Children: Title IV, Parts A and B of the Social Security Act.* Mimeographed. Washington, D.C., 1972.

Corwin, Ronald. *A Sociology of Education.* New York: Appleton-Century-Crofts, 1965.

Council on Social Work Education. *Personnel in Anti-Poverty Programs: Implications for Social Work Education.* New York: Council on Social Work Education, 1967.

Daly, Dorothy. *Closing the Gap . . . in Social Work Manpower.* Washington, D.C.: U.S. Department of Health, Education, and Welfare, 1965.

Danish, Steven J., and Hauer, Allen L. *Helping Skills: A Basic Training Program.* New York: Behavioral Publications, 1973.

Downs, Anthony. *Inside Bureaucracy.* Boston: Little Brown, 1967.

Eaton, J.W. *Stone Walls Not A Prison Make.* Springfield, Illinois: Thomas, 1962.

Ellsworth, Robert. *Nonprofessionals in Psychiatric Rehabilitation.* New York: Appleton-Century-Crofts, 1968.

Elston, P. *New Careers in Welfare for Professionals and Nonprofessionals: A Proposal for Staffing Reorganization Linked to Programs for the Improvement and Expansion of Welfare Services.* New York: New Careers Development Center, New York University, 1967.

Etzioni, Amitai. *A Comparative Analysis of Complex Organizations.* New York: Free Press, 1961.

Etzioni, Amitai. *Modern Organizations.* Englewood Cliffs, N.J.: Prentice-Hall, 1964.

Etzioni, Amitai. *The Semi-Professions and Their Organization.* New York: Free Press, 1969.

Ferman, L.A. *Job Development for the Hard-to-Employ.* Ann Arbor: Institute of Labor and Industrial Relations, University of Michigan —Wayne State University, 1968.

Fine, Sidney A. *A Systems Approach to Task Analysis and Job Design— Seminar Workshop Workbook.* Kalamazoo, Michigan: The W.F. Upjohn Institute for Employment Research, 1967.

Fine, Sidney A., and Wiley, Wretha W. *An Introduction to Functional Job Analysis.* Washington: The W.F. Upjohn Institute for Employment Research, 1971.

Fine, Sydney A., and Wiley, Wretha W. *An Introduction to Functional Job Analysis: A Scaling of Selected Tasks from the Social Welfare Field.* Kalamazoo, Michigan: The W.F. Upjohn Institute for Employment Research, 1971.

Fishman, Jacob; Pearl, Arthur; and MacLennan, Beryce. *New Careers: Ways Out of Poverty for Disadvantaged Youth.* Washington: Howard University, 1965.

Fishman, Jacob. *Training for New Careers.* Washington: Center for Youth and Community Studies, Howard University, 1965.

French, David G. *Needed Research on Social Work Manpower.* Report to the Task Force on Social Work Education and Manpower. Washington: U.S. Department of Health, Education, and Welfare, Welfare Administration, Bureau of Family Services, 1964.

Gans, Herbert. *The Urban Villagers.* New York: Free Press, 1962.

Gartner, Alan. *Do Paraprofessionals Improve Human Services: A First Critical Appraisal of the Data.* New York: New Careers Development Center, New York University, 1969.

Gartner, Alan. *Paraprofessionals and Their Performance.* New York: Praeger, 1971.

Gerth, H.H., and Mills, C.W. *Character and Social Structure.* New York: Harcourt Brace and World, 1953.

Gilbert, Neil. *Clients or Constituents: A Case Study of Pittsburgh's War on Poverty.* San Francisco: Jossey-Bass, 1970.

Ginsberg, Leon; Emery, Margaret; and Isaacson, John. *Syllabus on Orientation and Training of Beginning Workers to Provide Social and Rehabilitation Services.* Prepared for the Office of Manpower Development and Training, DHEW, Social and Rehabilitation Service. West Virginia: West Virginia University School of Social Work, 1971.

Goffman, Erving, *Presentation of Everyday Self.* New York: Doubleday, 1959.

Goffman, Erving. *Asylums.* New York: Doubleday, 1961.

Goldberg, Gertrude S. *New Careers: The Social Service Aide: A Manual for Trainees.* Washington: University Research Corporation, 1968.

Goodman, Paul. *Growing Up Absurd.* New York: Vintage Books, 1960.

Gould, Karolyn R. *Career Mobility for Paraprofessionals in Human Service Agencies.* Washington: U.S. Department of Labor, 1969.

Gould, Karolyn. *Where Do We Go From Here?* New York: National Committee on Employment of Youth, 1969.

Grant, Douglas. *Experiment in Culture Expansion: Norco Conference.* Sacramento: California Department of Corrections, 1963.

Gross, Neal; Mason, Ward; and McEachern, Alexander. *Explorations in Role Analysis.* New York: J. Wiley, 1958.

Grosser, Charles; Henry, William; and Kelly, James, eds. *Nonprofessionals in the Human Services.* San Francisco: Jossey-Bass, 1969.

Hall, Calvin, and Lindzey, Gardner. *Theories of Personality*. New York: J. Wiley, 1957.

Hall, Richard. *Occupations and the Social Structure*. Englewood Cliffs, N.J.: Prentice-Hall, 1969.

Harrington, Michael. *The Other American: Poverty in the United States*. New York: Macmillan, 1962.

Heberle, Rudolf. *Social Movements: An Introduction to Political Sociology*. New York: Appleton-Century-Crofts, 1951.

Higman, Howard. *The Colorado Story*. Boulder: University of Colorado, 1966.

Homans, George. *The Human Group*. New York: Harcourt Brace and World, 1950.

Howton, F. William. *Functionaries*. Chicago: Quadrangle Books, 1969.

Hughes, Everett. *Men and Their Work*. Glencoe, Illinois: Free Press, 1958.

Illich, Ivan. *Deschooling Society*. New York: Harper and Row, 1971.

Ingalls, John D. *A Trainer's Guide to Andragogy*. Washington: USD-HEW, Social and Rehabilitation Service, 1973.

Kahn, Alfred. *Theory and Practice of Social Planning*. New York: Russell Sage, 1969.

Kassel, Myrna Bordelon. *Career Systems in State Human Service Agencies*. Chicago: Human Services Manpower Career Center, 1971.

Katan, Yosef K. *The Utilization of Indigenous Nonprofessionals in Human Service Organizations and the Factors Affecting It—An Exploratory Study*. Ph.D. dissertation, University of Michigan, 1972.

Katz, Daniel and Kahn, Robert. *The Social Psychology of Organizations*. New York: J. Wiley, 1966.

Katz, Fred E. *Autonomy and Organization: The Limits of Social Control*. New York: Random House, 1968.

Katzell, Raymond A.; Korman, Abraham; and Levine, Edward. *Research Report No. 1: Overview Study of the Dynamics of Worker Job Mobility*. Washington: U.S. Government Printing Office, 1971.

King, C. Wendell. *Social Movements in the United States*. New York: Random House, 1956.

Knowles, Malcolm S. *The Modern Practice of Adult Education*. New York: Association Press, 1970.

Kogan, Leonard, ed. *Social Science Theory and Social Work Research*. New York: National Association of Social Workers, 1960.

Kornhauser, William. *Scientists in Industry: Conflict and Accommodation*. Berkeley: University of California Press, 1963.

Lang, Kurt, and Lang, Gladys. *Collective Dynamics*. New York: T.Y. Crowell, 1961.

Larson, P.; Belding, N; and Falk, R. *A Functional Model for the Use of Paraprofessional Personnel*. Mimeographed. Minneapolis: New Careers Research, University of Minnesota Center for Sociological Research, 1968.

Larson, P; Bible, M.; and Falk, R.F. *Down the Up Staircase: A Study of New Careers Dropouts*. Recommendations and summary reprinted in *New Careers Perspectives*. Reprint Series No. 10. Washington: University Research Corporation, 1969.

Lester, Richard. *Manpower Planning in a Free Society*. New York: Princeton University Press, 1966.

Levitan, Sar. *Antipoverty Work and Training Efforts: Goals and Reality*. Ann Arbor: University of Michigan, 1967.

Lewis, Michael D., and Stormer, G. Edward. *Human Services: A Common Core Curriculum for Human Service Workers*. Illinois: Governors State University, 1972.

Lowy, Louis. *Training Manual for Human Service Technicians Working with Older Persons*. Boston: United Community Services of Metropolitan Boston and Boston University School of Social Work, 1968.

Lubove, Roy. *The Professional Altruist*. Cambridge: Harvard University Press, 1965.

Lynton, E.F. *The Subprofessionals: From Concepts to Careers*. A Report of a Conference to Expand and Develop Subprofessional Roles in Health, Education, and Welfare. New York: National Conference on Employment of Youth, 1967.

Lynton, Roy P., and Pareek, Udai. *Training for Development*. Homewood, Illinois: The Dorsey Press, 1967.

March, James, and Simon, Herbert. *Organizations*. New York: J. Wiley, 1958.

Merton, Robert. *Social Theory and Social Structure*. Glencoe, Illinois: Free Press, 1959.

Meyer, Carol H. *Staff Development in Public Welfare Agencies*. New York: Columbia University Press, 1966.

Monahan, Fergus. *A Study of Non-Professional Personnel in Social Work*. Washington: Catholic University Press, 1960.

Moynihan, Daniel P. *Maximum Feasible Misunderstanding*. New York: Free Press, 1969.

Myrdal, Alva, and Klein, V. *Women's Two Roles*. London: Routledge and Kegan, 1956.

National Social Welfare Assembly. *The Use of Case Aides in Casework*. New York: National Social Welfare Assembly, 1959.

National Study Service. *Use of Volunteers in Public Welfare.* New York: Junior League of New York, 1963.

Novick, David, ed. *Program Budgeting.* Washington: Bureau of the Budget, 1965.

Pearl, Arthur, and Riessman, Frank. *New Careers for the Poor.* New York: Free Press, 1965.

Pearlman, Robert, and Jones, David. *Neighborhood Service Centers.* Washington: U.S. Department of Health, Education, and Welfare, 1967.

Queen, Betty. *A Reappraisal of the Use of Volunteers in Public Welfare.* Chicago: American Public Welfare Association, 1962.

Reiff, Robert, and Riessman, Frank. *The Indigenous Nonprofessional: A Strategy of Change in Community Action and Community Mental Health Programs.* New York: National Institute of Labor Education, 1964.

Ricci, Edmund. *Organizational and Professional Influences Upon Work-Role Conception and Work Interaction.* Ph.D. dissertation, University of Pittsburgh, 1967.

Richman, Mary. *Social Diagnosis.* New York: Harper and Row, 1917.

Riesman, David. *The Lonely Crowd.* New Haven: Yale University Press, 1950.

Riessman, Frank; Cohen, Jerome; and Pearl, Arthur, eds. *Mental Health of the Poor.* New York: Free Press, 1964.

Riessman, Frank, and Popper, Hermine, *Up From Poverty: New Career Ladders for Nonprofessionals.* New York: Harper and Row, 1968.

Rosenberg, Janet. *Breakfast: Two Jars of Paste: A Training Manual for Workers in the Human Services.* Cleveland: Case Western Reserve University, 1972.

Rosenthal, Seymour, J. *Curricula and Training of Paraprofessional Employees of Public Housing Authorities.* Washington: U.S. Department of Housing and Urban Development, 1972.

Schwartz, Edward E., ed. *Manpower in Social Welfare: Research Perspectives.* New York: National Association of Social Workers, 1966.

Schwartz, Edward E., and Sample, William C. *The Midway Office: An Experiment in the Organization of Work Groups.* New York: National Association of Social Workers, 1972.

Selznick, Philip, *Leadership in Administration.* New York: Row, Peterson and Co., 1957.

Shatz, Eunice. *New Careers: Generic Issues in the Human Services: A Sourcebook for Trainers.* Washington: University Research Corporation, 1968.

Sieder, Violet. *The Rehabilitation Agency and Community Work.* Washington: U.S. Department of Health, Education, and Welfare, Vocational Rehabilitation Administration, 1966.

Sills, David. *The Volunteers.* Glencoe, Illinois: Free Press, 1957.

Simon, Herbert. *Administrative Behavior.* New York: Free Press, 1957.

Smelser, Neil. *Theory of Collective Behavior.* New York: Free Press, 1963.

Social and Rehabilitative Services. *Operational Planning Manual: FY '73.* Washington: HEW, 1972.

Specht, Harry, and Pruger, Robert. *Job Creation: A Means for Implementing a Public Policy of Full Employment.* California: Contra Costa Council of Community Services, 1966.

Teare, Robert J., and McPheeters, Harold L. *Manpower Utilization in Social Welfare.* Atlanta: Southern Regional Education Board, 1970.

Thomas, Rose C. *Public Service Careers Program Training Manual for Case Aide Trainees.* New York: City of New York Department of Social Services, 1968.

Thompson, J. *Organizations in Action.* New York: McGraw-Hill, 1967.

Toch, H. *The Social-Psychology of Social Movements.* Indianapolis: Bobbs-Merrill, 1966.

University Research Corporation: *Human Resources and Manpower Development: A Curriculum Approach.* Washington: University Research Corporation, 1970.

Vollmer, Howard, and Mills, Donald, eds. *Professionalization.* Englewood Cliffs, N.J.: Prentice-Hall, 1966.

Whyte, W.F. *Street Corner Society.* Chciago: University of Chicago Press, 1955.

Whyte, William. *The Organization Man.* New York: Doubleday, 1956.

Wilensky, Harold. *Intellectuals in Labor Unions: Organizational Pressures on Professional Roles.* Glencoe, Illinois: Free Press, 1956.

Wilensky, Harold, and Lebeaux, Charles. *Industrial Society and Social Welfare.* New York: Free Press, 1958.

Wiley, Wretha W., and Fine, Sidney A. *A Systems Approach to New Careers: Two Papers.* Kalamazoo, Michigan: The W.F. Upjohn Institute for Employment Research, 1969.

Wilson, Jerusa D.; Fishman, Jacob R.; and Mitchell, Lonnie E. *An Assessment of Technical Assistance and Training Needs in New Careers Projects Being Sponsored by the United States Training and Employment Service, Manpower Administration, Department of Labor.* Washington: University Research Corporation, 1969.

Zander, Alvin; Cohen, Arthur; and Stotland, Ezra. *Role Relationships in Mental Health Professions.* Ann Arbor: University of Michigan Press, 1957.

Articles

Adelson, Gerald, and Kovner, Anthony R. "The Social Health Technician: a New Occupation." *Social Casework*, July 1969, pp. 395-401.

Ahearn, F.L., Jr. "Correlates of Job Status Among Indigenous Nonprofessionals in Community Action Programs," *Social Science Quarterly*, December 1969.

American Journal of Public Health, September 1969.

Anderson, D., and Dockhorn, J. "Differential Use of Staff: An Exploration with Job Trained Personnel." *Personnel Information* 8 (1965).

Andrade, Sally J., and Burnstein, Alvin G. "Social Congruence and Empathy in Paraprofessionals and Professional Mental Health Workers." *Community Mental Health Journal* 9 (Winter 1973).

Apel, Yetta. "The Utilization of Nonprofessional Personnel in Service Roles in the Provision of Mental Health Services." *Columbia University School of Social Work* (1967), mimeo.

Aptekar, Herbert H. "Supervision and the Development of Professional Responsibility: An Application of Systems Thought." Paper presented at Institute for Field Instructors, April 29, 1965, Yeshiva University.

Argyris, Chris. "Individual Actualization in Complex Organizations." In *Organizations and Human Behavior*, edited by G. Bell. Englewood Cliffs, N.J.: Prentice-Hall, 1967.

Austin, Lucille N. "Basic Principles of Supervision." *Social Casework* 34 (October 1958) :445.

Baker, E. Jo. "The Mental Health Associate: One Year Later." *Community Mental Health Journal* 9, (Fall 1973).

Baker, Mary R. "Approaches to a Differential Use of Staff." *Social Casework*, April 1966.

Barker, Robert L., and Briggs, Thomas L. "Trends in the Utilization of Social Work Personnel: An Evaluative Research of the Literature." Research Report No. 2. New York: NASW, 1966.

Barker, Robert L. "Differential Use of Social Work Personnel and Its Relationship to the Perception of Social Work Roles by Chiefs of State Mental Hospital Social Service Units." Ph.D. dissertation, Columbia University School of Social Work, 1967.

Barney, H.S. "The Use of Nutrition and Home Economics Aides in Maternity and Infant Care and Children and Youth Projects." *Journal of Home Economics,* February 1970.

Barr, Sherman. "Some Observations on the Practice of Indigenous Nonprofessional Workers." *Personnel in Anti-Poverty Programs.* New York: Council on Social Work Education, 1967.

Beck, Bertram. "Utilization of Personnel in Social Work: Those with Full Professional Education and Those Without." National Association of Social Workers, February, 1962.

Beck, Bertram. "Wanted Now: Social Work Associates," *Social Welfare Forum.* New York: Columbia University Press, 1963.

Beck, Bertram. "A Professional Approach to the Use of 'Nonprofessional' Social Work Personnel." American Psychological Association, May 1967.

Beck, Bertram M. "Nonprofessional Social Work Personnel." In *Nonprofessionals in the Human Services.* Edited by Grosser, Charles; Henry, William; and Kelly, James. San Francisco: Jossey-Bass, 1969.

Becker, Howard. "The Teacher in the Authority System of the Public School." In *Complex Organizations: A Sociology Reader.* Edited by Amitai Etzioni. New York: Holt, Rinehart, and Winston, 1967.

Bell, Gerald. "Formality Versus Flexibility in Complex Organizations." In *Organizations and Human Behavior.* Edited by Gerald Bell. Englewood Cliffs, N.J.: Prentice-Hall, 1967.

Berman, Gerald S., and Haug, Marie R. "New Careers: Bridges or Ladders." *Social Work* 18 (July 1973).

Bidwell, Charles. "The School as a Formal Organization," in *Handbook of Organizations.* Edited by J. March. Chicago: Rand McNally, 1965.

Birnbaum, Martin, and Jones, Chester. "Activities of the Social Work Aides." *Social Casework,* December 1967.

Block, Alvan. "An Analysis of Social Work Practice in Mental Hosptials as a Basis for Developing Manpower Policies." Ph.D. dissertation, University of Pittsburgh, 1967.

Blum, Arthur. "Differential Use of Manpower in Public Welfare." *Social Work,* January 1966.

Blum, Henrik. "The Multipurpose Worker and the Neighborhood Center." *American Journal of Public Health,* March 1968.

Boehm, Werner. "Relationship of Social Work to Other Professionals." In *Encyclopedia of Social Work.* Edited by H. Lurie. New York: NASW, 1965.

Boulding, Kenneth E. "The Concept of Need for Health Services." *Milbank Memorial Fund Quarterly,* October 1966.

Bowman, G., and Klopf, G. "Auxiliary School Personnel." In *Up From Poverty: New Career Ladders for Nonprofessionals*. Edited by F. Riessman, and H. Popper. New York: Harper and Row, 1968.

Brager, George. "The Indigenous Worker: A New Approach to the Social Work Technician." *Social Work*, April 1965.

Brennen, Earl. "College Students and Mental Health Programs for Children." *American Journal of Public Health*, October 1967.

Brody, Adele C.; Felton, Nadine; and Riessman, Frank. "A New Careers Approach to Training." In *Up From Poverty*. Edited by Riessman, and Popper. New York: Harper and Row, 1968.

Brozen, Y. "Toward an Ultimate Solution." *Saturday Review*, May 23, 1970 :30-61.

Bucher, Rue, and Stelling, J. "Characteristics of Professional Organizations." *Journal of Health and Social Behavior*, March 1969.

Bucher, Rue, and Strauss, Anselm. "Professions in Process." *American Journal of Sociology*, January, 1961.

Budner, Stanley; Chazin, Robert M.; and Young, Howard. "The Indigenous Nonprofessional in a Multiservice Center." *Social Casework*, June 1973.

Cain, Lillian, and Epstein, Doris. "The Utilization of Housewives as Volunteer Case Aides." *Social Casework*, May 1967.

Christman, June J. "Group Methods in Training and Practice: Nonprofessional Mental Health Personnel in a Deprived Community." *American Journal of Orthopsychiatry*, April 1966.

Clack, Frank, and Wishick, Caroline. "New Staff or Public Health." *Public Health Reports*, February 1968.

Clark, Burton R. "Organizational Adaptation and Precarious Values: A Case Study." *American Sociological Review*, June 1956.

Clark, Peter, and Wilson, James. "Incentive Systems: A Theory of Organizations." *Administrative Science Quarterly*, September 1961.

Cloward, Richard A., and Epstein, C. "Private Social Welfare's Disengagement from the Poor." In *Community Action Against Poverty*. Edited by G. Brager and F. Purcell. New Haven: College and University Press, 1967.

Cockerill, Eleanor. "The Interdependence of the Professions in Helping People." *Social Casework*, November 1953.

Cogan, M. "The Problem of Defining a Profession." *Annals of the American Academy of Political and Social Sciences*, January 1955.

Coggs, Pauline, and Robinson, Vivian. "Training Indigenous Community Leaders for Employment in Social Work." *Social Casework*, May 1967.

Cowen, Emory L.; Anntrost, Mary; and Izzo, Louis D. "Nonprofessional Human-Service Personnel in Consulting Roles." *Community Mental Health Journal* 9 (Winter 1973).

Cowen, Emory L.; Dorr, Darwin A.; and Pokraki, Francine. "Selection of Nonprofessional Child Aides for a School Mental Health Project." *Community Mental Health Journal* 8 (August 1972).

Cudaback, Dorothea. "Case Sharing in the AFDC Program: The Use of Welfare Service Aides." *Social Work*, April 1969.

Cudaback, Dorothea. "Training and Education of New Careerists in Public Welfare." *Public Welfare* 28 (April 1970).

David, Henry. "Manpower Theory and Conceptualization." In *Manpower for Mental Health*. Edited by F. Arnoff. Chicago: Aldine, 1969.

Davis, Donald A. "Teaching and Administrative Functions in Supervision." *Social Work*, April 1965 :83.

Day, R., and Hamblin, R. "Some Effects of Close and Punitive Styles of Supervision." *American Journal of Sociology*, March 1964.

DeHoyos, Arturo, and DeHoyos, Genevieve. "The Professional Mobility of Social Work and Its Middle-Class Orientation." *American Journal of Orthopsychiatry*, January 1968.

Denham, William. "Initial Experience in the Utilization of Indigenous Nonprofessionals as Manpower Resources in the Human Services: An Analytic Study." Ph.D. dissertation, Brandeis University, 1969.

Denham, William, and Shatz, Eunice. "Impact of the Indigenous Nonprofessional on the Professional's Role." In *Human Services and Social Work Responsibility*. Edited by W. Richan. New York: National Association of Social Work, 1969.

Dockhorn, Jean. "A Study of the Use of the Social Work Assistant in the Veterans Administration." *Veterans Administration*, July 1965:

Eaton, Joseph W. "Whence and Whither Social Work? A Sociological Analysis." *Social Work*, January 1956.

Eisdorfer, Carl, and Golann, Stuart. "Principles for the Training of 'New Professionals' in Mental Health." *American Psychological Association*, 1968.

Epstein, Doris W.; Lowenstein, Sophie F.; and Duggan, Mary M. "Issues in Training New Professionals." *Social Casework*, January 1974.

Epstein, Laura. "Differential Use of Staff: A Method to Expand Social Services." *Social Work*, October 1962.

Epstein, Norman, and Shainline, Anne. "Paraprofessional Parent-Aides and Disadvantaged Families." *Social Casework*, April 1974.

Euster, Gerald L. "Mental Health Workers: New Mental Hospital Personnel for the Seventies." *Mental Hygiene*, July 1971.

Farrar, Marcella, and Henem, Mary. "Use of Non-Professional Staff in Work with the Aged." *Social Work*, July 1963.

Finch, Wilbur A. "The Challenge of a New Careers Concept." *Public Welfare*, April 1970.

Fine, Jean Szalcozi. "Issues in Manpower Development Program Planning." *Working Papers No. 1*. Washington: Department of Health, Education, and Welfare, 1971.

Fine, Sidney. "Guidelines for the Design of New Careers." In *Up From Poverty: New Career Ladders for Nonprofessionals*. Edited by F. Riessman, and H. Popper. New York: Harper and Row, 1968.

Fine, Sidney A. "A Systems Approach to Manpower Development in Human Services." *Public Welfare*, January 1970.

Finestone, Samuel. "Major Dimensions and Alternatives in Differential Use of Casework Staff." In *Experimentation in Differential Use of Personnel in Social Welfare*. New York: NASW, 1964.

Fitzdale, Ruth, "Peer-Group Supervision." *Social Casework* 34 (December 1952) :415.

Flexner, Abraham. "Is Social Work a Profession?" *Proceedings of National Conference on Charities and Corrections*, 1915.

Fox, Raymond. "An Inservice Educational Program for the Paraprofessional." *Child Welfare*, May 1973.

Frankel, Charles. "Social Philosophy and the Professional Education of Social Workers." *Social Service Review*, December 1959.

Frontiers of Hospital Psychiatry. "Nonprofessionals: Key Workers in 'Attitude Therapy.' "*Roche Report*, May 1968.

Gannon, T.M. "The Role of the Nonprofessional in the Harlem Domestic Peace Corps." *Sociology and Social Research*, 1968.

Gartner, Alan. "The Use of the Paraprofessional and New Directions for the Social Service Agency." *Public Welfare*, April 1969.

Getzels, J.W., and Guba, E.G. "Role, Role Conflict, and Effectiveness." *American Sociological Review*, April 1954.

Ginzberg, Eli. "Manpower in a Service Economy." In *Training Health Service Workers: The Critical Challenge*. Edited by Lucy Kramer. Washington: Department of Labor and Department of Health, Education, and Welfare, 1966.

Ginzberg, Eli. "Forward." In *Upgrading Blue Collar and Service Workers*. Edited by Charles Brecher. Baltimore: John Hopkins University Press, 1972.

Glovinsky, A., and Johns, J.P. "Paraprofessionals: 26 Ways to Use Them." *School Management*, 1969.

Goldberg, Gertrude. "New Nonprofessionals in the Human Services: An Overview." *American Psychologist*, May 1967.

Goldman, Roy D., and Singer, Robert D. "How Do Mental Health Para-professionals Form Judgments about Patients? The Development of a Patient Evaluation Scale." *Community Mental Health Journal*, Fall 1974.

Goode, William J. "Community Within a Community: The Professions." *American Sociological Review*, April 1957.

Goode, William. "Encroachment, Charlatanism, and the Emerging Professions." *American Sociological Review*, December 1960.

Goode, William. "The Protection of the Inept." *American Sociological Review*, February 1967.

Gordon, Jesse E. "Project Cause, the Federal Anti-Poverty Program and Some Implications of Subprofessional Training." *American Psychologist*, May 1965.

Gottesfeld, Harry; Rhee, Chongic, and Parker, Glenn. "A Study of the Role of Paraprofessionals in Community Mental Health." *Community Mental Health Journal*, August 1970.

Gouldner, Alvin. "Cosmpolitans and Locals: Toward an Analysis of Latent Social Roles." *Administrative Science Quarterly*, December 1957 and March 1958.

Gouldner, Alvin. "Organizational Analysis." In *Sociology Today*. Edited by R. Merton. New York: Basic Books, 1959.

Green, A.D. "The Professional Social Worker in the Bureaucracy." *Social Science Review*, May 1968.

Greenwood, Ernest. "Attributes of a Profession." *Social Work*, July 1957.

Grosser, Charles. "Perceptions of Professionals, Indigenous Workers and Lower-Class Clients." Ph.D. dissertation, Columbia University School of Social Work, 1965.

Grosser, Charles. "Local Residents as Mediators Between Middle-Class Professional Workers and Lower-Class Clients." *Social Service Review*, March 1966.

Grosser, Charles. "The Role of the Nonprofessional in the Manpower Development Programs." U.S. Department of Labor, 1967.

Grosser, Charles F. "Manpower Development Programs." In *Nonprofessionals in the Human Services*. Edited by C. Grosser; W.E. Henry; and J.G. Kelly. San Francisco: Jossey-Bass, 1969.

Gurin, Arnold. "Outline of Recommendations on Curriculum Content for Community Organization." Council on Social Work Education, New York, December 1968.

Hadley, John M.; True, John E.; and Kepes, Sherwin Y. "An Experiment in the Education of the Preprofessional Mental Health

Worker: The Purdue Program." *Community Mental Health Journal*, February 1970.

Hall, Oswald. "Organization of Manpower in Some Helping Professions." In *Manpower in Social Welfare: Research Perspectives.* Edited by E. Schwartz. New York: NASW, 1966.

Hallowitz, Emanuel, and Riessman, Frank. "The Role of the Indigenous Nonprofessional in a Community Mental Health Neighborhood Service Center Program." *American Journal of Orthopsychiatry*, July 1967.

Halpern, Katherine S. "Navajo Health and Welfare Aides: A Field Study." *Social Service Review*, March 1971.

Hardcastle, David. "The Indigenous Nonprofessional in the Social Service Bureaucracy: A Critical Examination." *Social Work*, April 1971.

Hartog, Joseph. "A Classification of Mental Health Nonprofessionals." *Mental Hygiene*, October 1967.

Haug, Marie, and Sussman, Marvin B. "Professional Autonomy and the Revolt of the Client." *Social Problems* 17:153-161.

Heilig, S.M.; Farberow, Norman L.; and Litman, Robert E. "The Nonprofessional Volunteers in a Suicide Prevention Center." Los Angeles: Suicide Prevention Center, 1966.

Heyman, Margaret. "A Study of Effective Utilization of Social Workers in a Hospital Setting." *Social Work*, April 1961.

Heyman, Margaret. "Criteria for the Allocation of Cases According to Levels of Staff Skill." *Social Casework*, July 1961.

Hirschowitz, Ralph. "Aide-Therapist Programs—Where Do We Go From Here?" *Mental Hygiene*, October 1967.

Hodge, Robert W., Siegel, Paul M.; and Rossi, Peter H. "Occupational Prestige in the United States, 1925-1963." *American Journal of Sociology*, November 1964.

Hoff, Wilbur. "Health Manpower: Older Poor Adults Trained as Home Health Aides." *Public Health Report*, March 1968.

Houston, Laura Pires. "Black People, New Careers, and Humane Human Services." *Social Casework*, May 1970.

Ishiyama, Toaru; McCulley, Willa; and Rodriguez, Ozzie. "Does the Psychiatric Aide Have a Treatment Role?" *Mental Hygiene*, January 1967.

Jones, Betty L. "Nonprofessional Workers in Professional Foster Family Agencies." *Child Welfare*, June 1966.

Jones, Hettie. "The Use of Indigenous Personnel as Service Givers." In *Individual and Group Services in the Mobilization for Youth Experience.* Edited by Harold Weissman. New York: Association Press, 1969.

Jones, Hubert. "Beyond Romanticism: A Critical Look at the Use of Indigenous Workers." Mimeographed. NASW Second Symposium on Human Services and Professional Responsibility. San Francisco: May 1968.

Joy, A. "System and Role Conflict Inherent in the 'New Careers' Concept." Ph.D. dissertation, University of California, 1968.

Kadushin, Alfred. "The Knowledge Base of Social Work." In *Issues in American Social Work*. Edited by D. Kahn. New York: Columbia University Press, 1959.

Kadushin, Alfred. "Games People Play in Supervision." *Social Work* 13 (March 1968).

Kase, Harold M. "Purposeful Use of Indigenous Paraprofessionals." *Social Work*, March 1972.

Kelly, James G. "The Mental Health Agent in the Urban Community." *Urban America and the Planning of Mental Health Services*. Symposium No. 10, 1964.

Kidneigh, John. "Restructuring Practice for Better Manpower Use." *Social Work*, April 1968.

Kissick, William. "Effective Utilization: The Critical Factor in Health Manpower." *American Journal of Public Health*, January 1968.

Kohn, M.L., and Schooler, C. "Class, Occupation, and Orientation." *American Sociological Review*, October 1969.

Kramer, Phillip. "The Indigenous Worker: Homeowner, Striver, Activist." *Social Work*, January 1972.

Kurzman, Paul A. "The New Careers Movement and Social Change." *Social Casework*, January 1970.

Lambert, Camille, and Lambert, Leah. "Impact of Poverty Funds on Voluntary Agencies." *Social Work*, April 1970.

Lee, Ann. "The Training of Non-Professional Personnel." *Nursing Outlook*, April 1963.

Lenzer, Anthony. "New Health Careers for the Poor." *American Journal of Public Health*, January 1970.

Leon, Edwina T. "The MSW as a Supervisor of Paraprofessionals." In *Educating MSW Students to Work with Other Social Welfare Personnel*. Edited by Margaret Purvine. New York: Council on Social Work Education, 1973.

Levenson, D. "Role, Personality, and Social Structure in the Organizational Setting." *Journal of Abnormal and Social Psychology*, March 1959.

Levinson, Perry, and Schiller, Jeffrey. "The Indigenous Nonprofessional —Research Issues." U.S. Department of Health, Education, and Welfare, 1965.

Levitan, Sar, and Mangum, Garth. *Making Sense of Federal Manpower Policy*. Ann Arbor: University of Michigan (March 1967).

Levitt, Louis. "Case Aides and Administrative Penalties." *Public Welfare*, January 1970.

Lief, Harold. "Subprofessional Training in Mental Health." *Archives of General Psychiatry*, December 1966.

Lourie, Reginald; Rioch, Margaret; and Schwartz, Samuel. "The Concept of a Training Program for Child Development Counselors." *American Journal of Public Health*, October 1967.

Lowenberg, Frank M. "Toward A Systems Analysis of Social Welfare Manpower Utilization Patterns." *Child Welfare*, May 1970.

Lowenberg, Frank M. "On the Training of Paraprofessionals for Social Welfare Services." *Public Welfare*, Summer 1971.

Lurie, Harry. "The Responsibility of a Socially Oriented Profession." In *New Directions in Social Work*. Edited by C. Kasius. New York: Harper and Brothers, 1954.

MacLennon, Beryce. "New Careers as Human Service Aides." *Children*, September-October 1966.

MacLennon, Beryce; Klein, William; Pearl, Arthur; and Fishman, Jacob. "Training for New Careers." *Community Mental Health Journal*, Summer 1966.

Marler, Don C. "The Nonprofessionalization of the War on Mental Illness." *Mental Hygiene*, July 1971.

Marshall, Thomas. "Professionalism and Social Policy." In *Man, Work, and Society*. Edited by S. Nosow and W. Form. New York: Basic Books, 1962.

Meisels, Joseph F. "Self-Conception, Job-Perception, and Job Satisfaction of Social Workers." Ph.D. dissertation, University of Minnesota, 1962.

Mencher, Samuel. "Social Policy and Welfare Manpower." In *Manpower in Social Welfare: Research Perspectives*. Edited by E. Schwartz. NASW, 1966.

Meyer, Henry. "Professionalization and Social Work." In *Issues in American Social Work*. Edited by A. Kahn. New York: Columbia University Press, 1959.

Meyer, Henry. "The Effect of Social Work Professionalization on Manpower." In *Manpower in Social Welfare: Research Perspectives*. Edited by E. Schwartz. New York: NASW, 1966.

Meyer, Henry. "The Nonprofessional, the Agency, and the Social Work Profession: Some Sociological Comments." American Psychological Association, May 1967.

Miller, D. "Supervision: Evolution of an Organizational Role." In *Organizations and Human Behavior.* Edited by G. Bell. Englewood Cliffs, N.J.: Prentice-Hall, 1967.

Miller, Irving. "Supervision in Social Work." *Encyclopedia of Social Work.* New York: National Association of Social Workers, 1971.

Miller, S.M. "Breaking the Credentials Barrier." In *Managing People at Work.* Edited by D.S. Beach. New York: Macmillan, 1971.

Minuchin, Salvador. "The Paraprofessional and the Use of Confrontation in the Mental Health Field." *American Journal of Orthopsychiatry,* October 1969.

Misner, Gordon. "The Development of 'New Careerist' Positions in the Richmond Police Department." California: Contra Costa Council of Community Service, 1966.

Montgomery, Helen. "Differential Utilization of Social Work Personnel." *Children,* May-June 1964.

Morrison, Andrew P. "Consultation and Group Process with Indigenous Neighborhood Workers." *Community Mental Health Journal,* February 1970.

National Association of Social Work. *Experimentation in Differential Use of Personnel in Social Welfare.* New York: National Association of Social Workers, 1964.

Neiman, Lionel J., and Hughes, James W. "The Problem of the Concept of Role—A Resurvey of the Literature." In *Social Perspectives on Behavior.* Edited by Herman Stein, and Richard Cloward. Glencoe, Illinois: Free Press, 1958.

Orzack, Louis. "Social Change: Implications for Welfare Manpower." In *Manpower in Social Welfare: Research Perspectives.* Edited by E. Schwartz. New York: NASW, 1966.

Otis, Jack. "Problems and Promise in the Use of Indigenous Personnel." *Welfare in Review,* June 1965.

Palmbaum, Paul J. "Apprenticeship Revisited." *Archives of General Psychiatry,* October 1965.

Penningroth, Paul. "The Community College in Mental Health Training: Report of a Conference." Atlanta: Southern Regional Education Board, April 1966.

Perlmutter, Felice, and Durham, Dorothy. "Using Teen-Agers to Supplement Casework Services." *Social Work,* April 1965.

Perrow, Charles. "Hospitals: Technology, Structure, and Goals." *Handbook of Organizations.* Edited by J. March. Chicago: Rand McNally, 1965.

Piliavin, Irving. "Restructuring the Provision of Social Services." *Social Work,* January 1968.

Poovathumkal, Chacko. "Community Mental Health Ideology Scale Standing of Paraprofessionals." *Community Mental Health Journal*, Summer 1973.

Pruger, Robert, and Specht, Harry. "Establishing New Careers Programs: Organizational Barriers and Strategies." *Social Work*, October 1968.

Rapaport, Lydia. "In Defense of Social Work: An Examination of Stress in the Profession." *Social Service Review*, March 1960.

Reiff, Robert. "Dilemmas of Professionalism." In *Nonprofessionals in the Human Services*. Edited by Charles Grosser, William Henry, and James Kelly. San Francisco: Jossey-Bass, 1969.

Reiff, Robert, and Riessman,Frank. "The Indigenous Nonprofessional: A Strategy of Change in Community Action and Community Mental Health Programs." National Institute of Labor Education, New York, 1964.

Reinherz, Helen. "College Student Volunteers as Case Aides in State Hospitals for Children." *American Journal of Orthopsychiatry*, April 1963.

Riessman, Frank. "The 'Helper' Therapy Prinicple," *Social Work*, April 1965.

Riessman, Frank. "The Revolution in Social Work: The New Nonprofessional." *Trans-Action*, November-December 1964.

Riessman, Frank. "The New Community-Based Nonprofessional Mental Health Aide." *Journal of the Fort Logan Mental Health Center*, Winter 1965.

Riessman, Frank. "Blueprint for the Disadvantaged." Anti-Defamation Leage, 1967.

Riessman, Frank. "Strategies and Suggestions for Training Nonprofessionals." *Community Mental Health Journal*, Summer 1967.

Riessman, Leonard. "A Study of Role Conceptions in Bureaucracy." *Social Forces* 27 (1948-1949).

Richan, Willard. "A Theoretical Scheme for Determining Roles of Professional and Non-Professional Personnel." *Social Work*, October 1961.

Richan, Willard C. "Utilization of Personnel in Social Work: Those with Full Professional Education and Those Without." *Final Report of the Subcommittee on Utilization of Personnel*. New York: National Association of Social Workers, 1962.

Rioch, Margaret. "NIMH Pilot Study of Training Mental Health Counselors." *American Journal of Orthopsychiatry*, July 1963.

Rosinski, Edwin, and Spencer, Frederick. "The Training and Duties of the Medical Auxiliary Known as the Assistant Medical Officer." *American Journal of Public Health*, September 1967.

Schorr, Alvin. "The Retreat to the Technician." *Social Work,* January 1959.

Scherz, Frances. "A Concept of Supervision Based on Definition of Job Responsibility." *Social Casework* 39 (October 1958) : 440.

Schwartz, Charlotte. "Problems for Psychiatric Nurses in Playing a New Role on a Mental Hospital Ward." In *The Patient and the Mental Hospital.* Edited by Milton Greenblatt. Glencoe, Illinois: Free Press, 1957.

Schwartz, Edward E. "A Strategy of Research on Manpower Problems." In *Manpower in Social Welfare.* Edited by E.E. Schwartz. New York: National Association of Social Work, 1966.

Scott, W. Richard. "Professionals in Bureaucracies—Areas of Conflict." In *Professionalization.* Edited by H. Vollmer and D. Mills. Englewood Cliffs, N.J.: Prentice-Hall, 1956.

Scott, W. Richard. "Reactions to Supervision in a Heteronomous Pro-*Sociology.* Edited by R. Faris. Chicago: Rand McNally, 1964.

Scott, W.Richard. "Reactions to Supervision in a Heteronomous Professional Organization." *Administrative Science Quarterly,* June 1965 :65-81.

Seeman, Melvin. "Role Conflict and Ambivalent Leadership." *American Sociological Review,* June 1953.

Simpson, Richard, and Simpson, Ida. "The Psychiatric Attendant: Development of an Occupational Self Image in a Low Status Occupation." *American Sociological Review,* June 1959.

Smith, Dorothy. "Front-Line Organization of the State Mental Hospital." *Administrative Science Quarterly,* December 1965.

Smith, Philip. "Using Functional Job Analysis to Redesign Jobs." In *Statewide Career Planning in a Human Service Industry.* Edited by M. Austin and P. Smith. Tallahassee, Florida: Board of Regents, 1973.

Sobey, Francine. *The Nonprofessional Revolution in Mental Health.* New York: Columbia University Press, 1970.

Specht, Harry; Hawkins, Arthur; and McGee, Floyd. "The Neighborhood Sub-Professional Worker." *Children,* January-February, 1968.

Stein, L. I. "The Doctor-Nurse Game." *Archives of General Psychiatry,* June 1967 :699-703.

Suinn, Richard M. "Traits for Selections of Paraprofessionals for Behavior Modification Consultation Training." *Community Mental Health Journal,* Winter 1974.

Summers, David A., Faucher, Ted; and Chapman, Sue B. "A Note on Nonprofessional Judgments of Mental Health." *Community Mental Health Journal,* Summer 1973.

Szoloci, Jean. "Some Conceptual Issues in Social Welfare Manpower Statistics." *Welfare Review*, March 1967.

Tannenbaum, Robert, and Massarik, Fred. "Participation by Subordinate in the Mangerial Decision-Making Process." *Canadian Journal of Economics and Political Science*, August 1950.

Taran, Freeda B. "The Utilization of Nonprofessional Personnel in Social Work: A Review of Relevant Studies." Mimeographed. New York: Mobilization for Youth, 1963.

Teare, Robert J. "Roles and Functions of Different Levels of Social Welfare Workers." Mimeographed. University of Georgia, 1969.

Thompson, Margaret A. "The Professionalization of New Careerists." Master's thesis, University of Minnesota, 1969.

Thompson, Victor A. "Hierarchy, Specialization, and Organizational Conflict." *Administrative Science Quarterly*, March 1961.

Truax, Max. "The Training of Nonprofessional Personnel in Therapeutic Interpersonal Relationships." *American Journal of Public Health*, October 1967.

Udy, Stanley. "Comparative Analysis of Organizations." In *Handbook of Organizations*. Edited by J. March. Chicago: Rand McNally, 1965.

United States Civil Service Commission. *Interim Guidelines for Reevaluation of Employment Requirements and Practices Pursuant to Emergency Employment Act*. Washington: Government Printing Office, 1972.

United States Civil Service Commission. "Upward Mobility Through Job Restructuring," April 1972.

United States Department of Health, Education, and Welfare. "Utilization of Social Work Staff with Different Levels of Education." Welfare Administration, December 1965.

Wasserman, Harry. "The Professional Social Worker in a Bureaucracy." *Social Work* 16 (January 1971) :90-91.

Wattenberg, Esther. "Progress Report on Education: Minneapolis New Careers Programs." Mimeographed. University of Minnesota (September 1968.

Weber, G. "Conflicts Between Professional and Nonprofessional Personnel." In *Professionalization*. Edited by H. Vollmer and D. Mills. Englewood Cliffs, N.J.: Prentice-Hall, 1966.

Weed, Verne, and Denham, William H. "Toward More Effective Use of the Nonprofessional Worker: A Recent Experiment." *Social Work*, October 1961.

Wellner, Alfred. "A Statewide Survey of Community Needs for Mental Health Technicians." *Mental Hygiene*, April 1968.

Wilensky, Harold L. "The Professionalization of Everyone?" *American Journal of Sociology*, September 1964.

Willcox, Alanson F. "The New Professionals—Practical Aspects of the Use of New Careerists in Public Service Agencies." *Mental Hygiene*, July 1970.

Wilson, Jerusa C.; Jacob Fishman; and Lonnie Mitchell. "An Assessment of Technical Assistance and Training Needs in New Careers Projects." Washington: University Research Corporation, 1969.

Young, Carl E.; True, John E.; and Packard, Mary F. "A National Survey of Associate Degree Mental Health Programs." *Community Mental Health Journal*, Winter 1974.

INDEX